# Crime Prevention

# Crime Prevention
## Facts, Fallacies and the Future

Henry Shaftoe

First published 2004 by
PALGRAVE MACMILLAN
Houndmills, Basingstoke, Hampshire RG21 6XS and
175 Fifth Avenue, New York, N.Y. 10010
Companies and representatives throughout the world

PALGRAVE MACMILLAN is the global academic imprint of the Palgrave Macmillan division of St. Martin's Press LLC and of Palgrave Macmillan Ltd. Macmillan® is a registered trademark in the United States, United Kingdom and other countries. Palgrave is a registered trademark in the European Union and other countries.

ISBN 0–333–92127–5 hardcover
ISBN 0–333–92128–3 paperback

This book is printed on paper suitable for recycling and made from fully managed and sustained forest sources

A catalogue record for this book is available from the British Library.

Library of Congress Cataloging-in-Publication Data
Shaftoe, Henry.
    Crime prevention : facts, fallicies, and the future / Henry Shaftoe.
        p. cm.
    Includes bibliographical references and index.
    ISBN 0–333–92127–5 (cloth) — ISBN 0–333–92128–3 (pbk.)
        1. Criminology.    2. Criminal justice, Administration of.    I. Title.

    HV6025.S454 2004
    364.4–dc22                                                      2004052824

10   9   8   7   6   5   4   3   2   1
13  12  11  10  09  08  07  06  05  04

Transferred to digital printing in 2006.

# Contents

# List of Figures and Plates

# Acknowledgements

This book draws on the work of a number of people who have kindly conveyed their knowledge and thoughts to me in the past and present, most notably Steve Osborn, Laurie Taylor, Tim Read, and particularly John Pitts, who made substantial contributions to an earlier version of two of the chapters. Thanks to Catherine Gray and Beverley Tarquini at Palgrave Macmillan for encouragement and editing advice and Nancy Campbell and Paul Revell at UWE for technical assistance. Maggie Lythgoe helped considerably with the final editing, checking and correcting. I would also like to thank all the students who have submitted written work to me as part of the crime prevention courses I run. Cumulatively, I have probably learnt more from them than they have from me!

# Introduction

At 10.25 on a hot Wednesday evening the duty surveillance officer spotted an all-too-familiar sign. A red blip was showing quite clearly on the geographic information system (GIS) screen covering the north-west boundary segment of the Norville social housing scheme. A juvenile was clearly breaking the area curfew and was heading towards the upper income gated community of Eastbury. This was the first time that Billy Gardom had been left on his own in the control centre at Compliance Security Ltd; after all he had only been in the post for two weeks, having been dishonourably discharged from the armed forces after a random drug test found traces of cocaine in his system. However, drawing on his experience as a navigator in a third-generation Challenger tank, he adeptly scanned the bank of multiplex monitors and clicked to full screen mode to home in on the closest camera viewpoints. Feeding in the GIS coordinates to the camera software, Gardom panned, tilted and zoomed in on the miscreant. Scrolling through the facial recognition programme for all tagged juveniles in the northwest sector, the screen rapidly highlighted the name and previous convictions of Jamie Watt, aged 12, from Byard Crescent. Watt was a notorious crack addict who was almost certainly going to try to break into the fortified enclave at Eastbury, so that he could steal to raise cash for his next fix. Gardom immediately called up the social services rapid response van, which, as good fortune would have it, was already patrolling in the vicinity. Gardom was relieved that, as Watt was a juvenile, he could call social services, rather than the overstreched probation squad.

'Calling social services response team nine, this is Gardom. I've got another nipper for your secure unit. Our dog handler will hand him over to you on the corner of Byard and Surrey Street, as soon as you can get there.'

'OK but try not to bag too many more tonight', quipped the social worker. 'We're already over capacity in our northwest sector custody blocks.'

'Well you'll just have to convert another school into a secure unit', retorted Gardom, only half-jokingly. He'd read only earlier that day, in the local electronic bulletin, that prison expenditure had finally over-taken education as the largest budget drawn from local taxes.

The dystopian scenario above suggests the reality that could emerge from a particular set of policy choices for the control of crime. In this hypothetical instance, the policy route chosen has been one of repression and exclusion. Popular inclination often leads us to want to 'wipe out crime', 'stamp out' drug dealing, 'beat the burglar' and indulge in other similar warlike strategies to 'take out' villains. Becoming a victim or hearing of someone who has become a victim makes us angry and, as often as not, vindictive against known or alleged offenders. So it is quite understandable that a lot of crime control policy is established as a direct response to popular rage and frustration. In a democracy we all, directly or indirectly, influence policy through our attitudes and political expectations. Generally (yet with notable exceptions such as the resistance to reintroducing capital punishment in the UK) politicians will do what they think will get them re-elected and crime is the perennial political football that is kicked around by elected representatives eager to attract voters to their cause.

Unfortunately, much of the debate about how to prevent crime feeds off misinformation, moral panics and retributional rage. This book aims to introduce some cool pragmatism into the debate, without shying away from the broader moral, ethical and value-based issues that make crime such a complex yet fascinating social phenomenon. In 1970 Norval Morris and Gordon Hawkins, two eminent criminologists, published *The Honest Politician's Guide to Crime Control*, in which they tried to cut through the obfuscation and academic point-scoring of criminological research, to come up with some practical crime control implications for policy makers.

Although, with the wisdom of hindsight, their publication can now be seen as somewhat flawed, it was an admirable attempt to bridge the chasm that separated academic research and real-world practice.

This book has similar aims, but a broader canvas to work on. In the last 30 years a huge amount of research and experimental practice has been undertaken in the field of crime control. One of the overarching conclusions that can be deduced from all this work is that the prevention of crime requires the engagement of a whole range of actors, not just those employed by the police and other sections of the criminal justice system. Unlike Morris and Hawkins, who primarily concentrated their attentions on proposals to amend the functioning of the law and the criminal justice system, this book will indicate the key role to be played in the prevention of crime by such apparently unlikely professions as housing managers, planners, teachers, youth workers, social workers, community development officers and health visitors, and, equally importantly, lay citizens.

Hundreds of academic papers and government-sponsored reports from many countries have been published in the last 20 years. This book attempts to distil and comment on the most significant of this welter of information to produce a plain-speaking digest of the facts, fallacies, failures and future prospects in crime prevention. This is a hugely ambitious task made manageable by concentrating on what might be called 'locational' crimes – offences that occur in a particular place, usually the home, the street, workplace or town centre. They make up the vast majority of crimes that affect ordinary people – burglary, car crime, theft, criminal damage and crimes of violence against the person. But this does exclude some of the bigger crimes, including white-collar crimes such as fraud, libel and insider dealing, and international organised crime such as drug cartels and mafia groups. There are also crimes against humanity such as war, terrorism and environmental destruction. All these 'big' crimes are worthy of books in their own right and trying to incorporate them into this one would be superficial and inappropriate, because, to tackle them, a different approach is often required to that of dealing with locational crimes, so the focus of the book would be dissipated.

## Key themes and principles

The core thesis of this book is that the use of the criminal justice system to control crime has reached or exceeded saturation point. Increased investment in criminal justice activity (such as escalation of the drugs war or expanding the prison population) would be either ineffective or positively counterproductive. We should be directing our efforts towards *preventing* as much crime as possible through interventions that reduce opportunities and motivations to offend. Many interventions that prevent crime are valuable in their own right as improvers of the general quality of life for citizens, so should be promoted as good social policies rather than covert crime control mechanisms. Such social policies are generally integrative and inclusive ones, but they require long-term commitment and investment to enable them to succeed. The types of repressive and exclusive policies illustrated in the (barely) fictional scenario at the beginning of this chapter are expensive and unsustainable, even if they appear to 'hold' the situation in the short term.

To develop the above thesis, this book is premised on 14 overarching principles, which can help to clarify the complex debate about crime control:

1.  Crime is not a single entity, like a virus or fog, engulfing the population. It is a social construct, covering a multitude of sins, defined only by the legal system of a particular culture. However, there are certain acts that are almost universally defined as criminal or offensive, namely interpersonal violence, abuse of those less powerful than oneself, vandalism and theft.
2.  Many types of crime can be controlled solely by repressive measures, but this can lead to unacceptable reductions in civil liberties and the quality of everyday life.
3.  Deterrence has a role to play in crime prevention, but in most societies, deterrent measures (for example police patrolling, apprehension and punishment of offenders as a lesson to others) have reached saturation in their effect on crime levels, so that further investment in these alone is unlikely to be cost-effective.
4.  Crime control is not just a technical activity, it is usually influenced by political attitudes and strategies, but to blame

all crime problems on national and global politics is unhelpful to victims and communities suffering from the effects of crime and devalues the tangible progress that can be made at the local level.

5. No one criminological theory can explain crime, but most theories have at least some value in helping us to develop a comprehensive understanding of what causes certain types of offending in certain contexts.

6. Single solutions to crime problems are almost always less effective than cocktails of measures. Despite this, political expediency demands simple, quick-fix interventions and this has led to numerous failures in crime control practice.

7. Long-term preventive investments usually yield a better return than short-term reactive measures and actually save money over time.

8. Opportunity reduction (physical or 'situational' crime prevention) has to be complemented with criminality (social) prevention – reducing the *motivation* to offend.

9. If a measure can be reasonably evaluated as being successful in preventing crime, then as long as it does not infringe civil liberties or degrade the quality of life, it should be actively considered as part of a crime control strategy (that is, 'if it works, use it').

10. Although every state, town and neighbourhood has a particular set of security needs, there are proven, replicable measures that can be adapted to prevent crime in the majority of contexts.

11. The 'environment', in both its geographical and social-learning sense, is a key factor that can explain variations in crime and is a good focus for ameliorative intervention. Safe homes and neighbourhoods are characterised by strong social networks, familiarity, trust, stability and cohesion.

12. Enlightened measures that control crime are generally desirable as part of broader social policy, or, conversely, well-considered social policies may also help to reduce levels of offending.

13. In the long run, inclusive, integrative approaches to preventing crime will lead to a better quality of life for all, than exclusive, repressive approaches.

14.  Ultimately, a political decision has to be made to find the right balance between preventing crime and ensuring personal freedom and civil liberties.

These principles are not necessarily covered in separate sections of the book; they will emerge in various combinations at various points and are implicit in much of the discussion throughout.

## How the book is organised

Unlike some other publications about crime prevention that study it in relation to a particular theoretical or sociological phenomenon – postmodernism, the risk society or post-Fordism for example – this book takes a more eclectic approach, coming at the subject from a number of different angles. It could therefore be regarded as a matrix of facts and thoughts about crime prevention, rather than a closely argued thesis following a particular line of enquiry. This, of course, risks incoherence, but crime prevention is such a complex subject that trying to force it into a single frame of reference does not do it justice. In terms of theoretical analysis, much (but not all) of what is discussed could be placed at various points along a continuum that has repression at one end and integration at the other (see section 9.10 for an explanation of this). Along with the 14 principles discussed above, this is the closest I can get to providing a framework for what follows.

I do not claim to have written the definitive book on crime prevention – the subject has so many facets, angles and hidden depths that this would be impossible. Many excellent books and articles have been written about the subject and I have referred to and listed as many of these as possible (at the end of the book). Furthermore, this is a dynamic and evolving area of study and practice, so I can only look at the current picture, whilst merely guessing what will happen next (Chapter 9). One way to keep up to date is to refer to websites; there are a number that have useful crime prevention contents, which will continue to be updated after the publication of this book (also listed at the end of the book).

Trying to cover such a huge and complex topic presents numerous sequencing and categorising problems. As this book is a matrix of information rather than a threaded discussion, there is no ideal sequence. Sometimes a particular issue could have been placed at various stages in the discussion or under more than one heading. Despite this, I would still generally recommend that you start at the beginning and work your way through from there.

Chapter 1 is about our 'love/hate' fascination with crime and why we procrastinate in the face of it. Chapter 2 attempts to tease out the facts about crime. It asserts that much crime control policy is based on ignorance, blind faith and political opportunism and attempts to paint an authentic picture of the extent and nature of crime, fear and victimisation. Chapter 3 looks at crime and the individual offender. It explains and discusses some theories and approaches that attempt to explain why some individuals become criminals whereas others do not. Chapter 4 looks at the links between crime and the environment. Chapter 5 covers analytical models and frameworks for crime control. Chapter 6 leads us from theory into practice, while Chapter 7 looks at the politics of crime prevention and then uses the USA and the UK as two case studies of the emergence of different policies and priorities over a number of years. The examples of France and Japan are briefly discussed as a contrast to the American and British approaches. Chapter 8 investigates 'what works' and condenses and interprets the practical experience and evaluative research that can help point to the best and most cost-effective types of intervention to create safer communities. Chapter 9 attempts to look into the future and make recommendations for creating safer communities and societies. The book concludes with brief descriptions of recommended further reading and websites related to the whole area of crime prevention.

### Facts, assertions and opinions

The control of crime is by no means an exact science and there is no one-size-fits-all solution to the huge range of problems caused by crime and insecurity. What follows in this book is a mixture of facts, assertions (backed up as far as possible by evidence gleaned from referenced sources) and opinions. Trying to write a totally objective book about crime control would be a doomed endeavour. Even academics in the social sciences, who rigorously provide evidence and references for every statement and assertion, make subjective choices about emphasis (what they choose to cover and what to leave out), in order to put their own world view and political sympathies in the best light possible. In this book I have tried to be as balanced as I can, but my views, often based on first-hand experience, will inevitably seep through and may on occasion bring some fresh views or perspectives.

Academics Jeffrey Ross and Stephen Richards (2002) have written a survival guide to prison, claiming the accolade that they had both been behind bars (one as a prison worker, the other as a prisoner). They acidly observe, in their introduction, that:

> Most books about prison are written by academic criminologists, who know little about prisons because they have no first hand experience and simply parrot outdated correctional theories and so-called empirical evidence they learned from other sheltered scholars.

Unfortunately, for the credibility of this book, I cannot lay claim to having a criminal record, but I have spent many years supervising and getting to know the lives of offenders and victims. It is to be hoped that these observations and reflections contribute to an enlightened debate and subsequent action to prevent crime and create safer communities.

# 1

# Fascination and Procrastination

## 1.1 What is crime?

> Crime is man's second fear. The cataclysm of war is the first. Crime, not disease, is the second; it has a quality of aggression, generative of fear, which disease lacks. (Morris and Hawkins 1970: ix)

> Crime pervades our daily lives like a plague, affecting the way we think, the way we act, the way we respond to one another. Fear of crime has a corrosive effect on interpersonal relations, making us wary of small acts of friendliness towards strangers. (Walker 1998: 14)

To hear many people talk about crime, you would think it was some kind of alien force or sinister virus that was infiltrating our civilised and law-abiding world. People talk about fighting crime as though honest citizens and our agents (usually the police) have to don full battledress and fight the good fight before we are overwhelmed by the forces of darkness. In reality, crime is both more prosaic and more worrying than the simple perceived battle between good and evil. On the prosaic side, a crime is simply an act or omission punishable by law. On the worrying side is the fact that crime is potentially everywhere and potentially in all of us. Nobody can honestly say that they will never commit a crime, indeed most of us have already offended several, if not many, times! Equally we can never know when we might get caught up in a criminal incident as a victim or witness.

Crime is a social construct. By that I mean that the definition of
a certain act as a crime relies on a general consensus, or at least
recognition, that this act is criminal and contravenes the code of
law that is in force at that time in the particular society where the
act has occurred. (For a more philosophical discussion of social
constructions of reality, see Searle 1995.) This thing called crime
is not a physical entity like a lump of rock or a greenhouse,
although throwing the rock at a greenhouse could well result in a
crime occurring!

The law defines crime, but the complication is that criminal law
is a fluid social construct in itself. We tend to think (and are
encouraged by the establishment to do so) that criminal law is an
immutable benchmark against which we can assess, judge and act.
This may be because we confuse it with scientific laws (such as
laws relating to structural mechanics or the behaviour of physical
matter during temperature changes). For example, there is a fixed
scientific law guaranteeing that water will boil at 100°C, so similarly we may assume there is a fixed law guaranteeing that people
cannot drink alcohol in British pubs until they are 18. This misunderstanding is very convenient for the lawmakers as it means
that most people will accept the law (even if they don't always
comply with its proscriptions). In many cases this pressure to
accept the law is given extra weight by implicit or explicit claims
that they are in accordance with the edicts of God or other deities
and their wrath will descend on anyone who even questions them.
This has led, in many cultures, to an attempt to control crime by
the introduction of more and more laws and correspondingly
increased staff and resources to try and enforce them. We could
instantly solve the problem of crime by making everything legal,
but this would not eradicate most of the suffering consequent to
crime. So although crime is a social construct, most criminal acts
are tangible, usually having a physical impact on people and with
direct and often traumatic consequences. Having some philoso-
pher tell you that crime is a chimerical manifestation of institu-
tional symbolism is not going to soothe your bruises or
recompense your financial loss if you have just been mugged for
your wallet.

The very tangible impact of this social construct called crime is
evidenced in people's fears and experiences. Starting during the
1980s, crime and fear of victimisation have gradually risen up the

scale of people's social concerns. Surveys such as the one carried
out by Glasgow University's Quality of Life Group (Rogerson
et al. 1990) and the Centre for Housing Policy at the University of
York (Burrows and Rhodes 1998) indicate that perceived levels of
crime are the strongest factors in people's sense of satisfaction
or dissatisfaction with the areas in which they live. An evaluation
of Priority Estates Projects (Foster and Hope 1993) showed that as
housing management and physical living conditions were
improved, crime became the main residual problem for residents
on many housing estates. So, although we could have endless academic debates about the meaning of crime, people are suffering
from it, out there on the streets, and there is a clear need to reduce
this suffering if we aspire to a better world.

## 1.2   Our love/hate relationship with crime

We have a bizarre attitude towards crime. On the one hand we say
that crime is one of the worst blights of contemporary life and our
communities could be best improved by reducing the chances of
becoming a victim in them. On the other hand, crime seems to be
one of our most popular forms of entertainment. Our righteous
indignation (or is it voyeurism?) is catered for by acres of shock
horror newsprint, shelves full of crime fiction and ever more offensive portrayals on cinema screens. American journalists say about
the predilection for gory newspaper headlines: 'If it bleeds, it
leads.' On television, police series and thrillers are *the* most
popular form of viewing (Sparks 1992). The latest trend seems to
be for crime docudramas and reconstructions which offer
peepshow entertainment thinly disguised as educational or public
service broadcasting (Hebert 1993).

   As if there wasn't enough crime on network, cable and satellite
television, you can go to the local video shop or multiplex cinema
and choose from an overwhelming array of prerecorded assaults,
rapes and murders. And if you want to safely dabble in a bit of
crime yourself, you can even go on a crime weekend at a country
house hotel and play whodunnit in the midst of simulated
murders. Interestingly, some crimes are considered more entertaining than others, yet this seems to bear no relation to their seriousness or trauma inducement in real life. Murder – objectively
the worst crime of all – is considered much more entertaining,

when written about by Agatha Christie or Colin Dexter for example, than sexual assault, burglary or child abduction.

We seem to have a love/hate relationship with crime – we love to hear about it and discuss it, but we hate it happening to us. It is as though we need to be aware of evil so that we can appear good by contrast. Karl Menninger (1968: 153) suggests that, for the sake of some kind of surrogate catharsis, the public wants crime, needs crime and gains definite satisfactions from the present mishandling of it:

> We condemn crime; we punish offenders for it; but we need it. The crime and punishment ritual is part of our lives. We need crimes to wonder at, to enjoy vicariously, to discuss and specu-late about, and to publicly deplore. We need criminals to iden-tify ourselves with, to secretly envy, and to stoutly punish . . . They do for us the forbidden, illegal things we wish to do and, like scapegoats of old, they bear the burdens of our displaced guilt and punishment – the iniquities of us all.

The journalist Mark Lawson suggests that watching criminal and violent acts allows the safety-valve release of our own pent-up frustrations and deviant inclinations by proxy. He goes on to say:

> Whether this process by which people make themselves feel better has the result of making society worse is a matter for psychologists and moralists to debate. But somewhere deep inside, people want and need Bruce (Willis), Arnie (Schwarzenegger) and Tom (of Tom and Jerry) to do it for them. (Lawson 1995: 20)

So, maybe in a perverse way, we need crime, as a kind of scape-goat and catharsis. But where does it come from? Who does it and why? What *do* people think are the real causes of crime? It is quite remarkable how nearly everyone seems to be an expert on the causes of crime. Ask the average person in the street for their views on currency exchange rate mechanisms or advances in neuro-science, and some respondents will claim insufficient understanding of the topic. By contrast, the majority of the population will happily proffer fully formed opinions on the causes and drastic solutions for our burgeoning crime problem.

## 1.3 Crime and the media

Most of this popular knowledge about dealing with crime is culled from coverage and analysis offered by the media, particularly newspapers and television (Ditton and Duffy 1983; Sparks 1992). Very few people, outside the criminological fraternity, go to the trouble of digesting and analysing the vast amount of rigorous research into crime and its treatment. So popular understanding of the subject has been filtered through the mass media's need to simplify, sensationalise and entertain.

Newspapers don't just report incidents of crime, they often use crime as a topic to make moral judgements about the deteriorating state of the nation and the decline of civilisation. Newspapers have used crime as a social barometer for as long as there have been columns to fill. Here are some random examples from the last 50 years:

In 1958 the *News of the World* was asking: '**WHAT'S GONE WRONG WITH US?** What is to be done about the gangsters and their terror tactics?' Nineteen years later the *Birmingham Evening Post* headlined with the question: '**WHAT HAS HAPPENED?** More murder, rape and violence.' In 1993 the *Daily Mirror* was claiming that 'Nobody knows how to prevent crime' and by 1998 the *Sunday Times* was talking about a '**TEENAGE TIMEBOMB**: Juvenile crime is soaring in Britain and across the Continent. Are we witness to a European youth underclass?'

When not asking such rhetorical questions about the consequences of crime running out of control, newspapers like to fill their pages with accounts of exceptionally vicious and lurid offences. Research into crime reporting, carried out at Edinburgh University (Ditton and Duffy 1983), demonstrated that while only 5% of crime involves sex and violence, 46% of newspaper coverage is concerned with crimes of this type. This inevitably leads to a distorted view of crime and a heightened fear of certain categories of offence.

The exploitation by the media of crimes that are bizarre or exceptional doesn't just provide a frisson of excitement to viewers and readers, it also leads many viewers and readers to assume that these rare occurrences are endemic and to demand answers which are as dramatic and immediate as the crimes themselves (Sparks

1992). Politicians, mindful of their re-election potential, yield to the hype, and the demands of their constituents, by sometimes pushing through ill-considered responses to the public outcries fuelled by the media. A good example of this was the coverage in England of the murder of the young James Bulger by two other children. Tragic though this was, it rated as a most exceptional crime; yet the population as a whole seemed to be agonising about 'where have we gone wrong with the nation's children?' as though murder of children by other children had become an epidemic. (In fact, according to Home Office recorded crime statistics, child abduction and murder in England has remained at a rare and constant level for at least the last 50 years.) Tabloid panics about paedophiles, drug dealers at the school gates and out-of-control children have often led to unworkable or counterproductive legislation that politicians have pushed through to placate a baying electorate.

It's not just the news that manipulates our perceptions of crime; the fictional media of books, television and film often blur, in our minds, the line between fact and fantasy. Inspector Morse is a believable sort of character in many people's eyes, so what do we make of the murder rate on his beat in Oxford? *NYPD Blue* was a gripping American cop series, but it is doubtful whether the New York Tourist Authority was too keen on it. Ask most people what they associate with Chicago and they will say gangsters, even though it is one of America's most civilised cities.

The influence of film and television on violent and criminal behaviour is hotly debated, but if a manufacturer is prepared to spend millions of pounds on lifestyle advertising to persuade us to buy its brand of lager, car or perfume, some people have clearly discovered a connection between imagery and behaviour. A huge amount of research has been carried out over the years to try and establish what links there might be between violent portrayals on TV and films and people's subsequent behaviour (for an overview see Gauntlett 1995). The jury is still out, but there is a suggestion that people with pre-existing violent or criminal intentions might use media precedents to copy particular techniques and normalise their behaviour. This blaming of the popular media for provoking crime and violence is not a new phenomenon. As long ago as 1917 the National Council of Public Morals pronounced that: 'The picture house is responsible for the increase in juvenile crime and boys are often led to imitate crimes which they have seen in the pictures.'

On the one hand, this media assault may reduce our sensitivity to scenes of violence and destruction, and in some cases may even make crime look attractively exciting (car chases for instance). On the other hand, what a very substantial number of people gain from all these criminal reports and scenes is a drastically heightened fear about their own risk of becoming victims (Sparks 1992; Toynbee 1994). This is vividly illustrated in England and Holland where, although the overall crime rates have fallen for several years starting in the mid-1990s, surveys by the Dutch Ministry of Justice and the Home Office showed that people's fear of crime continued to rise (see, for example, Home Office 2000). The implications and consequences of heightened fear are discussed in section 2.11.

## 1.4 Closing the stable door after the horse has bolted

Another problem with many popular media accounts of crime investigation and detection (both real-life and fictional) is the suggestion that the most effective way to control crime is to arrest offenders. A recent spin-off from the *Crimewatch* BBC TV series was called *Crimes Solved* – where viewer tip-offs had led to an offender being arrested. The programme title implies that crime is solved by arresting people – end of story. Most detective stories end with the criminal captured and incarcerated. Yet in some ways this is only the beginning of a range of problems. For example, what will happen when the prisoner is eventually released? Will his detention deter others or will it just create a vacancy for other criminals to step into his shoes? Until recently, many police forces used as their main indicators of success the number of crimes they cleared up, by arresting and convicting someone, and the speed with which they responded to a 999 call. Yet as a retired assistant commissioner of the police (writing in *Police News* May 2000) noted, these are both indicators of a *failure* to have prevented those crimes being committed.

To slightly caricature it, the criminal justice approach to crime control seems to entail waiting for a crime to happen and then responding rapidly and forcefully with a huge range of expensive resources and facilities, including high-powered cars (to get the police to the incident very quickly), huge teams of personnel to process the apprehended offenders (lawyers, psychologists, probation officers, social workers, magistrates, custody staff and victim support workers) and high security prisons (to keep the criminals they catch under guaranteed custody). This would be a bit like the NHS waiting for people to get ill, but then providing surgeons with state-of-the-art scalpels, huge teams of operating staff and hospital beds where patients could stay as long as they wanted. To their credit, health strategists have, for at least the last 150 years, put a huge investment into preventing people getting ill in the first place, by ensuring healthy environmental factors (such as clean drinking water and sewerage disposal) and promoting healthy individual living, through the provision of education, guidance and practical support.

The fire brigades, quite rightly, put a huge amount of energy and resources into ensuring that, as far as possible, buildings do not go up in flames. In terms of accidents in the home and outdoors, in the UK we even have a Royal Society for their prevention. Yet when it comes to crime problems, good detective work in solving crimes that have occurred is still seen as the apotheosis of crime control and attracts the best police minds and status. Quite apart from the extravagance and inefficiency of this approach (section 2.10), it means that citizens have to become *victims* of crime before anything is done. In much media reporting and fictional portrayal of crime, victims are presented as sacrifical lambs in order to stoke up our retributive rage and righteous indignation. If a crime is solved and an offender is successfully prosecuted, justice can then be applied (usually through punishment) and this is somehow supposed to recompense the victim and make everything alright. In reality, it may doubly exacerbate the problem by damaging the life of the offender and his or her family without really taking away the trauma or injury suffered by the victim.

Figures 1.1 and 1.2 compare the reactive criminal justice approach to crime control, with an alternative model based on the public health approach. Given the tautology that the chances of most offences occurring are dependent on whether or not an individual commits a crime, the figures are centred around the biographical timeline of an imaginary individual. In each case the horizontal axis represents developmental stages from birth to about 25 years old and the vertical axis represents variations from a neutral norm in the middle to either a pro-social condition (upwards) or an antisocial state (downwards). The thick line going from left to right could be anyone's individual developmental career. As we will discuss in Chapter 3, the criminal justice trajectory is based on the notion of sacrificing some individuals to a career of punishment and disenfranchisement to discourage others from following the same route. The potential and actuality of a public health-style alternative for controlling crime, which obviates the use of sacrificial lambs, will be developed in later chapters.

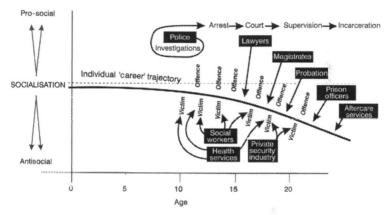

**Figure 1.1** Crime control: the criminal justice approach

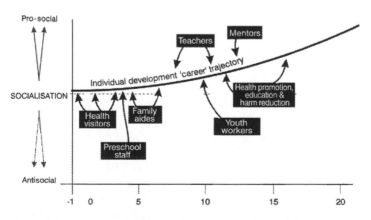

**Figure 1.2** Crime control: a preventive (public health model) approach

## 1.5  Why wait?

We now know so much about what could help to prevent people (and particularly young people in their formative years) from turning to antisocial behaviour and criminal activities (see, for example, Home Office 1998), yet we put several hundred times more precious resources into processing crime and punishing offenders than we do trying to prevent it in the first place (Home Office RDS Directorate 1999b). This would be all very well if processing crime and punishing offenders reduced crime levels in the long term – but it doesn't, as we shall see later.

After the barren 'nothing works' era of the 1970s and early 1980s (see, for example, Martinson 1974), there is now a growing interest in the rehabilitative treatment of offenders (McGuire and Priestley 1995; Vennard and Hedderman 1998). But why wait for people to offend? Why wait for them to go a very long way down the offending path before you intervene to help them back onto the straight and narrow? There are perhaps three explanations of why we take this reactive stance to dealing with crime and offenders. Firstly, there is a (correct) concern about civil liberties and 'net widening' (Cohen 1969) if we intervene at an early stage to prevent people turning to crime. But this presumes that crime prevention must involve some oppressive and restrictive interventions. Yet, when taking an integrative approach, as argued for in this book, the opposite is true – crime prevention is (or should be) about raising people's self-esteem, giving them wider opportunities, helping them to take control of their lives and so on. To quote Morris and Hawkins (1970: 52):

> We have never regarded poor educational facilities, unemployment, broken homes, slums, poverty, or grossly adverse social conditions of any kind as desirable features of our society. We wish to get rid of slums, not particularly because they are productive of delinquency and crime, but because we think they are a despicable way for people to live. We wish to facilitate happy and stable family lives not because we wish to reduce delinquency but because, all in all, we think that is the better way for people to live. In brief, the insights that we have gained from criminological research into the causes of crime and delinquency have not led us to want to do anything that we wouldn't have wished without such insights.

Secondly, too many people's jobs depend on maintaining the criminal justice system as it is (see Christie 1993). Even when professionals have more altruistic intentions than merely making a living out of crime (probation officers and social workers hopefully), their job descriptions and statutory requirements may give them little scope to do much more than stoke the boilers of the crime control factory. Performance appraisals of professionals involved in the criminal justice system tend to measure success by the number of individuals processed through the system, rather than whether crime, insecurity and victimisation have been reduced. As I was told by one probation officer some years ago, when I was trying to enthuse them about criminality prevention approaches: 'We're far too busy trying to catch up with the backlog of court reports and aftercare interviews to take on anything else.' In general, public servants are not encouraged to be reflective practitioners – they are expected to deliver the statutory requirements that their department or agency was set up for. Even senior members of the criminal justice establishment, such as judges and prison inspectors, rarely look beyond the confines of their own particular fiefdom to consider the efficacy of the whole system of which they are a part. It was only after he retired that Scotland's chief inspector of prisons reflected that:

> Having been for locking them up and throwing away the keys, I now believe that a much more profound shift is needed away from imprisonment. There should be a gradual transfer of resources towards failing primary schools in deprived areas and providing more opportunities for youth sport and youth organisations in the community. The time to address potential offending is when individuals are much, much younger. (Clive Fairweather, quoted in *Scotland on Sunday* 27/10/02)

Thirdly, political quick fixes are needed. As we shall see later (Chapter 8), a lot of effective crime prevention practices require investment now for benefits which only become apparent in the long term – sometimes even a generation or more – and politicians, looking to the next election, can't wait that long. The general public is baying (quite understandably) for immediate relief from their sense of insecurity and victimisation and want to see justice being done. So the politicians and their public servants feel under pressure to jerk their knees in the direction of whatever is the crime-stopping magic bullet of the time, be this rapid response units, saturation CCTV or short sharp shocks for juveniles.

But there must be some leeway, some space, some possibilities for doing a bit more than trying to close the stable door after the horse has bolted. For example, why can't we try and make the stable a place that the horse will feel happy with, rather than mere containment? Why don't we help the horse to learn about the consequences of bolting? Why don't we give the horse a sense of pride, self-esteem and responsibility for the stable, whether or not the door has been left open? In fact let's leave the door open to creative possibilities and reorientations.

We need to convince politicians of the waste of spending so much on the criminal justice system in proportion to prevention (use the health promotion/education versus illness treatment analogy). As a senior police officer from the home counties once remarked: 'If the criminal justice system was run as a business, it would have gone bankrupt years ago.' Furthermore, we need to recognise that the popular media are not the best source of information on offending and crime control. If we can't get rid of this lust for reading about and viewing the dastardly deeds of others, we need to separate fact from fiction.

### 1.6   What's gone wrong?

So, given the widespread and escalating concern about crime, what's gone wrong? Is it just that there are more opportunities to commit crimes – more consumer items to steal from shops, offices, homes and cars parked in the street? Are there (as one undergraduate suggested to me) more people walking the earth, so there is bound to be more crime and insecurity? Or are we in the throes of some moral and social decline of which rising crime is the inevitable corollary?

In the 1990s there was a renaissance of the view that the deterioration of society's moral fibre is responsible for the increase in crime. As the wrath of God has become a less dominant feature in many people's everyday lives, it is claimed that notions such as 'evil', 'wrong', 'bad' and 'sinful' no longer carry any moral weight, so that people will do what they think they can get away with. Right-wing thinkers claim this is a legacy of the permissive 1960s and 70s, while those on the left blame the 'me' generation of the Thatcherite 1980s. But in addition to moral degeneration, a whole host of other causes – bad genes, lack of discipline, unemployment, school truancy, video nasties, birth complications, junk food, relative poverty, badly designed housing estates, more portable goods, single parents, broken homes and latchkey childhoods – are still on hand as likely candidates for an explanation of why crime is still such a problem.

So who can we turn to to help us sort the wheat from the chaff, the facts from the fictions? Nobody could complain that there has been any shortage of experts trying to give us the real answers. For over a century, criminologists, psychologists and sociologists have been relentlessly publishing their contradictory findings on the causes of crime. In the 1970s, Morris and Hawkins were so exasperated by the priorities of their criminological colleagues, they suggested that research into the causes of crime should be prohibited, and redirected into the evaluation of crime prevention programmes. They proposed that we would be much better off trying to identify 'what works and how' (discussed in Chapter 8) rather than agonising about 'what's gone wrong and why' (discussed in Chapter 7). It could be argued that now, at the beginning of the new millennium, we have gone too far in the other direction and are only interested in what works, without trying to understand the political and cultural roots of the problems (Crawford 1998; Garland 2001).

Although much nonsense has been written about crime, and it is apparent that much of the research into the causes of crime has not yet translated into a significant reduction in levels of man's second greatest fear, it would be foolish not to trawl through and take stock of the vast body of knowledge and theory on the subject. Part of the problem seems to be a disconnection between criminological findings and crime prevention practice. Criminologists are expected to be academically erudite, and frontline workers in the public services need practical information on how to act effectively. In between these two positions there appears to be a gulf. As a contribution to bridging this gulf, the remainder of this book will attempt to intertwine theory with research and practice.

# 2

# The Facts about Crime, Offenders and Victimisation

## 2.1 Cutting through the chaff and bluff

'Law and order' is an emotive political rallying cry, but people interested in controlling crime and creating safer communities must go beyond the rhetoric to discover the reality. Yet what is this reality? Is there a body of politically neutral information upon which we can draw? Given that crime is a socially constructed phenomenon based on what the prevailing statutes of a particular state determine are illegal acts or omissions, the facts about crime always have been and will be slippery (see Maguire 1997; Davies et al. 1998 Chapter 3). Additionally, the agents of law and order have their own vested interest in ensuring that the facts about crime are either enhanced or reduced in order to safeguard their reputation and employment (Taylor 1999). However, for most citizens, crime is something they have experienced at first or second hand in increasing quantities over the last 50 years (Burrows and Rhodes 1998; Home Office RDS Directorate 2000b), even if the number of criminal incidents appear to have been stabilising or actually decreasing at the turn of the century.

During the 1980s there was some dispute as to whether crime was really on the increase or whether we were just reporting more to the police. However, the continued escalation of reported crime, along with the evidence from victimisation surveys of steadily increasing numbers of offences, has made it irrefutably apparent that over the last 25 years or so we have experienced the biggest crime wave of the twentieth century. Even though official recorded crime rates levelled off in the mid-1990s, the public perception was that crime was still increasing – only 4% of the respondents in the 1996 British Crime Survey thought recorded crime had fallen in the previous two years. And the recorded crime figures released in 2000 showed a substantial increase in violent crime in England and Wales, even though property crimes (the vast majority of offences) were down. In France, after major successes in the 1980s and level pegging in the 1990s, the first recorded crime figures for the new millennium showed a 5% increase on 1999. A similar picture has emerged in Holland.

## 2.2 Reporting crime

Much of the data upon which the criminal statistics are based is furnished by people who report behaviour or events, which they believe to be illegal, to the police. However, some of the things which people find most disturbing, like antisocial neighbours or rowdy youths hanging around street corners, are not illegal. I have been told by some police officers that the *majority* of incidents reported to them by the public are not crimes (for example 50% of all the calls made to the police in south Bristol in 1999 were about youth nuisance). Indeed, many of the complaints made against the police each year concern police inaction in situations where no offence had been committed. On the other hand, people may witness criminal acts and be unaware that they are illegal. For example, every day, assaults, extortion, threatening behaviour and robbery occur in the school playgrounds of Britain, but because they are not normally recognised as criminal acts, they are not reported to the police. Witnesses or victims of crime may be aware that a crime has been committed but may regard it as so trivial, like the theft of a scarf left on a park bench, that they fail to report it. Some crimes, often involving financial deception or assault, are committed against people who are drunk or drugged and may subsequently have little recollection of what happened. Some victims will not report a crime because it puts them in a compromising position – men looking for prostitutes who are subsequently robbed, for example. Victims are sometimes frightened to report an offence. This is often so in the case of domestic violence, racist attacks, child abuse or youth violence and bullying. A minority of ethnic minority victims may be reluctant to attract the attention of the police in case they decide to investigate their immigration

status. Beyond this, the victim may be sceptical about police effectiveness. They may also be hostile towards the police or subscribe
to a different code of ethics. Changing patterns of reporting will
also reflect changing social norms. As long ago as 1963,
McClintock went so far as to suggest that:

> One of the main causes for an increase in the recording of violent
> crime appears to be a decrease in the toleration of aggressive
> and violent behaviour, even in those slum and poor tenement
> areas where violence has always been regarded as a normal and
> acceptable way of settling quarrels, jealousies or even quite
> trivial arguments. (McClintock 1963: 74)

Reporting rates can be increased by improvements in practice. In
recent years the establishment of special rape and domestic violence units staffed by specially trained women police officers has
boosted the levels of reporting. Similarly whole-school anti-bullying
initiatives have been successful in raising reporting rates of play-
ground violence and sexual and racial harassment (Linklater et al.
1994). So, to some extent, official crime rates are a reflection of
citizens' faith in the authorities (most notably the police) as well
as giving us a crude indication of the amount of crime actually
going on.

## 2.3   Recording crime

When we look at the criminal statistics, what exactly are we
looking at? The criminal statistics emerge from an elaborate set of
interactions between people who commit offences, the public, the
police, politicians, the media and the courts. At each stage, the
values, beliefs and attitudes of the people involved in the criminal
justice system will have an impact upon the statistics.

Many crimes are never reported to the police. But not all
crimes which are reported go on the official records and those
that do may be recorded differently from area to area. Depite the
best efforts of the Home Office in England and Wales to stan-
dardise everything, there can still be variations between the
recording systems of different police forces, so what may appear
to be a high crime area may, in fact, be one in which police

recording techniques are more efficient. Reports in which the account is vague, or seems unlikely to result in any action, may also remain unrecorded. On the other hand, people who report an offence may subsequently withdraw their complaint. This inconsistency between police forces in one country becomes even more magnified if you try to compare crime levels between countries.

Getting a single snapshot of crime levels is difficult enough, but when you want to measure crime trends over time, it gets even more complicated. In the last ten years or so police counting rules have changed, categories of crime have been adjusted and a new ethical recording system has been introduced, so that reports that might previously have been dismissed are now faithfully recorded. At the neighbourhood level, police beat boundaries have often changed, as have electoral wards, so that trying to reconcile crime levels as a proportion of the victim population is a statistical nightmare.

Although crude, recorded crime figures can at least give us a rough picture of crime trends over a number of years. They can also make for interesting international comparisons (Council of Europe 1999). For Figure 2.1 I have selected England and Wales and two near neighbours and, using recorded crime figures for each country, tracked crime levels over the last 50 years. It is significant to note that the three countries display similar patterns despite different political and legal arrangements.

Figure 2.1 shows that the most dramatic crime rises took place from the 1970s through to the mid-1990s. Indeed, in 1991 the 16% rise recorded for that year was equal to all the crime recorded in 1950. The only noticeable dip in this upward trend was the decrease in recorded crime in France in the 1980s; the significance and explanation for this will be dealt with in section 7.8. Since 1993 there has been a levelling off and then a small drop in the number of crimes recorded, but the figures remain vastly higher than those of two decades ago. (For useful comparisons of international recorded crime, see Barclay et al. 2001.)

It is clear that the official criminal statistics alone will not necessarily give us the kind of information we may need to develop an effective community safety strategy (Bottoms and Pease 1986). To get a more accurate picture of the amount of crime that people are experiencing we really need to ask the people themselves.

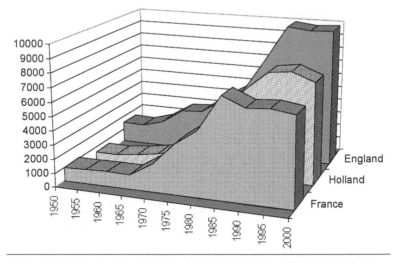

*Source*: Adapted from government statistics for each country, Home Office data and Barclay et al. 2001

**Figure 2.1** Crime trends recorded by the police in England and Wales, France and Holland (per 100,000 of the population)

## 2.4    Victimisation studies

Crime surveys carried out periodically during the last 20 years have given us a better picture of actual victimisation rates nationally and internationally, and a number of *local* crime surveys have given us a better understanding of crime at county, district and neighbourhood level.

Between 1982 and 2002 nine national crime surveys (known cumulatively as the British Crime Survey – see www.homeoffice. gov.uk/rds/bcs1.html for more information) were organised by the Home Office in England and Wales. They interviewed a representative sample of approximately 19,000 people about their experience of crime. What these surveys revealed is that there is much more crime going on than is recorded by the police. Overall only about a quarter of the crimes that victims had experienced were recorded by the police. There is considerable variation according to crime category, with, for example, a high recording level for the theft of cars (presumably for insurance purposes), but a low recording level for vandalism and, more alarmingly, violent crime. On a more positive note, what the British Crime Survey (BCS) reveals is that the increase in crime over the last 20 years has been less dramatic than the police-based statistics suggest. To reconcile the two findings one must conclude that part of the apparent increase in crime shown by the police figures is in fact increased reporting and recording of crime. To put a positive spin on it, this suggests that there might be increased faith in the police; on the other hand, the cynic might say that more people are reporting crime for insurance purposes or simply because more people have telephones, thus making it easy to report a crime.

Because it consists of household surveys, the BCS does not cover non-residential crimes such as shoplifting, fraud, commercial burglary and drug offences. Here are some key findings from the BCS:

- For those crime types that can be compared (including burglary, car crime, thefts from the person, assaults and vandalism), between 1981 and 1991 the police-based criminal statistics recorded a 100% increase, whereas the BCS suggested a 50% increase. Between 1991 and 1999 the BCS showed a levelling off and then small reduction in crime rates (by 15% between 1995 and 1997 and 10% between 1997 and 1999), which mirrored the recorded crime statistics, but at a lower level.
- Despite the recent falls in crime, people's concern about crime has not reduced. In fact a third of those interviewed in the 2000 BCS thought crime had increased 'a lot' between 1997 and 1999.
- Recorded crime has shown larger increases than the BCS largely because more crimes committed are now reported to the police. For comparable crimes, 36% were reported in 1981 and 50% in 1991.
- The BCS estimated a total of 15 million crimes against individuals and their property in 1991, going down to 14.7 million in 1999. By 1999, the only types of crime that were still increasing (from the categories covered by the BCS) were robbery and theft from the person.
- Vehicles are a very common target: one in five owners were victims of some sort of vehicle offence in 1991, but this risk had gone down to about one in eight by 1999. Of all BCS crimes,

36% involved vehicles. By 2000, theft of vehicles was down 11% and theft *from* vehicles was down 16% compared with 1997.

- Serious crimes of violence – wounding, robbery and sexual offences – accounted for only 5% of all crime. Less serious assaults – what are usually called 'common assaults' and are not regarded as serious enough for inclusion in the criminal statistics – accounted for another 12%. Overall, the great majority of criminal incidents, about eight in every ten, involved offences against property rather than against people. Despite national concern about the increase in violent crime, the 2000 BCS found that violence was down by 4% (wounding down by 11%) since the previous survey.
- The 2000 survey showed that burglary was down 21% from the1997 figures, to its lowest level since 1991.

Victimisation surveys have helped us to understand that we are not all equally at risk from crime. Young people are more likely to be victims than the elderly, and black people more than white. The British Crime Surveys suggest that about a quarter of all violent crimes are accounted for by domestic violence against women (Cabinet Office 1999). Young men are most likely to be victims of violent crime in streets and public places, probably because they venture out more and put themselves in risky situations such as football matches and gatherings outside pubs at closing time (Muncie 1999). Elderly women face a comparatively low risk, even allowing for the fact that they go out less (Mayhew et al. 1992).

Even within a comparatively compact country like Britain, there are dramatic regional variations, particularly between urban and rural areas. In 1999 the metropolitan police district of London recorded 23 robberies per 10,000 population, compared with the mostly rural Lincolnshire police district which recorded only 1 robbery per 10,000 – a twenty-fold difference (Home Office 2000).

Putting all this into perspective, it is worth pointing out that in any one year, even nowadays, over 97% of the population will *not* become a victim of street crime (excluding vehicle thefts) (van Dijk et al. 1990; Home Office 1992, 1994; Home Office RDS Directorate 2000b). Robberies (or muggings as they are popularly known – probably the most traumatic type of street crime after rape, assault and murder) still accounted for less than 2% of all recorded crimes in 1999 (Home Office RDS Directorate 2000b).

But this in itself is not enough to allay the fear of going out onto a darkened street at night.

The old adage that lightning never strikes twice in the same place does not appear to apply to the chances of being a victim of the same crime more than once. Farrell and Pease (1993) found that if you have been a victim once of burglary, you are much more likely to suffer the same crime again. Burglars are wise enough to know that, after a few weeks, you will have replaced your stolen video, TV and so on, so there will be brand new stock waiting for them if they make a return visit. For different reasons it has been found that bullying, domestic violence and racial intimidation/attacks are likely to be repeated against the same victims and, if not dealt with, will escalate in their ferocity.

## 2.5 People from minorities and particular groups

The British Crime Survey has questioned a booster sample of people from Afro-Caribbean and Asian backgrounds in order to find out whether they are disproportionately victims of crime and the extent to which there is a racial element in the offences they experience. A booster sample was necessary because the numbers picked up in a nationally representative sample were not large enough to get a good picture. (White people still constitute over 90% of the population of England and Wales, according to the census.) The key findings from this booster were that:

- Both Afro-Caribbeans and Asians tend to be more at risk than whites for many types of crime. This can be partly explained by social and demographic factors, particularly the areas in which they live – many black people have to live in inner-city areas and housing estates where crime is more prevalent. However, taking account of this, ethnic minority risks still tend to be higher. Asians in particular face a greater than average risk of becoming victims of vandalism, robbery and theft.
- Afro-Caribbeans and particularly Asians see many offences against them as being racially motivated. Being threatened and assaulted because of race is common. For Asians, evidence or suspicion of a racial element in property offences is relatively frequent.
- For offences involving property theft and damage, both Asians

and Afro-Caribbeans were slightly more likely than whites to suffer higher monetary losses.

• Asian victims are more vulnerable to victimisation by groups of strangers and suffer rather more serious victimisations. Afro-Caribbeans were more likely to know the person victimising them. Afro-Caribbeans were more likely than Asians, and much more likely than whites, to be victimised by other Afro-Caribbeans.

Lea and Young (1985: 26) wrote:

a young black male [aged 12–15] is twenty-two times more likely to have a violent crime committed against him than an elderly white woman [over 65] and seven times more likely to have something stolen from him. Thus the objective likelihood of serious crime occurring to a person is sharply focused by locality and social characteristics of a person.

In the USA, black male teenagers are the category most likely to be victims of violent street crime; in some parts of America this is the most common reason for death among black youngsters, above illness or accidents (Dryfoos 1990).

Lesbians and gay men are likely to be underrepresented as official victims of crime; they are more at risk of abuse and harassment than the heterosexual majority and in many cases will be reluctant to report an offence occurring (see, for example, Scottish Executive 2000).

Local crime surveys have also given us a better understanding of the dramatic affect that crime can have on how people go about their daily lives. For example, in Islington, London, where one of the first local crime surveys was carried out (Jones et al. 1986), a quarter of the residents said they avoided going out after dark for fear of crime, and over half of all the women surveyed were afraid to be out at night. Many subsequent local crime surveys, often carried out as part of the audits required under the British Crime and Disorder Act 1998, have revealed similar and enduring levels of self-curfew among women and people from ethnic minorities.

Local crime surveys can also be used to gauge what local people's priorities are in terms of improving community safety and it has been found that these are often out of kilter with the priorities of the police and public services. For example, people in Islington were clear about what they wanted the local police to concentrate on: robbery with violence on the street, sexual assaults on women, the use of hard drugs, burglary, drunken driving and racist attacks. They were equally clear that the police spent too much time on other kinds of crime, such as prostitution, the use of cannabis and shoplifting.

Victimisation studies have revealed some of the quirks of official statistics. In most areas domestic burglary is an offence which has a relatively high reporting rate. This is not because people who report burglaries expect the burglar to be caught or their goods returned. They report it because they need a crime number from the police in order to make an insurance claim. However, this is not a universal pattern. As insurance premiums in high crime neighbourhoods have risen, many poorer people have been unable to afford the premiums and so, when they are burgled, have nothing to gain by reporting it. Victimisation studies have shown that sometimes a falling rate of officially recorded burglary in a high crime neighbourhood can mask the reality that burglary is actually rising, but insurance policies are decreasing.

Even victimisation surveys cannot give us a truly accurate picture of the quantity and quality of crime, as they rely on respondents' memories and understanding of definitions of crime. In the case of offences which cause personal humiliation and embarrassment (such as sexual assaults and domestic violence), respondents may be reluctant to divulge information to interviewers, and sometimes the offender may be in earshot of the interview.

## 2.6   European and international comparisons

In recent years a number of international studies of comparative crime levels have been undertaken (see, for example, Barclay et al. 2001). The International Crime Victims Surveys (ICVS), coordinated from the Dutch Ministry of Justice, have attempted a standardised telephone interview technique with a sample of residents in a number of countries. Over the 12 years that the ICVS have been organised, over 200,000 people have been interviewed worldwide (van Kesteren et al. 2000). Although subject to a number of methodological weaknesses (such as varying understandings and categories of crime between different countries), the ICVS can give us a rough guide to variations in levels and types of crime between countries.

Over the last 25 years there appears to have been a general increase in crime in all European and Western countries. Although there have been plateaux where the crime rate has levelled off in some countries for a few years and occasional reductions, it is impossible to find any European country where the crime rate is now lower than it was 20 years ago. On the plus side, both official government figures and the 2000 ICVS (van Kesteren et al. 2000) suggest that crime levels have fallen slightly in many countries since the mid-1990s (after very large increases in previous years). Between 1993 and 2000 France, England and Holland had modest falls in recorded crime, along with many other Western European countries and the USA. On the other hand, over the same period recorded crime rates rose in Italy and Portugal and Eastern European countries. It may not be insignificant that the countries experiencing these recent falls in crime have more developed crime prevention strategies than those where crime continues to increase.

To some extent, the increase in crime over the last 25 years or so is substantially weighted by increases in reporting, rather than absolute increases in criminal events. Victims and witnesses may nowadays be more inclined to report crime because with more access to telephones (particularly mobile phones) it is easier to report and the public may feel more comfortable about contacting the police than they did previously. This latter point may explain why a country such as Sweden appears to have such a high crime rate – more victims in Sweden report crimes to the police than in any other European country, according to the 1996 ICVS. Conversely, France has one of the lowest reporting rates, which may be to do with the historically poor rapport between the French police and public.

A crude compilation of figures from the ICVS suggest that the highest risk countries (of those surveyed) are Australia, England and the Netherlands; average countries for crime include the USA, Canada, Denmark and France; and those with low rates of crime include Japan, Finland, Norway, Switzerland and Northern Ireland. These categories do not reveal crime *trends*; for example between 1988 and 1991 victimisation risk increased in England by 56% whereas in Belgium over the same period it only increased by 9%. Conversely between 1995 and 1999 *recorded* crime statistics for the two countries suggested that the opposite had taken place, with crime decreasing in England and Wales by 21% and increasing in Belgium by 18% (Barclay et al. 2001). In France the crime rate fell in the early 1980s, as it has in England and the Netherlands from 1993 onwards.

The ICVS suggests significant victimisation risk variations between countries according to types of crime. For example, England is the car crime capital of Europe (although Poland has a higher rate of theft *from* cars, whereas (unsurprisingly perhaps) the flat countries of Denmark, the Netherlands and the southern half of Sweden are top for bicycle theft. In the 1989 ICVS (van Dijk ct al. 1990) 2.5% of respondents said they had been robbed at some time in the previous five years. However, for those respondents from Northern Ireland the rate was 1.5%, while for the Spanish the rate was 9%. According to this survey you are three times more likely to get robbed in the USA than you are in Britain.

Self-report criminality surveys can give us yet another dimension to the crime picture. Like crime victimisation surveys, they bypass official recorded statistics and rely on people giving an honest response in return for confidentiality. An international self-report delinquency study (Junger-Tas et al. 1994) found that in most European countries 40–70% of young people admitted to delinquent behaviour in the previous 12 months.

There are many likely explanations for the absolute increase in crime in the West. Briefly, it is likely that the following factors in particular may have contributed to the dramatic increase in crime rates over the last 25 years: the huge increase in drug misuse and related offending, the profusion of portable consumer goods (including cars and their contents) and people's increased mobility, leading to a decline in traditional stable communities. These issues will be revisited in Chapters 4 and 9.

## 2.7  The impact of crime

What emerges unequivocally from victimisation studies is that the poor and most vulnerable bear the brunt of crime. It is they who are most frequently victimised, are required to pay the highest insurance premiums, can least afford security devices and whose lives are most damaged. People living in the poorest areas are also most likely to suffer repeated offences of the same kind (usually

burglary, racial attacks or domestic violence), often committed by
the same offenders (see Farrell and Pease 1993). Over the longer
term, the impact of crime on individual lives can be shattering.
Studies indicate that the life expectancy of a recently widowed
woman may be reduced significantly if she is the victim of a burglary. The offence itself may be fairly trivial, just young boys trying
their luck, but its impact may be fatal (Lea and Young 1985).

The impact of being a victim of crime will also depend on the
victim's circumstances, materially, physically and emotionally. A
reasonably well-off, middle-class male may be able to shrug off the
inconvenience of having his car broken into and his car radio and
briefcase stolen. He will almost certainly be able to claim on his
insurance. By contrast, for an older woman living on her pension
in a run-down inner-city area, having her house broken into and
her television stolen may be the last straw that tips her into trauma
and depression. Likewise, a youth may be able to live with a few
scars caused by being the loser in a bottle fight in a pub, whereas
the effect on an older person of receiving an injury, as a result of
being robbed in the street, could be devastating. These relative
impacts of crime partly explain the disparities between fear and
actual victimisation risk.

On the whole there is a remarkable symmetry between those
who commit crime and their victims. By and large, it is young
working-class white men who attack and rob young working-class
white men, and young black men who attack and rob other young
black men (see Maguire et al. 1997; Croall 1998). If we consider
property crime it is clear that, by and large, it is the poor who steal
from the poor. In a study of burglary on a housing estate in the
north of England, the majority of offenders lived within 200 yards
of their victims (Pease 1991).

## 2.8   Crimes of the powerful

Critics of victimisation studies maintain that although they tend to
fill in many of the gaps in the picture of crime, they nevertheless
reinforce the impression that crime is simply a problem generated
by lower class criminals. As Box (1981: 62) observes:

> People can report having been a victim of crime only if they
> know they have been victimised. However, in many instances of

corporate crime, white-collar crime and other forms of respectable and not so respectable crimes, persons remain totally unaware that they are victims.

Indeed, to ignore the crimes of the powerful distorts the picture dramatically. As Pearce (1973) notes, while the estimated cost of crime in the USA in the 1970s was $7 billion per annum, the cost of tax evasion by the wealthiest 1% of the population in the same period was estimated to have cost the nation over $9 billion. (For a more extensive discussion of white-collar and corporate crime, see Croall 1992 and Shover 1998.)

The crimes of the powerful set a bad example to all of us and bring many statutory institutions (including the criminal justice system) into disrepute. If you are already wealthy, you can hire the best defence lawyers and buy people's silence. So apart from the financial damage caused by white-collar and corporate crime, there is the risk that it legitimates offending: 'If the captains of industry are at it, then why don't we try a bit of it.' Crimes such as tax evasion also erode the public money that could be available to raise the quality of life in impoverished areas, traditionally the breeding grounds of petty crime.

However, we should be wary of measuring the seriousness of crime by its financial magnitude. An offence with little or no financial loss, such as an attempted burglary in an elderly person's flat or a racially motivated minor assault on an Asian woman, could precipitate the victim into a permanent state of trauma and disability. White-collar and corporate crimes require a different preventive approach to the high volume crimes that are the focus of this book. The offender/victim relationship is less clear, as are the locational/environmental issues (internet fraud or insider dealing, for example). However, the influence of personal morality and ethics can apply just as much to whether someone steals from a neighbour or a large company swindles the exchequer.

## 2.9  Targeting certain types of crime

In addition to the crime that is reported by the public, much of the crime recorded by the police is crime they have targeted. Such targeting is determined by a range of factors including complaints from the public, pressure from the media, new criminal intelligence and political pressure to improve the clear-up rate. Thus a blitz on car crime, prostitution, pornography, drug dealing or street robbery may well skew the statistics, by giving the impression that, for the duration of the blitz, the offence in question has reached epidemic proportions.

In Britain in the late 1990s, public, political and media concerns about paedophilia, rape and domestic violence meant that the police, in order to appear responsive, had to encourage victims of these heinous crimes to come forward. Special suites in police stations for victims of sexual crimes, publicity and dedicated telephone lines for victims of domestic violence and child abuse, police proactively seeking possible victims of abuse amongst former residents of children's homes; all enabled previously hidden victims to come forward and add their names to the crime statistics. Greater police sensitivity to racist and homophobic incidents means that such crimes are now more likely to find their way into the official statistics. The irony of all this is that, as the police force becomes more of an equal opportunities organisation, in terms of its sensitivity of response to all sectors of the population, it will look as though crime is getting worse in many previously under-reported categories.

Critics have claimed that the criminal statistics are essentially a police fabrication which exaggerates the involvement of the poor in crime and understates the involvement of the rich and powerful. While there may be some truth in this charge, we have to ask why, if the police are able to manipulate official statistics as easily as their critics claim, they do not manipulate their low clear-up rate (as they appear to do in some Eastern European countries).

## 2.10 The clear-up rate

An offence is said to be cleared up when an offender admits a crime or is found guilty after trial. Research suggests that this is seldom a product of Inspector Morse-style detective work, however. A proportion of the clear-up rate is accounted for by offences which an offender asks to be taken into account during his or her interrogation at the police station. The lion's share of the rest is generated by eyewitnesses who either know the culprit themselves or are able to describe a culprit who is already known to the police. The clear-up rate for different offences varies enormously. The clear-up rate for murder is high because the offender is usually a member of the victim's family or somebody the victim knows well. The offence usually arises out of domestic conflict or an argument outside a pub, and offenders usually admit the offence and often turn themselves in. Most people who murder are not experienced criminals and don't commit further offences. Bag snatching, by contrast, has a low clear-up rate. It is an offence that is committed frequently by a relatively small number of people. It occurs at great speed and, as a result, the victim can seldom identify the offender.

Crime victim surveys have revealed that less than half of all known crimes are reported to the police. Of these, only about two-thirds are officially recorded and of these only about a quarter are eventually cleared up (Lea and Young 1985; Jones et al. 1986). After all this attrition, only about one crime in thirty results in the perpetrator being cautioned or convicted and for every 200 known crimes, only one person is imprisoned (Figure 2.2).

These figures seriously call into question the value of pumping more money and resources into traditional crime control measures such as policing and deterrent sentencing. Even if police detection

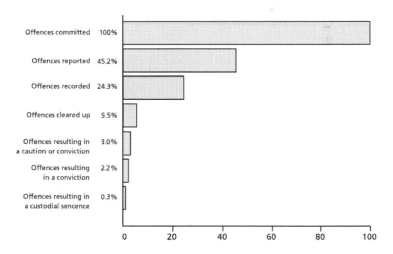

Source: Adapted, with permission, from Home Office RDS Directorate 1999b

**Figure 2.2**   Attrition within the criminal justice system

and court conviction rates improved by 100%, over 90% of offenders would still get away with their crimes. And if we doubled the number of prison places (each one costing at least £500 per prisoner per week) available in Britain, still only 1% of known offences would end up with a perpetrator behind bars.

## 2.11   Fear of crime – a problem in its own right

Fear of crime is not necessarily linked to the actual risk of victimisation. According to the ICVSs, the British are twice as worried about crime as the Swiss, but they are not twice as likely to become victims. Balvig (1987) suggests that this disparity may be partly to do with the media's coverage or neglect of crime as an issue. Through their national crime surveys, the Dutch have noted that, although crime rates have stabilised or fallen in the Netherlands over the last few years, the *fear* of crime has gone on increasing. Now they are having to tackle the important business of fear reduction, as irrational levels of fear can be seriously detrimental to people's quality of life.

As well as the sheer unpleasantness of the sensation, fear can significantly constrain people's choice of actions. For example, many people, particularly women and the elderly in run-down urban areas, live under a self-imposed night-time curfew because of fear of crime. In the 1996 BCS, one of the questions was: 'How safe do you feel walking alone in the area after dark?' Of women over the age of 60, 60% said they felt unsafe, while only 10% of men under 60 said they felt unsafe. Even in the case of fear about having your house burgled, where statistically men and women should face a similar risk, an earlier survey revealed that 27% of women were very worried, compared with only 18% for men. Feeling very worried about becoming a victim of sexual harrassment or assault affects the lives of over a quarter of all women, and for women in the 16–30 age band, 41% feel very worried about being raped, according to the BCS. Subsequent research in four inner-city areas (Leitner et al. 1993) revealed that almost half of all residents surveyed never walked out alone after dark for fear of their safety. For some Asian women living in high crime areas, all the above fears, plus the risk of racial abuse, means that they are terrified to leave their homes alone at any time.

Despite substantial variations in levels of crime between differing locations and environments, fear blankets the whole population, so that low-risk groups in low-risk areas take unnecessary precautions (Standing Conference on Crime Prevention 1989). Contradictorily, some groups such as young males put themselves at considerable risk of being victimised by frequenting volatile areas such as town centres late at night and post-football match gatherings. According to an analysis of the BCS, males aged 16–24 make up 21% of the victims of violent crime, compared with only 0.8% of females aged 65–74. Some critics have argued that low-risk groups such as elderly women are rarely victimised, simply because they hardly ever dare to venture out. The BCS analysed the fortunes of a sample of elderly women who *did* go out a lot (they nicknamed them the 'old ravers') and found that they were *still* a low-risk group. However, some people, such as those from ethnic minority groups in certain locations, have a justifiable fear based on a realistic risk of victimisation.

Ironically, young men, the category of people most at risk from violence in the street, appear to be the least fearful (although this could be ascribed to macho posturing). So we can see that tackling the problem of fear is a separate issue from preventing people becoming victims, in cases where fear and actual risk are at variance. It is not entirely clear why there should be this apparent mismatch between risk and perception, but media sensationalism, the etching into people's memories of certain appalling incidents and the threatening appearance of some urban environments may all be contributing factors. However, it may also be the case that our definition of 'risk' is inadequate, in that it only takes account of the likely *frequency* of incidents and not the potential *impact*. And so, whilst elderly people may be less frequent victims, they may judge (quite rationally) that the likely impact of any incident could have serious consequences (in terms of physical and psychological injuries), far in excess of the consequences for younger people, and that this justifies their greater caution.

This fear, justified or otherwise, can affect the functioning and viability of urban centres perceived as unsafe, and can become a self-fulfilling prophecy, as the streets are abandoned to the intoxicated and the desperate. This scenario stretches from the square outside the central library in Stockholm, to Saturday nights in central Nottingham. An audit of Nottingham's crime problems (KPMG/SNU 1990) estimated that the city centre retail and leisure services were losing £24 million of potential annual turnover as a result of 'avoidance' by people who thought the area was unsafe. As part of the Nottingham audit, a survey of 1,000 residents found that 45% of users of the city centre in the evening said that they felt unsafe. Some even avoided the city centre during the day (3% on weekdays and 7% at weekends) through fear of crime. About half said that they worried about mugging and being attacked by strangers. A survey of users of Coventry city centre (Ramsay 1989) found considerable levels of concern about personal victimisation: 63% sometimes avoided the city centre to minimise their chances of being victimised; females more so than males and older people more often than younger people.

## 2.12  The real criminals

Criminality is a normal aspect of the social structure, a permanent feature of any complex society, an ongoing social activity like the practice of medicine or police work or university teaching or stevedoring. (Mack 1964: 52)

So, who are the offenders, creating this wave of crime, fear and victimisation? There is a popular stereotype of what we think a typical criminal looks like, exemplified by the Burglar Bill character in the children's book series and the burly masked intruder portrayed in advertisements for security hardware. But if we want to get away from the stereotype and form a more accurate picture of the average criminal, we need to ask two questions. What kind of people commit crime and who, of these people, gets caught? If you ask 'who commits crime?', the answer has to be most of us, if not all of us. How many of us haven't at some time taken office stationery home or used the workplace phone for personal calls? – both strictly criminal acts, but in practice rarely leading to arrest and conviction. However, if you ask the question 'who gets caught?', you arrive at a different answer.

Most of the offences we know about are committed by young males – more than 8 in every 10 apprehended offenders are male (Graham and Bowling 1995; Muncie 1999). In fact, Home Office statistics reveal that nearly a third of all men in England and Wales have a criminal record by the time they're 30 and that's excluding motoring offences. The peak age for males caught offending is around 17, and the 10–25 age range accounts for 50% of all crime apprehensions. Of course it could be argued that it is young inexperienced males who are targeted by the police and get caught, whereas older criminals and females get away undetected. However, there is no substantial evidence to support this argument. The results of self-report offending surveys are difficult to rely on, but where they have been attempted (for example Jones 1990; Home Office RDS Directorate 2000a), they suggest that young males are widely involved in offending and the peak age may be 15. Some kinds of crime are more popular with young people – burglary, for instance, where over three-quarters of those caught are under 21. Breaking into cars and taking them without their owners' consent ('twoccing' or joy-riding) is almost exclusively a young male activity.

Offenders tend to come from poor families, where unemployment is commonplace and the parents have often been in trouble with the law themselves. They will often be having difficulties at school, keeping up with the work, being bullied or perhaps truanting and they will often start offending at a very early age – well below the age of criminal responsibility. Lastly, the typical young caught offender is proportionally more likely to live in a large urban area, rather than a small town or the country (West and Farrington 1973, 1977; West 1982).

So the average caught criminal is a young man or boy with time on his hands, perhaps because he's been excluded or is truanting from school, or is out of work. His self-esteem is low; he sees himself as a failure in conventional terms, feeling excluded from legitimate means of achieving success and status. For him crime is not a profession. It is an activity he indulges in, sometimes on the spur of the moment, when he spots an opportunity to do something exciting (or acquire something to fund his addiction), because he's got nothing better to do, or because he is under pressure to keep up with his mates' tough behaviour. There's certainly little financial reward – BCS findings suggest that a quarter of all burglaries involve no loss to the victim and a half involve losses of less than £25.

Drugs are often the bridge that carry the bored young opportunist over into more determined criminal activity, as they start stealing to support their habit. But why did they start taking drugs in the first place? Probably because they were bored and excluded, with low self-esteem and virtually no prospects for the future. In these circumstances drugs are a delightful and delirious escape into another world and level of consciousness (Gray 2002); you'd be a fool *not* to take them, especially when your mates are high on them.

## 2.13 Summing up

So we know quite a lot about crime, where it happens, who it happens to, who does it and why they do it. Better information should, on the face of it, help us to develop more effective ways of dealing with crime. That's as long as we overcome what appears to be an inherent perverseness when it comes to developing policy on the basis of the facts. After all, we've known for a long time that prisons are expensive and ineffective, so what do we do? We build more prisons and lock more people up (Stern 1998). We know that more police doesn't equal less crime (Walker 1998), so what do we do? We clamour for more police and faster response times. We know from American (Rosenbaum et al. 1998) and British (Husain 1990) research that neighbourhood watch is least likely to work where it is most needed – in high crime areas – so we make it a major plank of our national crime prevention programmes. We know that crime prevention publicity campaigns have little impact (Rosenbaum et al. 1998), yet we still spend high proportions of precious crime prevention funding on expensive media campaigns and advertisements.

> Waging 'war' is the wrong way to fight crime. The truth is, we are not facing a foreign enemy. We are up against ourselves. We need to deal with our own social institutions, our own values, our own habits and our own crime control policies. The weight loss problem offers a useful comparison. The solution does not lie in a miracle cure. Instead it involves difficult long-term changes in your own behaviour: eating less, eating less fattening food and exercising more. By the same token, we will reduce crime when we make basic changes in all of our social policies that affect families, employment and neighbourhoods. There is no quick, easy 'miracle' cure for crime. (Walker 1998: 15)

We can see from the dismal outcome of the detection, clear-up and reconviction rates that no one involved in attempts to control crime by catching criminals should feel complacent about the effectiveness of their work. In order to develop rational crime prevention policies and strategies, in addition to crime rates and prevalence data, we need to understand *why* crime occurs. In the next chapter we will look at some of the theories and research findings that suggest why some people commit offences whereas others don't. Then in Chapter 4 we will look in more detail at *where* crime occurs and what might be significant about locational variations.

# 3

# Crime, Deviance and the Individual Offender

## 3.1 Introduction

Without understanding what motivates some people to commit offences and what causes crimes to occur, we risk treating only the symptoms and thus will fail to prevent the problem occurring in the first place. If put on the spot, most people will proffer their own pet theory of what causes crime. As often as not these theories will be based on gossip, rumour and innuendo rather than careful study of research and criminological theory. Unfortunately, because crime is such an emotive topic, politicians, under pressure to curry favour with the electorate, are usually only too happy to legislate the most irrational policies for crime control.

If we want to be logical and rational, we should really base our policies and practices on the huge amount of research that has gone into the causes of crime, deviance and offending. Over the years, thousands of experts, be they philosophers, natural and social scientists, politicians, journalists or the clergy, have attempted to account for why people break the law. Their endeavours have led us up some blind alleys but have supplied some useful clues as well. This chapter introduces a number of theoretical perspectives on crime and the ways we might use them to gain a better understanding of the crime we encounter.

It is important to bear in mind that crime covers a multitude of sins so that, despite the claims of the proponents of particular theories, no one theory is going to explain all types of law breaking. Fundamentally, the causes of crime are laws declaring that certain acts or omissions are criminal. Theoretically we could eliminate

44

crime by repealing all laws. But, in democratic societies at least, laws are there to uphold the norms of acceptable behaviour. Criminal acts or omissions are perceived as unacceptable deviations from the codes of conduct to which the particular society in question has agreed (see Henry and Lanier 2001). To be more semantically accurate, therefore, we should perhaps be looking for the causes of deviance in this chapter, rather than the causes of crime. (For a more detailed discussion of the relationship between deviance and crime, see Rock and McIntosh 1973; Downes and Rock 1982.)

But before we get too lost within wheels within other wheels, let's assume, for the purposes of this discussion, that there are certain universally proscribed offences or deviant behaviours, such as theft of another person's legitimate property and violence against another person, that are at the core of crime and criminal behaviour. It is an understanding of these behaviours and the way the state has responded to them that is a key area of criminological investigation, so it is to criminology that we should initially look for underlying causal factors that will provide the foundations for developing crime prevention policies and practices.

One would assume that the people at the forefront of crime prevention policy and practice would be those who have made a career out of studying and researching the causes of crime – criminologists. Yet, with notable exceptions, most criminologists remain in the safe haven of their academic studies. The main reason for this is that there is little incentive in universities to help develop effective social policy; indeed academics are rated according to how many articles they get published in peer-reviewed journals rather than whether they have had a beneficial impact on the quality of life of the person in the street. Cynics would assert that, like so many other criminal justice-related occupations, criminologists need crime to feed off – the more crime, the richer the menu. One senior police officer and part-time academic scathingly refers to 'the dismal science of criminology which has until recently deliberately ignored the role of the individual, family and community in effective crime prevention' (Williamson 2000). This is a sad state of affairs, as the application of well-researched criminological theories to the delivery of effective crime control policies would act as a welcome counter to policies based on political dogma and populist hysteria.

What follows in this chapter is a brief overview of some of the most widely referred-to theories for explaining criminality and deviance at the individual or social group level. Another theory (or cluster of theories) suggests that environmental factors influence whether or not crime occurs. This *environmental* criminology does overlap with some of the individual/social theories covered in this chapter, but will be dealt with separately in Chapter 4. (For a more detailed discussion of the various criminological theories, see Maguire et al. 1997, Vold and Bernard 1986 and Walklate 1998.)

Criminologists and crime theorists fall into two broad schools of thought: the classical school and the positivist school. Classicism has been described as a non-theory because it is based on the notion of free will – nothing *causes* someone to offend, they just decide to. Positivism, on the other hand, assumes that an individual is not an isolated free spirit, but is in some way or another influenced, shaped or driven by external factors. These factors can be environmental, biological, sociological or psychological, as we shall see below. Within the positivist camp there is wide disagreement about which factors actually are influential. All the theories, apart from classicism, come under the positivist school of thought because they are all premised on the assumption that individual behaviour is subject to external or predisposing forces.

There have been attempts to reconcile classicist and positivist thinking under a general theory of crime (see Gottfredson and Hirschi 1990), but even the authors admit that this is a flawed enterprise. Many other criminologists have attempted to synthesise various theories or have created a new theory out of the seeds from other theories, so we end up with a patchwork of overlapping structures and categories, rather than a neat and definitive classification system (see Vold and Bernard 1986; Joyce 2001).

Nine categories of criminogenic theory are covered separately in the following sections, so that we can draw our own conclusions about their relative strengths and weaknesses in terms of informing crime control. The theories are: classicism (or rational choice), biogenetic, learning (or behaviourism), psychoanalytic, labelling, social control, social disorganisation, social strain and conflict.

## 3.2 Classicism or rational choice theory

Classicism was founded on the early notion of the rational and con-sistent application of the law as a means of circumscribing people's unacceptable desires and urges. Classicism assumes that people act rationally all the time, wishing to maximise their pleasures and min-imise their personal pain. We would all behave antisocially if we thought it would provide us with more pleasure and we could get away with it (for example helping yourself to somebody else's Mercedes sports coupé, knowing you're most unlikely to get caught). The law is drawn up and imposed as a means to constrain these criminal tendencies that are in all of us. The theory is that, without the force of the law, society would descend into anarchy.

Because we all have to coexist in society, we must enter a social contract with those around us. The rules which dictate how we should fulfill this contract are enshrined in law. Thus the job of the government is to referee these contracts and provide laws and penalties which will deter present and future wrongdoers and ensure their compliance with the law (Taylor et al. 1973). Of course some people, children and the mentally ill for example, aren't sufficiently rational to either enter, or be held to, a contract. Therefore the law also recognises the principle that in cases where offenders cannot be held fully responsible for their actions, the punishment should fit the criminal rather than the crime. Things get a bit more muddy when crimes are committed while the offender is in an irrational state of mind induced by rage or intoxi-cation. If you beat up your partner after a night out of heavy drinking and you come home to discover them with an attractive neighbour on the sofa, where does classicism stand?

Proponents of the classical approach to crime control will point out that there has been a huge increase in the temptation and absolute number of opportunities to misbehave: particularly the ease of stealing portable consumer goods such as video recorders, car radios and mobile phones either from their owners or the retailers who stock them in open-plan shops (Newman et al. 1997). The classical response to this is twofold: to make the crime more difficult to commit (opportunity reduction) and increase the certainty of apprehension and punishment (deterrence) (Cornish and Clarke 1986). We shall critically revisit these policies later in the book.

The past 20 years has seen a return to classical principles in Britain and the USA under the banner of New Right criminological thinking (Joyce 2001). The Back to Justice movement has challenged the belief that there is a link between poverty and crime, and that the provision of welfare or the administration of treatment can change criminals (Wilson 1975; Morris et al. 1980). It has stressed the essential rationality of offenders and championed their right to the due process of law and, if necessary, punishment. Its influence could be seen in government emphasis on the importance of punishment and 'zero tolerance'.

Classicism provides the theoretical underpinning to justify the criminal justice system as the principal means of controlling crime. The assumption is that if there is a sufficient threat and likelihood of apprehension and subsequent punishment for any misdemeanour we are tempted to indulge in, we will be deterred from acting illegally or antisocially. Having weighed up the potential gains and benefits against the pain, suffering and humiliation consequent to getting caught, we will make a rational choice to desist from the offensive act (Cohen and Felson 1979; Clarke and Felson 1993; Felson 1994).

It is likely that most of us, to a greater or lesser extent, will at times act or restrain from acting according to rational deliberation about the consequences. However, in the crime field, for classicism to work effectively, there has to be a certainty about apprehension and punishment if we overstep the mark. This certainty does not exist under the present criminal justice system and is unlikely to be significantly improved upon (as we saw in the last chapter).

### 3.3  Biogenetic theories

At the other end of the spectrum of theorising about crime causation lies positivism. At its most extreme, positivism draws a direct quasi-scientific line, connecting cause and effect (see Garland 1997). So, for example, in the same way as steam is caused by raising the temperature of water to 100°C, hardline positivists would claim that criminal behaviour can be caused by growing up on a council estate as the illegitimate son of single mother of low intelligence who only feeds her children with junk food.

It should be apparent from the contrast between classicism and positivism that we are in the criminological equivalent of the perennial 'nature/nurture' or 'free will versus products of our genes/environment' dichotomy. As ever the truth is likely to lie somewhere in the middle, but this hasn't stopped some purists campaigning for the merits of one extreme. Nowhere is this polarity more blatantly apparent than in the theories of biogeneticist criminologists.

This body of theory locates the drive towards criminality in the genetic or biological inheritance of the individual. At its core is a notion of behaviour as an expression of the actor's dysfunctional chemical constitution or peculiar DNA. People afflicted in this way are seen to career through the world, bound for an inevitable collision with a victim. Biogenetic man, like other animate species, behaves rather than acts and such behaviour can only be changed, it is argued, by the application of drugs, surgery or an elaborate process of reconditioning.

For Lombroso (1911), the original articulator of biogenetic theories of criminality, the delinquent was a throwback, a creature stuck at an earlier stage of development than other members of their species. In the 1950s the Gluecks ran extensive tests on groups of boys in reformatories, to ascertain whether a relationship exists between body type and criminality (Glueck and Glueck 1956). They demonstrated that a disproportionately large number of inmates were hard and round (mesomorphs) and that far fewer were soft and round (endomorphs) or fragile and thin (ectomorphs). From this data they concluded that body type had a significant bearing upon a person's criminality and that, as Lombroso had believed, criminality was genetically or biologically determined.

Critics noted that perhaps boys who looked tough were more likely to be sent to a reformatory than those who looked, for example, like scholars. They also suggested that the realities of working-class life, with its low protein diet and emphasis upon physical prowess and hard physical labour, meant that there were more short muscular boys in this traditionally arrest-prone population. Undeterred, Hans Eysenck continued with this line of enquiry and, in the 1960s, demonstrated a relationship between biological type, personality and criminality (Eysenck 1964).

Critics of biogeneticism will point out that if criminality is simply a product of the actor's biogenetic inheritance, how do we account for the massive concentration of identified criminals in the lowest reaches of the social structure, irrespective of height, weight or hat size? Self-report studies demonstrate that undetected crime is universal. Indeed Belson and Didcott (1968) indicate that the actual incidence of juvenile crime is over 90%. Are so many of us 'programmed to offend', and if we are, why do most of us grow out of it when we reach the age of 17 or 18 (Rutherford 1986)? Social disorganisation theorists have observed that the offending rates of social groups that move out of the inner city drop dramatically. If this is so, it appears that biogenetic determinism can be neutralised by upward social mobility.

This wealth/location connection may also explain why people from ethnic minorities, and particularly black people, are disproportionately involved in the criminal justice system, both as offenders and victims. Racists will argue that black people must be genetically more criminal, but this labelling increases the chances that people from ethnic minorities will be discriminated against and forced to live in poverty in the least desirable areas of our conurbations, the very areas where crime and victimisation are highest anyway. Also, given the fact that the majority of us offend but don't get caught, police targeting of any particular social or ethnic group will almost inevitably yield a substantial catch of offenders.

While crude biogenetic explanations of criminality are out of fashion today, criminologists, judges and magistrates are still prone to explaining female criminality as an effect of the menopause, premenstrual tension or impaired rationality (Heidenson 1985; Gelsthorpe and Morris 1990). It could also be argued that the disproportionately higher male involvement in crime, and particularly violence, could be explained by the stronger build and higher metabolic rate of boys and men. Males are much more likely to take risks than females (whether its overtaking on blind corners or robbing banks). Could this be an inherited biogenetic trait (evolutionary adaption for the role of hunter and territory defender) or do males merely *learn* to take more risks and beat other people up?

Finally, it could be argued that we are all genetically prone to be offensive and antisocial and that it is only through the application of effective social controls and learning that we become law-abiding and pro-social. One only has to observe the self-centred behaviour and lack of consideration of others expressed by babies and young children to realise that there could be a strong element of truth in this. Biogenetic theories could be used to reinforce the importance of personal and social education and behaviour management as a means of civilising the aggressive and selfish beast that lurks within all of us. It could also justify the use of sports and adventure activities as ways of constructively channelling aggressive and risk-taking drives, particularly amongst young males.

### 3.4 Learning theory or behaviourism

Learning theory assumes that all behaviour, criminal and non-criminal, is learned; what we do is a result of our nurture rather than our nature. Behaviour refers to any activity, mental, physical or emotional, which is observable and acquired as a result of experience. Learning theorists, or behaviourists as they are sometimes known, are not interested in speculating about events and activities which cannot be observed. (For the classic exposition of this theory, see Sutherland and Cressey 1943, and for an overview, see Nettler 1984.)

The process of learning is explained somewhat differently by different theorists. The idea of conditioning is usually associated with Pavlov and his justly famous salivating dogs. Pavlov observed that the presentation of a stimulus (dog food) caused his dogs to salivate. When the stimulus was consistently accompanied by a conditioned stimulus (a ringing bell) over a period of time, the presentation of the conditioned stimulus on its own would eventually be sufficient to cause the dogs to salivate. The dogs were then said to have learned a conditioned response. Throughout this process the dog remains an involuntary and passive subject.

Operant conditioning, by contrast, is a process in which learning takes place as a direct result of actions initiated by people themselves. Skinner's rats were confined in a cage with a lever which, when depressed, released a food pellet. Initially the rat depressed the lever by accident but eventually came to learn that there was a cause and effect relationship between depressing the lever and the arrival of the food pellet. In this scenario the rats who make the connection are not credited with having worked it out for themselves since the learning is seen to be an almost inevitable consequence of the environment in which they are placed (Skinner 1953). When we translate these ideas into the realm of human criminality, it follows that such behaviour will not have arisen as a result of a deliberate moral choice on the part of the actor but as a conditioned response to their environment. As such, attributions of blame are irrelevant.

Other learning theorists ascribe a more active role to the learner's thinking processes. Thus in Thorndyke's (1898) experiment a caged ape was confronted with a banana which was outside its cage and a stick which was inside. At first the ape could see no relationship between the two objects. When, however, the stick was placed in a line of vision between the ape and the banana, the ape was able to work out that the stick could be used as a tool to hook the banana and drag it into the cage. Such conceptual learning has been shown to be enhanced by opportunities to observe others and imitate or model oneself upon them. In this perspective, criminality is seen to be learned by exposure to models who illustrate criminal solutions to problems. The assumption that the behaviour of rats, dogs, apes and humans are essentially similar and may be changed in similar ways has exposed learning theorists to the criticism that the crucial difference between human beings and other species is their capacity to reflect upon their behaviour and make choices. On the other hand, there is no getting away from the fact that we are just another (highly evolved) species of animal (Gray 2002). Therefore we should not regard ourselves as being exempt from the learning and conditioning that all animals experience as part of their development, so that they can adapt, survive and thrive in the social and physical environment they find themselves in.

From birth onwards we all learn, whether by behavioural reinforcement or reflective experience; the crucial factor, in terms of criminality prevention, is *what* we learn. Edwin Sutherland coined the term 'differential association' to describe the process whereby delinquents learnt values and knowledge from others they associated with, which favoured criminal behaviour in preference to law-abiding behaviour (Sutherland and Cressey 1943).

Learning theory can be used to justify the importance of interventions to support parents with young children and direct play and educational work with children themselves. It can also justify mentoring and peer education schemes for older children and adolescents. All these types of intervention can help the developing young person to grow into a pro-social teenager and adult.

However, this does raise the sticky issue of what constitutes pro-social behaviour and who defines it. History is littered with cases of citizens being taught to be obedient, unquestioning conformists to norms that may or may not be acceptable from a philosophical and moral point of view.

### 3.5 Psychoanalytic theory

Psychoanalytic theory tends to be synonymous with Freudian theory, although other psychoanalysts, most notably Alfred Adler, may offer more valuable insights into the origins of criminality. Freud believed that the development of a healthy civilisation and a healthy individual were both dependent upon the successful reso-lution of the conflict between people's instinctual drives (their id or unconsciousness) and the demands of the social world. For Freud, the arbiter between these two sets of demands is the con-scious ego. In his view the development of a healthy ego is depen-dent upon positive formative experiences in the first five years of life. If these experiences are negative and abusive, Freud suggested that psychological illness may follow, which could be expressed in deviant or criminal behaviour (see Toch 1979).

The remedy Freud offers for such illness is psychoanalysis. The aim of psychoanalysis is to discover experiences which haunt the patient's memory but are so painful that they have been repressed into the unconscious. The practical problem is what to do with these revelations of a messed up early life once they have been drawn out, which may explain why many people stay in analysis almost indefinitely. Psychoanalytic theories of criminal motivation tend to regard criminal behaviour as a symptom, or the acting out, of unresolved conflicts or traumas rather than freely chosen behav-iour, and thus lie within the positivist school of theory.

Bowlby (1946) locates the need to steal from others as an attempt on the part of boys who experienced maternal deprivation to symbolically reappropriate their mothers' care and sustenance. Subsequent commentators have suggested that boys from father-less families who steal cars are, in fact, engaged in a form of com-pulsive masculinity as an overcompensation for their lack of an immediate father figure.

Alfred Adler (1931) was the definer of the inferiority complex. He suggested that the need to overcompensate for feelings of inferiority could lead some to act in attention-seeking ways that are also illegal. The person with an inferiority complex may also strive to hurt back the person or system that has made them feel inferior.

A major problem with psychoanalytic explanations of crime is that they fail to account for why similarly neurotic or traumatised people do not inevitably turn to crime, and why so few women, who are, presumably, equally vulnerable to early trauma and disorders, are involved in crime. Nevertheless, it must be said that the formative years of many of the people on the caseloads of probation officers or in prisons were disrupted or traumatic and their behaviour cannot easily be explained in terms of rational choice.

Beyond this, if crime is simply a symptom of individual pathology, we can only account for the significant differences in levels and patterns of crime between nations in terms of the differential capacities of parents of different nationalities to rear their children effectively. And indeed there may be a germ of truth here. Is it significant that Japan, which has low crime rates, has a very tight and rigorous nuclear and extended family system, which ensures that children are given intense, enduring, consistent and affectionate upbringings? The downside for many libertarian westerners is that this can lead to a suffocating pressure to conform. So perhaps we can overcome the problem of psychoanalysis being unable to undo the consequences of early childhood disturbances by doing our best to prevent the developmental problems occurring in the first place. And indeed this is what Adler (1931: 196) suggested:

> If we could train our children to the right degree of co-operation and if we could develop their social interest, the number of criminals would drop very considerably and the effects would be seen in the near future. These children could not be incited or lured into crime . . . Independent, forward-looking, optimistic and well developed children are a help and comfort to their parents . . . At the same time as we influence the children we should also concentrate on influencing parents and teachers.

This quote makes an interesting link to learning theory; it could be claimed that psychological disturbances could, in many cases, be ascribed to bad learning experiences in early childhood. Therefore psychoanalytic theory could be described as a particular version of learning theory. Bowlby (1953) stressed the crucial importance of ensuring that young children are given a healthy, happy, loving and secure start to their lives in order to prevent problems in the future. Thus psychoanalytic theory can be used to justify investment in parenting support interventions, early years education and family therapy as valid methods for preventing future criminality.

### 3.6 Labelling theory

Labelling theorists locate the stigmatisation associated with the imposition of a deviant label, a court appearance for example, as the process which spoils identity and projects the person so labelled into a deviant career (Goffman 1961; Becker 1963; Cicourel 1968). Thus labelled, the deviant is forced to associate with those who are similarly stigmatised and their predicament is compounded by increased surveillance from the police, probation officers or psychiatrists, serving to amplify their deviance by reinforcing the label and closing off non-deviant options (Young 1971).

There are a number of problems with labelling theory. While describing the processes whereby offenders, once apprehended, are inducted into a deviant career, it fails to explain why they might commit offences in the first place. It explains secondary not primary deviance. It also exaggerates the impact of labelling. It is simply not true that everybody who appears in court, for example, is inducted into a deviant career; the majority of people who appear in court only do so once. It also fails to address those factors in the social structure and in the lives of individuals that might push some people into a life of crime more readily than others. There is also a dubious implication at the heart of this perspective that crime would cease to be a problem if state officials stopped reacting to it!

This said, prison staff and probation officers often encounter people to whom a deviant label has been successfully applied and who are, as a consequence, unable to break out of a self-defeating pattern of behaviour which can often involve frequent institutionalisation. In such cases the deviant label 'con', 'villain', 'nutter' and so on has become, in Goffman's term, their master role. Similar labelling can occur in the home and at school when impressionable youngsters can feel the sting of being referred to as the 'bad apple' in the family or the class troublemaker. In line with learning theory, if these labels are applied unyieldingly by careless adults, the child may permanently adopt the role that has been allocated to him or her. Adults who think they can reform erring youngsters by scapegoating risk the backlash of self-fulfilling prophecies. The child who has been told that he or she is a liar (when he or she was actually trying to tell the truth) may decide that there is no point in being truthful. If you're told you're no good, you might as well make the best of a bad job.

Labelling is particularly apparent in the case of negative racial stereotyping. One of the reasons that black people are disproportionately represented in the criminal justice system may be that they are perceived (labelled) by the police as more likely to be offending. Famous black pop, film and football stars frequently mention in media interviews that they have been stopped and questioned by the police who cannot believe that they have acquired their Porsche or Ferrari legitimately.

In terms of crime prevention practice, labelling theory suggests that we should not make self-fulfilling prophecies by stigmatising and subsequently excluding individuals or whole neighbourhood populations on the basis of one-off or piecemeal transgressions. People should not be stereotyped on the basis of their race, class or social circumstances. We need to remind ourselves that every individual and community is different and capable of change and that the best way to achieve change for the better is often to invest trust and responsibility in those who might otherwise be written off.

### 3.7  Social control theory

Social control is what institutions of the state and religions apply to keep the masses docile and obedient. Social control can be mostly benign (Buddhism, the Danish government) or mostly repressive (Stalinism, McCarthyism, the Spanish Inquisition). Formal social control is not so necessary when informal social controls are active (as, for example, in Japan where self-control and social responsibility are learnt and internalised during childhood development). Some commentators claim that crime is such a problem in the West these days because the decline in religion-based morality and the loosening of public and private discipline (the permissive society) have led to a moral vacuum where people will do anything they can get away with. This has been compounded by the ethics of free-market capitalism which appear to encourage greed, material achievement by any means possible (see Reiman 1995) and subsequent increases in income inequality and social exclusion. The socially excluded then feel that they are beyond normal social controls and have nothing to lose by offending. Indeed they may even regard certain types of misdemeanour (vandalism, joy-riding) as a justifiable response to their exclusion from the rewards of mainstream society.

Box (1983) argues that were it not for a combination of moral constraints (learnt) upon our behaviour and the fear of getting caught (rational choice), most of us would break the law far more often. Conformity, he argues, is ensured by moral standards and external surveillance. Thus the question of why people desist from crime is as important to control theorists as the question of why some people engage in it. Control theorists identify the loosening or neutralisation of moral and normative constraints as the factor which allows the actor to drift towards a subculture of delinquency which is the flip side of the conventional moral order.

Matza (1964) notes that for 23 hours a day, six days a week, the delinquent leads a completely conventional, law-abiding life. So how is it that so many people manage to neutralise these moral constraints and commit criminal acts? Lower class young men, says Matza, live a great deal of their lives feeling that they are acted upon; feeling that things happen to them, not that they make things happen. This, he says, makes them fatalistic and this sometimes becomes hard for them to bear. They want to restore a mood of humanism by taking control of events, but they are held to the conventional moral order by the normative pressures of social control. It is, at this point, Matza argues, that they engage in a process of 'sounding' in which they devise reasons why the criminal activity with which they are flirting is permissable – 'They're probably insured', 'They can afford it', 'They probably stole it themselves'. In this way they neutralise the conventional moral bind and move into a state which Matza describes as 'drift', a state somewhere between conformity and illegality; in a state of readiness to commit themselves to the criminal opportunity which next presents itself.

Whereas most of the perspectives presented here view the criminal as radically different from the law-abiding citizen, social control theory believes that the terms 'criminal' and 'law-abiding', when applied to people, refer to moments in their lives rather than enduring characteristics. The problem with social control theories is that they fail to account for the fact that in the real world a small minority of people are persistently involved in serious, and sometimes highly dangerous, crime and the overwhelming majority of people are not. The fact that we may all misappropriate the firm's paper clips gets us nowhere nearer to an understanding of the origins of persistent child molestation, rape or aggravated burglary. It seems evident that something more than a temporary loosening of the moral bind is at work in these cases.

However, social control theory may go some way to explaining why there has been such a huge rise in criminal activity in Eastern Europe since the collapse of communism. Whatever else they may or may not have achieved, there can be no doubt that communist administrations kept a pretty tight reign on their citizens. At the other end of the political spectrum, it may be no coincidence that the USA (the land of the free), where personal freedom from oppressive governance extends to the right to carry loaded firearms in your handbag, has one of the highest violent crime rates in the West. This would appear to suggest that crime is the price we pay for fewer politically imposed social controls.

Social control theories offer us a useful insight into the nature of rules and moral codes, but offer, at best, a partial account of deviant motivation. In terms of crime prevention, social control theory suggests that we need rules to abide by, whether these are national laws, school rules or personal codes of conduct, so that we are clear about the boundaries between acceptable and unacceptable behaviour. Crucially though, rules, regulations and laws must be understood by and acceptable to the majority, if not all, of those they affect. Ideally, social control is a consensual activity, defined, mandated and informally enforced by citizens going about their everyday business (*self*-control – see Gottfredson and Hirschi 1990). Social control theory can thus be used to justify community development, social cohesion strategies and neighbourhood agreements as having crime prevention pay-offs. However, if social control measures are imposed by threat or force on an unwilling populace, there is a danger that resistance, subversive criminality and, ultimately, violence will emerge.

## 3.8 Social disorganisation theory

Social disorganisation theory could be viewed as a micro-level variant of social control theory; it considers the criminogenic implications of loosened geographical and cultural ties. This theory arose out of the research of a group of academics known as the Chicago School (see Park 1936). They saw the zone of transition as a place peopled by groups that were losing the social norms of their culture of origin but had yet to take on those of their new culture. Thus norms of behaviour were in a state of flux and this resulted in social disorganisation.

Their study of different rates of crime in different zones of Chicago set the foundations for environmental criminology and subsequent theories about crime and the environment. However, the concept of social disorganisation does not have to be a geographically rooted phenomenon; it can also be a result of familial, cultural or religious changes. The combination of loosening extended family networks, cultural rejection and religious abandonment have undoubtedly led to a new generation of people from all ethnic groups (including the majority white ethnic grouping) feeling isolated and alienated from mainstream social organisations and structures, which may make them feel less concerned about contravening laws which have been set up to protect the interests of the society and networks from which they have been excluded. It is significant that the two ethnic groups in Britain that are proportionately least likely to feature in offender statistics (people of Asian Indian or Chinese descent) are the two groups who have clung most tightly to their cultural, religious and familial antecedents. However, in many countries, there are new generations of people born in those countries who are floundering in a kind of no-man's-land somewhere between their parents' original ethnic mores and the values of the dominant white culture that has not fully accepted them. Young people in France whose parents originated in North Africa, young people of Pakistani descent in the UK and young Turks in Germany are all examples of groups likely to be suffering the consequences of social disorganisation (compounded by the negative effects of labelling).

Social disorganisation weakens the possibility for informal social control (Bursik and Grasmik 1993; Hirschfield and Bowers 1997) and the risk is that this vacuum will be filled by either unfettered lawbreaking or repressive state intervention (usually by the police). Matza (1969) suggests that there is no such thing as social disorganisation, only sociologists who can't figure out how a given form of social organisation actually works. It is also possible that as members of a low status social group, residents of certain ethnic groups or certain locations got more attention from the police and, as such, were prone to labelling by them.

In terms of crime prevention policy and practice, this theory supports the importance of facilitating stable, integrated and socially cohesive communities. This can be achieved through planning policy (for example urban villages), housing development and management (for example mixed tenure, local lettings), resident control (for example cooperatives, neighbourhood panels) and community development activities that build up *social capital* (Putnam 1995, see p. 76 for an explanation of social capital) in particular localities.

### 3.9   Social strain theory

Social strain occurs when you are told that certain material possessions and conditions are required to achieve happiness and high status, yet you are denied the legitimate means to acquire them. The popular media and in particular the advertising industry put huge social strain on people with low incomes. Turn on your TV in your crumbling council flat and you will doubtless see many happy, shiny, successful people living in the lap of luxury, particularly if you watch the adverts. In America, and to varying degrees in other countries, the prevailing notion is that anyone can be rich, successful and, by implication, happy, if they put their minds to it and work hard. In a free enterprise democracy, it is claimed that there are no barriers to anyone becoming president of a profitable company or indeed president of the United States. This is known as 'the American dream'.

Based on the earlier work of Robert Merton (1968), Messner and Rosenfeld (1997) argue that in the USA the fantasy of an open society, the American dream, masks the reality of a lack of access to legitimate opportunity for the poorest. They argue that 'The criminogenic tendencies of the American Dream derive from its exaggerated emphasis on monetary success' (Messner and Rosenfeld 1997). In such a situation, argue Cloward and Ohlin (1960), people trapped at the bottom of the social structure, who are encouraged to achieve socially valued material goals but denied legitimate opportunities to do so, will experience strain. Their response to this strain will be to form subcultural groupings in which solutions to the problem of status frustration can be developed. These solutions can take a variety of forms, but for disaffected youths they tend to coalesce around property and vehicle crime, if a sufficiently organised criminal infrastructure exists, violent gang rivalry if it does not, or a retreat into drink or drugs. Strain theories underwent a revival in the wake of the British inner-city disturbances of 1981 since it seemed clear that the young black and white participants in these events were exactly the kinds of people that Cloward and Ohlin had been talking about 20 years before (Lea and Young 1985).

Given that so many young people are the subjects of oppression, status frustration and social strain, how is it that they aren't all persistently criminal, violent or retreatist? As Matza (1964) has pointed out, while these young people may possibly drift in and out of crime depending upon how they are feeling about their predicament at any given time, they are not wedded to a delinquent subculture in the way that Cloward and Ohlin suggest. Social strain is tied to economic inequality and the prevailing social values. Nations and cultures that equate success and happiness with material wealth and conspicuous consumption, yet simultaneously drive a deepening chasm between rich and poor, inevitably run risks. Some members of the disaffected poor will use any means possible to bridge that chasm, leading to conflict (see Reiman 1995).

An interesting extension of social strain theory, although with shades of learning and psychoanalytic theory too, is the notion of delinquency as fashion. The idea is that young people in particular make certain lifestyle choices to fit in with prevailing fashions and subcultures with which they wish to be identified. In many circumstances the fashionable thing has been for a youth to join a gang. But fashions change over time and it has been suggested that delinquent gangs may no longer be seen as 'cool' or fashionable (Gladwell 2001). Tough guys, such as 'gangsta rappers', who took risks were, for many years, the high status role models in their neighbourhoods. But some young people have seen the long-term damage this has inflicted on their elder siblings (drug addiction, injury and incarceration) and in the USA, at least, there is anecdotal evidence to suggest that crime is no longer as cool as it used to be.

Social strain theory has implications for crime control policy. Consequent to this theory, anything that reduces inequalities of opportunity, and enables all people to acquire their desired status by legitimate means, should reduce the overall amount of criminal behaviour. Thus, inclusive education, training and employment policies as well as income redistribution programmes should reduce the amount of social strain. Equally, giving people from disadvantaged backgrounds the opportunity to achieve legitimate status (through systems which promote cooperatives, peer education and community leadership) should prevent many of them from seeking status through antisocial means. At a broader policy level, we could also perhaps benefit from a reappraisal of the widely promoted assumption that happiness is principally achieved through the single-minded accumulation of wealth and material goods. We tend to point an accusing finger at the media (for example *Who wants to be a Millionaire*, *Hello* magazine) and particularly the advertising industry for encouraging greed and envy, but (hopefully) these are not the only ways that we learn about life choices and aspirations. Education and sociocultural interactions should at least be able to counterbalance the propaganda of those who want to sell things to a gullible population.

### 3.10   Conflict theory

Conflict theory is rooted in Marxist thinking and may therefore, at first sight, appear to be rather dated. After all aren't we all capitalists now? Well most of us may be, but in our struggle to buy up shares in Rio Tinto and a holiday villa in Spain, we've left behind a significant minority, formerly labelled the 'underclass' but more recently christened the 'socially excluded'. It is no coincidence that the socially excluded are disproportionately involved in crime; after all they've got nothing to lose but their claims (for state benefits).

Conflict theorists maintain that, in advanced capitalist societies, there is an inevitable conflict between the owners of capital and the state, on the one hand, and those who are at the mercy of the capricious labour market on the other (Taylor et al. 1973; Platt and Takagi 1981). The criminal justice system, they argue, represents the repressive arm of state power which acts in the interests of the ruling class (Mathiesen 1974). Crime perpetrated by working-class people may be, on the one hand, a form of resistance to oppression and, on the other, particularly if it is committed against other working-class people, a confusion about who is responsible for their plight.

This analysis led to some fruitful work. Stuart Hall and his colleagues (1978) explored the origins and political function of the mugging panics that periodically spread through the UK. Taylor and Taylor (1971) also utilised a class analysis in locating football hooliganism as a product of the hijacking of the game by big business. In a similar vein, John Clarke (1976) located the emergence of skinheads as an attempt by groups of dispossessed working-class young people to resuscitate symbolically a real working-class community which was eroded by economic recession.

Paul Gilroy (1982) argued that the criminalisation of black young people as a result of unwarranted intensive policing and prosecution must ultimately be explained in terms of the need of a state in crisis to transform economic problems into racial conflict, thus displacing the problem and dividing the working class. Lea and Young (1985, 1993) enjoin conflict theorists to abandon their left idealism, which they define as an engagement with the world as it ought to be, in favour of a left realism which engages with the world as it is, however politically inconvenient that may be (Matthews and Young 1986, 1991). Left realism is in part a rejoinder to a group of highly influential American right-wing commentators of whom James Wilson (1975) is the best known. Wilson noted that those most likely to be victimised by crime were the poorest and most defenceless members of society. Because of this, these people, whom socialist parties had traditionally viewed as their natural constituency, had the biggest investment in the election of a party which took crime itself, rather than the behaviour of the agents of the criminal justice system, seriously. It is for this reason (vote catching) that law and order has become such a political football.

Conflict theory would imply that expressive crime (such as vandalism, stealing and burning cars, looting of shops, riots and so on) could be reduced if government and governance (both at the national and local level) was seen to be aimed at the interests of all the people rather than the cronies of those in power. Corrupt governments and public administrations should not expect their constituents and service users to be paradigms of virtue. The riots and violent demonstrations that periodically erupt in the poorer areas of Britain, France and the USA are effectively, if not explicitly articulated as such, a group expression of a sense of injustice and desperation against the state and its policy impacts, even though many try to dismiss them as a bunch of hooligans getting out of control (Beaud and Pialoux 2001).

## 3.11    Feminist criminology

Feminist criminology does not give us a new theory of crime but it does give us a new *perspective*. In the 1970s and 80s feminist criminology averred that women and children were far more prone to fear and criminal victimisation than men and that, contrary to popular opinion, for many women home was a very dangerous place. Indeed, had it not been for the research undertaken within feminist criminology, it is unlikely that any of the following would have assumed the importance they did in the 1980s: investigations into sexual and physical abuse of children, police responses to the survivors of rape and sexual assault and sexual harassment in the workplace (Gelsthorpe and Morris 1990).

Beyond this rediscovery of the victim and the exploration of the ways in which female crime is pathologised by both criminologists and agents of the justice and penal systems, feminist criminology asked a central, but previously unasked, criminological question. Why do women seem to commit so few crimes, appear in court and enter prison much less often than men? Why, if they are subject to social strain, do they not form delinquent subcultures or drift into crime when norms are weakened or surveillance reduced? Why do they not learn criminal responses to criminogenic stimuli (Heidenson 1985; Gelsthorpe and Morris 1990)?

The answer, asserted by many, is that girls and boys are socialised differently, encouraged to express, or not express, anger, frustration and disappointment differently and rewarded or not rewarded for sallying forth to take what they want from the world. What emerged from this analysis was that gender socialisation was a key variable in many of the theoretical explanations of crime discussed in this chapter. Indeed, in most of them, the explanation only works if one is not a woman. However, this last point hints at the biogenetic differences between men and women. Could it be that, because males are biogenetically larger, stronger and with higher metabolic rates than females, they are more prone to take risks, use force to achieve their ends and more easily resort to agressive behaviour? As ever, in the nature/nurture debate, it is likely that genetic predispositions and learnt behaviour are both influential factors in our make-up. But it is important to note that learning can override biology. As Nye said in 1958:

> The human infant has no sense of 'right' dress, safe driving speeds, moral sex behaviour, private property or any other norms of society, whether custom or law. Conformity, not deviation, must be *learned*.

### 3.12 Levels of explanation

There are, of course, conflicts between these theoretical perspectives. Freudians who contend that 'it's all in the mind' will never be able to find a point of accommodation with learning theorists who dispute the very existence of an entity called 'mind'. Similarly, classicists who celebrate the possibility of human autonomy cannot compromise with the determinist strain theories that appear to regard human intentionality as an illusion. Yet to see these theoretical schools simply as conflicting explanations of the same thing is an oversimplification. They do not merely give different answers to the same question, rather they attempt to answer different questions, directed at different levels of the phenomenon of criminality and thus the explanations they offer may, in fact, be complementary. So an accumulation of predisposing factors and influences may precipitate an individual into criminality, as the pastiche below indicates.

**How to be a criminal**

Criminals are made not born (although being born male gives you the edge), but it helps if you start preparing yourself as early as possible. A good start is to make sure that one, or preferably both, of your parents has a criminal record. In this case you can immerse yourself in deviance as you grow up, perhaps meet other criminal associates and experience the disruption of absent parents, while they are incarcerated. If your parents aren't fully fledged criminals, it would be a good idea if they had addictions, especially alcoholism. This will ensure that you experience irrational behaviour and violence at regular but inconsistent intervals. If your parents make it clear that they don't love you and generally mistreat you, so much the better – this will toughen you up and get you off to a bad start at school. A disrupted family life where your primary carers fluctuate (for example a sequence of 'stepfathers', various relatives looking after you or being fostered by frequently changing families) is excellent for toughening you up and giving you low self-esteem (it seems like nobody wants you). Inconsistent discipline is best of all – not knowing which way your parents or guardians will react really messes up your psyche.

A bad start at school is helpful in preparing you for future delinquency – it means you will be picked on by teachers and ostracised by your peers. If you have difficulty learning for whatever reasons (be they a learning disability, having difficulty concentrating because of the distress at home or even because you are too bright for your cohort), your status as a 'problem' will blossom and this will ensure that you do not get sucked into the mainstream system that produces law-abiding citizens. Once you have become slightly deviant at primary school, it is much easier to amplify your outsider status as you move into secondary education.

At school make sure you get in with the bad crowd. Seek out fellow outsiders who get their status from being tough and difficult. If you get bullied, look upon this as an advantage because it means you can learn how to bully others in turn. Hopefully, your parents will not be bothered about where you are or what you do, so you will be able to spend a lot of time out on the streets getting bored and staying out late. This will give you the opportunity to try your hand at small bits of vandalism, antisocial behaviour and petty crime, such as stealing sweets from newsagents. The earlier you start offending, the higher the chances that you will become a successful recidivist. You can then gradually get into more serious offending, but don't do this too rapidly as it may attract unwanted attention from the police. If you have been allocated a social worker or education welfare officer because of your behavioural difficulties, don't worry – they will mostly leave you alone so that they can get on with all the reports and performance indicator forms they have to complete.

As part of your criminal benefits package, it is worth considering drug addiction. Heroin is the preferred drug of mature offenders – it is great for blotting out the awfulness of life on the margins and means you will have to keep your hand in daily at stealing, in order to fund your habit. If you really want to live dangerously, try crack cocaine or a cocktail of any drugs you can lay your hands on.

For serious careers advice, your best bet is to get yourself admitted into a Young Offenders Institution (YOI), where you will meet lots of more experienced offenders who can offer numerous tips about how to make your crimes more serious. YOIs have a very good graduate record, with about two-thirds of all former inmates being reconvicted within a year, so you can be confident of a substantial career ahead.

To get into a YOI, you will need to have been caught for an offence, so you may have to be quite blatant in order to get arrested. This is easier if you have experience of provoking the negative attention of authority figures, such as parents, teachers and youth workers. Having spent time in care (either in an institution or through fostering) substantially increases your chances of successfully graduating into a delinquent career.

If you are able to, consider moving to a run-down housing estate on the edge of a big city (although chances are, you will already be living in one). You will meet other like-minded souls and there will be plenty of opportunities to commit crimes without being challenged. The chances are that physical security will be poor and the design and layout of the neighbourhood will offer plenty of opportunities to steal from or mug your neighbours.

Fortunately penal institutions do not try too hard to prepare you for a normal life after you are released, and there is very little aftercare follow-through which might put pressure on you to find a boringly legal occupation and shackle you with your own accommodation. You will also be pleased to know that the various public service agencies, who you may have had a brush with, are unlikely to talk with each other about your individual case, so it is quite easy to play them off against each other and get them off your back. They're also so understaffed that if you ignore them they'll go away. This is particularly worth remembering if you are unfortunate enough to be put on probation or parole.

A word of caution – when you envisage a lifetime of crime, don't raise your expectations too high. Admittedly some criminals lead charmed lives of untold wealth in villas on the Costa Brava, but most villains lead unrewarding lives of poverty, boredom and low self-esteem. Furthermore, as a card-carrying criminal you will be reviled by the moral majority, and you will rarely be forgiven or given the opportunity to go straight (even assuming you wanted to).

## 3.13   Why aren't we all criminals?

In the 1960s a 17-year-old youth was walking up Haverstock Hill in north London when he spotted a £1 note lying on the pavement. He immediately picked it up and handed it in at the nearest police station. Allowing for inflation, many, but not all, people would do the same nowadays if they found a £10 pound note in the street, particularly if it was in an identifiable envelope or purse. Given all the possible pressures (described above) to behave deviantly and dishonestly, how come this teenage male (a member of the highest offender risk group) still acted in a law-abiding manner? In these days of pervasive crime, we tend to assume that our only protection from total lawlessness is the deterrent effect of an ever harsher criminal justice system that promises tougher sentences and zero-tolerant police officers. Yet a large number of people, as with the aforementioned youth, appear to be innately law-abiding.

It is shocking that, according to Home Office statistics, one-third of all males will have a criminal record by the age of 30. Yet this still means that two-thirds of males and the majority of females will have no criminal record. We tend to put a vast amount of effort into trying to understand the motives and do battle with the minority of people who do commit crimes. We rarely try to understand the motives of the majority who do *not* commit crimes, with a view to figuring out how to nurture and facilitate such pro-social behaviour. One analytical model might consist of putting law-abiding people into two crude categories that we could call the self-regulators and the rational choosers. The self-regulators are like our youth who hands in money at the police station – they want to do right and will not offend because it is morally wrong. Braithwaite (1989, 1998) describes such people as 'self-sanctioning with pangs of conscience'. By contrast, the rational choosers accord to rational choice theory: they are people who behave in a manner that maximises their pleasure and minimises their pain. These are the people who would pocket a found £10 note if they were reasonably confident that there was no chance they would be caught and prosecuted for theft. Their conscience would not be pricked by the internal guilt that would restrain the self-righteous.

There is a third crude category of the population: the outlaws. These are the minority of people who break the law regardless of the deterrence of possible capture and harsh punishment – recidivists and chronic addicts among them (see Bennett and Wright 1984). The three responses to the temptation to offend can thus be summarised as:

1. *The self-regulator:* 'I abide by the law of the land because it's wrong to break the law. I don't want to cause any distress or suffering. My conscience restrains me from the temptation to offend.'
2. *The rational chooser:* 'I usually abide by the law because I don't want to get a criminal record. I have too much to lose if I got caught and it would be humiliating. I sometimes break the law if I am certain I can get away with it.'
3. *The outlaw:* 'I break the law because I'm a criminal. I'll get arrested sooner or later, so I might as well carry on offending in the meantime. What have I got to lose? I've got no hope of making it in the conventional system.'

It is important (and crucial in terms of policy) to note that these categories, as applied to individuals, are permeable and interchangeable over time and according to context. Yet so much crime control policy assumes that one's behaviour is fixed, with the result that we hear slogans such as 'beating the criminal', as though criminals were a separate species of animal. In reality, outlaws at 16 could quite feasibly become self-righteous pillars of society, by the age of 30, if they got the right breaks and weren't stereotyped. Equally, people who behave outlandishly in one context (at a football match, for example) could be exemplars of propriety at their grandparents' silver wedding anniversary.

Current crime control policy is aimed almost exclusively at deterring the rational choosers, on the assumption that this is the only way to staunch the floodgates of criminality supposedly inherent in us all. With regard to the outlaws, the criminal justice system incarcerates the few it catches, on the basis that as they are and forever will be criminals, they must be kept out of circulation as the only means of preventing them reoffending. We spend billions of pounds annually maximising the pain potential and minimising the pleasure potential of crime, as our sole defence. We think we can control crime almost exclusively through deterrence and incapacitation. This undoubtedly curbs the behaviour of a significant quantity of the population, but has no effect on the majority of outlaws who don't get arrested and is of total irrelevance to the self-regulators. Quite apart from the fact that this approach only hits part of the target, it gives a very demeaning message to all of us: that we are all incapable of behaving *ourselves*.

There is the old platitude that law-abiding (self-regulating) people have nothing to fear when they see themselves being tracked by CCTV cameras in the street, followed by uniformed security staff around the aisles of supermarkets, frisked by bouncers at city centre pubs and curtain-twitched by neighbourhood watch coordinators, but for many (myself included) it is unsettling and occasionally initimidating. This does not imply that we should abandon all measures aimed at reducing the opportunities for crime, increasing the likelihood of apprehension and guaranteeing just sentencing. But it is problematic and ultimately fruitless to think we can reduce crime merely by applying these measures with more vigour, ubiquity and harshness (Currie 1998). More of the same, only harder, is like hammering a nail that has already sunk into the wood.

In addition to deterrence and apprehension, we need to think about how we deal with the outlaws (give them something to lose? intensive rehabilitation programmes if they are caught, rather than just locking them up?). And most importantly of all, we need to think about how we can increase the numbers of the self-regulating group – the people who police themselves (parenting guidance? child support networks? early personal and social education?). Braithwaite suggests that conscience-building, in which people police themselves, can be achieved through social movements that highlight the shamefulness of deviant acts such as domestic violence, fraud or drink-driving, so that social disapproval leads to its internalisation through conscience (Braithwaite 1998). Just think how much money and wasted effort (not to mention wasted lives) we could save if the majority of people returned £10 notes to their rightful owners because *it would be wrong not to do so.*

Finally, it is important to point out that citizens will be more inclined to *do the right thing* if our social, economic and political system is perceived as fair and just. Corrupt governments and agents of the state, dishonest politicians and divisive policies are much more likely to prompt the citizenry to do crime if they can get away with it and, in many cases, to become righteous outlaws.

## 3.14  Summing up

The theories outlined here offer a range of perspectives from which to view crime and deviance. They are not prescriptions but attempts to understand a complex phenomenon. What they suggest is that, if we are to reduce the problems of crime and disorder, we must engage simultaneously with the individual and their experience, the culture of the social group of which they are a part, the position of that group in the social and political structure, and the laws, rules and values of the society we live in (Figure 3.1).

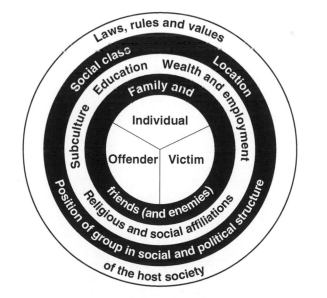

**Figure 3.1**   The individual's position within broader spheres of influence

Unfortunately, this multicausal understanding of crime does not curry much favour with the majority of politicians who in turn feel accountable to the views of the people who elect them. Most of these views are based on emotional responses to the suffering caused by crime rather than a cool rationality based on proven criminological theories. As Vold and Bernard (1986: 356) note:

> People adhere to theories of crime because those theories are consistent with preferred crime policies. Adherence to the theory then determines the nature of empirical research, which is designed to discover facts to support the preferred theory and discredit competing theories.

Brigitte Koch, in her study of crime control developments in Britain through the 1980s and 90s, comments that crime prevention policy has not necessarily been based on research findings, but rather on personal convictions (Koch 1998). Thus we have a policy approach which is exactly the reverse of rational scientific method and may be the reason why we have, so far, been remarkably ineffective in controlling and preventing crime.

# 4

# Crime and the Environment

Space is the stage on which man's behaviour unfolds. Space provides the occasions for motives – the opportunities, temptations and pressures. Space conditions human relationships, brings people together and separates them. Space undergirds social climate, sets limits, inspires, beckons, frustrates, isolates, crowds, intrudes, liberates. (Toch 1980: xi)

**Plate 4.1**   Child's play, South Wales

## 4.1   Introduction

Figure 3.1 illustrated how the condition of the individual, whether offender or victim, can be understood as being within a wider social, political, cultural and economic context. There is another set of circles of influence that surround and influence individual circumstances; this set recognises the spatial and environmental context within which we all exist:

- the nature of the buildings in which we live, work, play or study
- that building's relationship to its surrounding spaces and location in the neighbourhood
- the neighbourhood's relationship to the rest of the town or countryside
- the location of the region and nation in which we live.

The two sets of circles are complementary, overlapping and interactive and, ideally, would be better illustrated as axes of a three-dimensional sphere. This chapter will address this second axis – the environmental one.

The experiences and actions of the individual are generally mediated by his or her immediate environment, but the condition of that environment is, in turn, affected by broader local, regional, national and global influences. However, unlike the outward journeying ripples generated by a stone being thrown into the water, these environmental ripples converge on the individual, but are filtered through the various rings of influence.

It makes sense to look for the causes of crime by studying environmental circumstances as well as the individual proclivities, discussed in the last chapter. After all, nearly all crimes occur in a place, so it may be worth trying to find out what it is about certain situations and locations that make crimes more likely to occur there (see Eck 2002). Furthermore, it would be worth finding out if there are significant variations or concentrations of where offenders and victims live or occupy, as, if there is more than a random distribution, then this will have implications for preventive interventions.

Unsurprisingly in view of the above, there has been a huge amount of theorising and research about crime and the environment, spanning at least the last seven decades (see, for example,

Shaw 1929; Shaw and McKay 1942; Baldwin and Bottoms, 1976; Georges-Abeyie and Harries 1980; Davidson 1981; Bursik and Grasmick 1993). Environmental criminology draws on a number of theories, both classicist and positivist, some of which were covered in the last chapter. From the former category are drawn rational choice and routine activity theory, which underpin situational crime prevention approaches (discussed in detail later). Routine activity theory asserts that, for a crime to take place, there must be an opportunity (potential victim or physical target), a criminally motivated person and the absence of a capable guardian (someone who would respond if a crime was attempted). Ameliorating any one of these three factors would proportionately reduce the chance of an offence actually taking place (see Cohen and Felson 1979).

From the positivist camp, social disorganisation theory and its subsequent offspring have offered sound theoretical foundations for studying the links between crime and the environment. Social disorganisation was used as an explanation of the persistence of higher levels of recorded juvenile crime in 'zones of transition' – districts inhabited by successive waves of new immigrants (see Shaw 1929). Park (1936) and his colleagues depicted the city as an ecological system in which symbiotic (interdependent) social and economic relations existed between social groups who occupied different zones of the city. Thus a geographic structure and a socioeconomic pecking order developed on the basis of wealth, race and length of time in the country.

Perhaps the major contemporary significance of the work of the Chicago School of environmental psychologists is their observation that the movement from the zone of transition signalled upward social mobility and was invariably accompanied by a reduction in the rate of recorded juvenile crime amongst the socially mobile group. Put another way, the crime rate appeared to be a function of the zone rather than its inhabitants and this has important implications for the race and crime debate. Seen this way, it is apparent that disadvantaged people from ethnic minorities may be found in high crime areas because those are the only areas they can afford to live in or are able to find accommodation in, because all the more privileged people, higher up in the pecking order, have moved out to safer areas. These high crime areas then become reinforced (just like the reinforcement of individual labelling theory), as pimps and drug dealers find that they are attractive business locations. By their transitional nature they have low levels of social control – most of the people who might have resisted crime in the streets have fled to safer areas.

The early work of the Chicago School fed into later studies which looked at the effect of community cohesiveness on levels of crime (Bursik and Grasmick 1993). Areas that were unsettled, with high resident turnover and unclear subcultural norms, were predictably found to be less bonded (people didn't recognise each other, interact and support each other). This lack of bonding or cohesiveness meant that criminals could operate with more anonymity and less likelihood of interference from residents. The potential for 'resident interference' is viewed by Sampson et al. (1997) as a positive antidote to crime, particularly violent street crime, and has been developed more broadly by theorists such as Putnam (1993, 1995) into the notion of 'social capital'. Social capital, in essence, is the accumulation of trust between people who know each other through mutual activity, aid and communication. Putnam and others' thesis is that this social capital has eroded as we have become a more individualised, fragmented and mobile society and this has resulted in a range of social ills, including increased crime and aggression (see also Sennett 1996).

So what has all this research and theorising led to, in practice? Commencing in the 1970s there was a huge interest in Britain and the USA in reducing crime in specific locations by designing the environment in such a way that a potential offender will decide not to commit a crime and reducing the opportunities for crime to occur. These two approaches – crime prevention through environmental design and situational crime prevention (both based to some extent on classical interpretations of crime and deviance) – will be covered in the next two sections. The chapter will then look at environmental issues which are premised on a positivist approach, particularly social disorganisation theory.

### 4.2   Crime prevention through environmental design

A number of planned environments of the last 40 years have produced unforeseen criminogenic side effects. Notable examples of this are single use area zoning, which has resulted in various parts of conurbations being unoccupied at certain times of the day or week, and traffic/pedestrian segregation schemes such as Radburn. The Radburn layout is based on the laudable principle of separating traffic from pedestrians in housing developments. An access road and garaging would be provided down one side of a row of houses, whilst the other side would front onto a purely pedestrian area characterised by gardens, communal spaces and footpaths. Unfortunately this has resulted in making many houses vulnerable to burglaries on one side and car theft on the other and, as a result, many Radburn estates have been reorientated to turn them back into conventional houses on streets. Pedestrian subways are another example of well-intentioned designs that may have prevented some traffic accidents but have provided opportune locations for street crime and offender escape routes.

The notion that 'bad design breeds crime' prompted a number of people to start looking at whether the reverse could be applied – that we might be able to 'design out' crime. Following Jeffery's (1971) investigations into links between crime and environmental design and Newman's (1972) work on defensible space, 'crime prevention through environmental design' (CPTED) has been widely promoted as a cure for crime. Based on the findings from a controlled design improvement programme on a high crime housing estate in the New York area, Newman proposed a system of 'defensible spaces' designed to encourage householders to supervise and take on responsibility for the areas in which they live. He distilled this into four key design measures to overcome the failures of existing mass housing provision:

1. *Territoriality* – the subdivision of buildings and grounds into zones of influence to discourage outsiders from entering and encourage residents to defend their areas
2. *Surveillance* – the design of buildings to allow easy observation of the related territory
3. *Image* – the design of public housing to avoid stigma
4. *Environment* – the juxtaposing of public housing projects with safe zones in adjacent areas.

Although Newman (1980) stressed the parallel importance of social issues such as family networks, community development and good housing management in creating and maintaining safer neighbourhoods, it was his first two commandments that people latched on to. These notions of territoriality and surveillance were further purified by Coleman (1985), who, after studying numerous English housing estates, produced a 'design disadvantagement' index against which one could measure and then rectify design faults that were supposedly causing crime and antisocial behaviour. Despite a number of criticisms of such a simplistic, design determinist view of crime and its prevention, this approach has proved to be attractive; possibly because of its very simplicity – all you have to do is redesign buildings and communal spaces according to a fixed formula and crime will wither away!

There is much common sense in this designing for security approach (see Schneider and Kitchen 2002), but also a danger of overstating its impact and slipping into a design determinist philosophy, whereby people are seen as mere automatons whose behaviour is entirely conditioned by the environment in which they find themselves. There are examples of well-designed environments where crime levels have been high (for example Meadowell on Tyneside and Kirkholt in Rochdale) and badly designed environments where the disadvantage of the surroundings has not manifested itself in high levels of crime (for example Lillington Gardens in Victoria, London and many housing estates in Continental Europe).

Planning and urban design measures *alone* cannot significantly and durably reduce crime and insecurity (Crouch et al. 1999). In some cases they may merely displace the problem. Layouts and designs that work in some areas can be a criminogenic disaster in others. The Tuscan hill village concept of stuccoed clusters of housing, walled gardens and winding alleyways has not worked the way the architect intended at the Maiden Lane Estate in Camden, north London. The design of the upper west side skyscraper apartments in Manhattan does not prove to be so appealing when it is realised on a cloud-scraping hillside above Dundee. Even the nicest 'Tudorbethan' developments such as St Mellon's in Cardiff can become ghettos of fear and discontent if their residents live in poverty and boredom.

Part of the problem associated with attempts to design out crime may be that offenders just don't get the message (Hillier and Shu 2002; Shaftoe and James 2004). Defensible space and natural surveillance concepts rely on psychological signals being transmitted to potential miscreants that they are not supposed to be in defined spaces and will be spotted if they try to offend. Outlaws, macho risk-takers and the heavily intoxicated are unlikely to read, or take heed of, these signals.

The Scottish Office (1994: 9) proselytised the principle of 'planning in a broader context' for crime prevention in their Planning Advice Note:

> Environmental improvement alone or in conjunction with improved security measures is unlikely to be successful in preventing crime in areas which suffer from profound social and economic distress where fundamental issues such as housing management and maintenance, job creation and community development also require to be addressed.

At best the results of physical planning and urban design provide the backdrop against which changing social activities and dynamics evolve. There is little evidence to suggest that the design of the physical environment determines people's behaviour in such a direct cause and effect relationship. After all, it is people that commit offences, not environments. Social planning (involving other disciplines and agencies) should complement physical planning, so that other human needs, not necessarily directly related to shelter and the use of space, are catered for (Osborn and Shaftoe 1995).

These reservations about the shortcomings of pure design determinism have not deterred the blossoming, particularly in North America, of CPTED as an orthodoxy with its own professional association and consultants. In Britain, Secured by Design (SBD) awards for homes and car parks have been actively promoted by the police. Although some research has suggested that SBD schemes actually do experience lower crime rates (see Armitage 2000), victimisation (and particularly repeat victimisation) still does occur and certain crimes (such as domestic violence and distraction thefts, for example) will be unaffected by design modifications. Secured By Design is a worthy approach, but there are questions as to what extent any design can be made definitively secure. Perhaps it might be more honest to describe SBD developments as 'burglary resistant' or (in the case of SBD car parks) 'unattractive to car thieves', rather than claiming that crime in its entirety has been designed out. As the woman who was brutally attacked in an SBD car park in Bristol discovered to her cost, the car was safer but she wasn't.

## 4.3   Situational crime prevention

Situational crime prevention is probably the purest application of classical/rational choice theory. The idea is that we should simply make crime harder to commit and, in the process, reduce the pleasure and profit gained from the criminal act. In the face of the daunting psychological and socioeconomic circumstances that may have to be altered to reduce people's *motivation* to offend, such simpler solutions to the crime problem are bound to have political appeal. To this end, in the late 1970s and early 1980s government resources were directed away from social intervention and towards situational crime prevention. *Designing Out Crime* (Mayhew 1980) identified eight situational measures which could be effective in reducing crime:

1.  *Target hardening*, for example stronger locks/building materials
2.  *Target removal*, for example cheque or card payment instead of cash
3.  *Removal of means*, for example gun control, knife amnesties
4.  *Reducing the payoff*, for example property marking, dye release into stolen items
5.  *Formal surveillance*, for example police or security patrols
6.  *Natural surveillance*, for example residents able to keep watch during normal activities
7.  *Employee surveillance*, for example by doormen/concierges/caretakers and so on
8.  *Environmental management*, for example reducing vandalism by limiting the allocation of young families to estates

Proponents of situational crime prevention argue that such a strategy does not require us to know what makes the offender tick in order to make the victim safer. As Mayhew once observed, we don't need to understand the motivation of the speeding motorist to know that placing a sleeping policemen in the road will slow him or her down. But as John Lea (1992: 81) argued, while it is undoubtedly true that situational crime prevention measures can be effective, they:

> always have a crucial social element ... A purely 'technicist' attitude to crime prevention is incapable of understanding why the same technical innovation works on some occasions and not others because it fails to grasp how technical 'effects' are always mediated through social relations between people.

This leads us to the problem of human ingenuity overcoming what at first seems an infallible adjustment to the situation. An example would be the increase in the use of credit and debit cards, which initially promised more security than the carrying of cash. As a result, ingenious offenders have found ever more sophisticated ways of electronically stealing other people's money, whilst the more desperate criminals just hold people up at cashpoints.

Allatt (1982) was one of the first academics to rigorously test the effectiveness of some aspects of the situational approach. A housing estate was surveyed before and after a comprehensive range of physical security improvements. In the short term, burglaries were reduced, but there were problems of displacement of crimes to neighbouring areas and and unimproved homes. Also it was found that a significant minority of residents did not use the extra security devices fitted, and poor installation and maintenance weakened their effectiveness. Possibly in response to such critiques of situational prevention, by 1997 one of the original thinkers behind situational crime prevention had doubled the list of opportunity-reducing measures to 16 (Clarke 1997). Some of these new measures relied more on an awareness of a socially responsive behaviour on the part of the individual and included 'rule setting', 'facilitating compliance' and 'stimulating conscience'.

The implicit object of the situational crime prevention initiatives of the early 1980s was the 'opportunistic criminal'. The opportunistic criminal, characteristically, spots an open window or an unlocked car and promptly hops through the window or into the driving seat. However, many people walking along that same street would not avail themselves of such opportunities, even if they believed that they would not be caught – the self-regulators discussed in the previous chapter. It would also suggest that the opportunistic criminal, rather than happening upon opportunity, might well have been out looking for it. For in real life people are different. This difference is dictated by their social and economic position, their culture or subculture, their upbringing, and their beliefs and values (Mills 1959; Critcher 1975). Thus, even if the pessimistic theories of human motivation which underpin the situational approach are correct, it could still be true that for some people the attainment of virtue would constitute the maximisation of pleasure and profit. At the other extreme there are people who are so irrational, demented, intoxicated or desperate that the normal restraints of pleasure and pain become irrelevant (the outlaws described in the previous chapter), as many observers of behaviour in front of CCTV cameras have discovered to their amazement.

This complication posed a significant problem for crime prevention initiatives based solely on a situational strategy. In areas where situational initiatives were attempted, it became evident that although victimisation dropped in the targeted area (at least temporarily), it rose in adjacent areas, indicating that opportunity-seeking offenders existed and that, if thwarted in one place, they would set off in search of softer targets elsewhere. More dangerously, if adjacent areas were also secured, it was found that 'determined offenders' would either use more force to get their way or change the type of offending they indulged in, for example from burglary to mugging. It also emerged that there were relatively few of these opportunity-seeking offenders who, nonetheless, tended to be involved in a large number of offences. This suggested that situational approaches had to be revised to take in the social dimension and return to the question of the motivation of offenders (see Osborn 1993).

This psychosocial context has been recognised by the proponents of situational crime prevention who, as noted, have added 'stimulating conscience' to their list of opportunity-reducing techniques (see Clarke 1997). It is difficult to see how stimulating conscience is qualitatively different to the inculcation of moral values inherent in social crime prevention – if you don't have a moral view of what is right and wrong, your conscience cannot be pricked. Situational crime prevention has thus been criticised for its assumption that the problem of crime can be solved by technical and administrative means while ignoring the broader normative, political and economic contexts that make crime such a slippery phenomenon (see Hughes 1998).

## 4.4   Location, location, location

As we have already discussed, crime covers a multitude of sins, perpetrated in many ways in a range of contexts. However, the majority of individual offender/victim crimes (where one person acts violently towards or steals from another person) occur in residential neighbourhoods or town centres and in each case they can occur either inside buildings or on the streets. Location, therefore, must be worth looking at to understand why there are significant geographical variations in the rates and density of the various categories of crime (see Pain 2001). What is clear from such enquiry is that crime is unevenly distributed and tends to be concentrated (according to type) in town centres and low-income residential areas of big cities.

As with the biological/social/psychological theories of crime, environmental criminology is a hotly debated subject. Depending on their political, ideological or theoretical perspectives, various commentators suggest that unsafe neighbourhoods and town centres are caused by:

- Poor design of streets, estates and city centres; inadequate lighting and hidden corners; monolithic use of areas and ill-conceived structures such as multistorey car parks and warren-like subways or footpaths
- Mismanagement and deterioration of the urban fabric; dereliction, rubbish, graffiti, inadequate policing, abandonment and blighting of areas, lack of civic pride and services
- The individualisation and privatisation of spaces and enclosures, so that buildings and businesses turn their backs on communal and public areas, leaving uncontrolled hinterlands such as service areas, access routes and parking spaces; people scuttle from one enclave to another rather than using the street as a valuable space in its own right
- Moral and social decline in individual and group behaviour, leading to yob culture, violence, predatory behaviour; loss of mutual support and community spirit, so that people do not intervene to thwart crimes and will often look the other way; mistrust of the police and other authorities
- Streets awash with the flotsam and jetsam of human problems: alcoholics, the homeless, young beggars excluded from welfare

benefits, squeegee merchants, drug addicts, dealers, hustlers, pimps, prostitutes, people discharged into community care, the long-term unemployed, thieves, runaways and truants.

Each one of these represents an extreme and inadequate appraisal of the problems associated with the lived-in environment, but a more moderated view, incorporating elements of all these viewpoints, may get us closer to the truth. It is likely that the roots of the problem of unsafe neighbourhoods, streets and urban centres lie somewhere in a mire of poor design and management, individual criminal proclivities and social deprivation. But a significant set of facts, worthy of the attention of anybody interested in controlling crime, is the huge and consistent variation between urban and rural crime rates.

One of the British Crime Surveys looked at where crime was most common. It divided the country up into 11 different kinds of area, according to the type of housing, employment and occupancy, and found that the high-risk areas were generally the poorest urban neighbourhoods. On what the BCS described as the 'poorest council estates', as many as one in six homes were subject to the attentions of burglars during the course of one year. People's homes were four times more likely to be broken into than the homes of people living in the leafy suburbs and rural areas. This contradicts the common perception that villains steal from the rich. The bleak reality is that the poorest and most vulnerable people are also the most likely to be victims of crime. This is partly to do with their sheer vulnerability; they are probably unable to secure their homes adequately and, as the geography of crime is very localised, they probably live in close proximity to offenders (see Baldwin and Bottoms 1976; Davidson 1981; Pain 2001). There was an assumption that, as mobility and availability of cars increased, offenders would travel further to commit their crimes. Popular tales of 'awayday' criminals, journeying from the big cities to target holiday resorts and sleepy market towns, have abounded, but Home Office research (Wiles and Costello 2000) found very little evidence to support this rumour. The same localisation scenario is true for other kinds of crime. The level of robbery (street crime or mugging) in some poor inner-city areas is almost five times as high as it is in suburban and rural areas. Even motorcars are three times more likely to be broken into or stolen on the poorest council estates than in areas of affluent sub-urban housing.

## 4.5 Crime and urbanisation

This pattern of higher per capita crime rates in urban areas seems to apply internationally. Chaline and Dubois-Maury (1994) quote French national police statistics for the number of crimes per 1,000 inhabitants, as shown below:

| | |
|---|---:|
| Paris | 139.95 |
| Cities with more than 250,000 inhabitants | 100.3 |
| Cities with between 100,000 to 250,000 inhabitants | 73.0 |
| Towns with between 50,000 and 100,000 inhabitants | 69.6 |
| Towns with between 25,000 and 50,000 inhabitants | 67.5 |
| Towns and villages with less than 25,000 inhabitants | 53.3 |

Interpol statistics (quoted in European Forum for Urban Security 1996) compare national crime rates per 1,000 inhabitants with rates for their respective capital cities, as shown below.

| Country | National rate | Capital city rate |
|---|---|---|
| Germany | 80 | 159 |
| France | 67 | 140 |
| Italy | 38 | 67 |
| Spain | 22 | 42 |

In each case, capital cities have approximately twice the crime rate of the national average. Some, *but not all* this difference could be accounted for by the extra number of visiting, transient offenders that they may host.

Generally speaking there is a direct correlation between population concentration and crime rates – the larger the city, the higher the per capita crime rate; the more rural the area, the lower the per capita crime rate. For example, according to Home Office annual crime statistics, the people in the predominantly urbanised South

Wales police force area (which includes Cardiff and Swansea) experience more than double the number of crimes per head than neighbouring Dyfed/Powys, which is almost entirely rural. Moreover, the crime rate in rural Dyfed/Powys also experienced one of the sharpest drops in crime rates of anywhere during the late 1990s. A similar contrast can be found between many other urban and neighbouring rural locations. The 'white flight' from many inner-city areas of the USA has now moved beyond the suburbs and out into more rural locations, as those who can afford to venture ever further to find a safe haven for their families. It is unlikely to be pure chance that gives predominantly rural Norway a much lower per capita crime level than densely urbanised Holland.

The irony of all this is that cities were originally built as places of safety. The early cities of Roman, Greek and other civilisations were safe refuges from the threats and violence of their rural hinterlands. Up until the seventeenth century most European cities were still walled to guard against ill-intentioned outsiders (Schneider and Kitchen 2002). And yet by the mid-nineteenth century the enemy was within and the burghers of inner-city London had to set up the first police force to control the rising tide of theft and thuggery in the city's streets.

It has been suggested (see, for example, Ravetz 1980) that twentieth-century cities actually provoke criminal behaviour amongst their citizens, who, alienated by the bleak, impersonal and oppressive built environment, turn to vandalism and violence in response.

Today the lesson seems to be: if you want to reduce your chances of being a victim of crime, go and live in the country, and many of those who can afford to, do exactly this. Clearly, for practical reasons, this is not a feasible option for the majority of the population. So perhaps our task should be to, firstly, identify what factors in the rural environment appear to make them more secure against crime and, secondly, see what we could do to re-create these factors in an urban environment.

### 4.6   Why is there less crime in rural areas?

First of all a clarification – crime is not just less in rural areas because there are less people: *per capita* rates are significantly lower. In 1995 the police recorded about 328,000 crimes in the Greater Manchester area, whereas in mid-Wales, the Dyfed/Powys police had only about 19,400 crimes on their books. Even comparing them on a per capita basis, Manchester clocked 12 crimes per 100 residents as against mid-Wales' 4 crimes per 100 – a threefold difference. However, all is not perfect in the country, for example racist attitudes are often more entrenched in rural areas, which on occasion can lead to violent outbursts against ethnic minority people who have settled or trade in villages and small towns.

There could be a number of explanations for the urban/rural variation in crime rates. Here are some of the claims made to account for the differences:

1. *Maybe urban police forces record more crime, whereas there is more 'hidden' crime in rural areas.* There is evidence (in the BCS) to suggest that much more crime occurs than is ever recorded by the police, but nothing to suggest that this is proportionately more likely to be the case in rural areas. In fact, if anything, less crime might be reported in urban areas, where the police are more likely to be overstretched and less accessible to residents.

2. *There is more poverty in urban areas, so people are more likely to steal to get what they want or need.* There *are* heavier concentrations of poverty in urban areas (on large housing estates and inner-city areas) but there are many poor people living in rural areas too – agricultural work is one of the lowest paid industries and there are relatively high levels of rural unemployment in many countries.

3. *There is more relative inequality in cities, so people steal to get even.* Partly true, but the difference between the landed gentry in their country seats and the farm labourers in their council houses and tied cottages could hardly be more polarised.

4. *There is more to steal in towns and cities.* In absolute terms this is true, but there are still plenty of pickings for the determined rural thief and the items in question are often less secured or supervised (for example farm equipment and livestock, or the contents of holiday cottages).

5. *Everything is too spread out in the country. This makes crime more difficult to commit, particularly as offenders and victims*

*tend, statistically, to reside a short distance from each other.* Yes, research has established that 'journeys to crime' are comparatively short (for example Davidson 1981; Wiles and Costello 2000) and rural areas are more dispersed than urban areas. But within these dispersed areas the dispossessed and the affluent often live in close proximity (think of the typical village or hamlet with the manor house and the tied cottages or the executive commuter homes and the council houses) and the motorcar has effectively reduced journey times for almost everyone.

6. *Cities attract deviants, drug addicts and ne'er-do-wells who thrive in the urban anonymity and are less visible in densely populated environments. Such people therefore migrate from the rural to the urban.* Yes, there is an element of truth in this – people who deviate from the norm are more visible in rural areas and can often be better supervised, formally or informally, in such an environment. However, it is important to recognise that many types of deviation are perfectly legal (for example growing dreadlocks or being a traveller) and the innate conservatism of many rural areas can be prejudicial and repressive.

7. *Everyone knows everyone else and their business in villages and rural areas, so any suspicious activity is likely to be visible and noted.* Yes, this kind of informal surveillance is much stronger in small communities, whereas in the big city there are too many goings-on and higher densities of movement, both of which impede the building up of informal surveillance and social control. Although, conversely, in spatial terms, there are potentially more hidden corners in rural areas where, at the far end of a farm track, it may be possible to engage unseen in some illicit activity.

8. *There is a much bigger turnover of residents and visitors in towns and cities, so routine, predictable and legal activity is less likely to be the dominant pattern; rural communities tend to be much more stable, so anything out-of-the-ordinary or unpredictable (and possibly illegal) will stand out.* Yes, indeed this links to and reinforces point 6, although the downside could be rural intolerance (as in 5).

9. *Urban living is more stressful so people get violent.* Yes, urbanites tend to live faster, more pressurised existences that are more likely to bring them into confrontational proximity with other

stressed-out urbanites (see Newman and Lonsdale 1996). However, it may be significant that the two worst massacres in Great Britain during the last 50 years (Hungerford and Dunblane) both occurred in semi-rural areas.

10. *There are more escape routes and hiding places in the confused maze of the big city.* Yes, this seems to be true; geographically, rural areas offer more possibilities for secretion yet, paradoxically, they are more visible. It is significant that the IRA, when preparing for terrorist bombing campaigns on the UK mainland, generally (but not exclusively) chose to hide its arms and explosives in anonymous urban locations.

11. *Residents feel more proprietorial in villages and rural areas; in towns and cities many people feel the neighbourhoods and public spaces are outside their control.* Yes, this seems to be generally the case; there is often a stronger sense of community and unity in self-contained villages, reinforced by the village pub, store and hall. As a result, residents are more likely to take combined action against a perceived threat.

The real picture that makes up the difference between urban and rural crime rates is likely to be made up of elements from most of the above statements, as well as other possible factors not discovered. In terms of crime and social conditions, nothing is ever simple!

## 4.7    Re-creating rural qualities in urban environments

If we can't all go to the country, can the country come to the city? It should be possible to bring many of the social and situational factors that benefit rural living (and relative safety) into the urban fabric, thus creating actual neighbourhoods as opposed to seamless tracts of urban development where people live and work. The points made in items 6–11 in the above list could all have implications for the way we plan, design and manage our towns and cities. As Lynch (1981) summarises:

the pleasures of living in an identifiable district which has quiet, safe streets and daily services easily accessible nearby, and within which one can organise politically when the need for control arises, are surely a legitimate feature of good settlement.

Although it was grounded in a different motivational source, the Urban Villages movement (known as the 'New Urbanism' in the USA; see Katz 1994) appears to address many of these issues and could therefore lead to the unintended, but welcome, added benefits of less crime and fear for residents. The Urban Villages movement in the UK was an attempt to tackle ecological and design problems in the bland suburban sprawls that were enveloping most British cities during the 1970s and 80s (Urban Villages Forum 1992). Instead of single use and single tenure housing estates, the Urban Villages Forum (along with the New Urbanists) argues for a wider mix of uses, activities and tenures within new developments, in order to encourage people to interact more easily and discourage unnecessary car journeys. Although proposed as a form of development to facilitate economic, environmental and social sustainability, it becomes obvious from the points raised in the previous section that such an environment should also lead to sustainable reductions in crime and improvements in community safety.

In *A Pattern Language* Alexander et al. (1977) anticipated the notion of the urban village with their pattern for a community of 7,000. They proposed to: 'Decentralise city governments in a way that gives local control to communities of 5,000 to 10,000 persons. As nearly as possible, use natural and historical boundaries to mark these communities.' Alexander et al. then propose the 'neighbourhood' as a smaller residential unit of about 500 inhabitants, with a cluster of neighbourhoods grouped to form a community (or, in the new terminology, an 'urban village').

Specifically, an urban village or 'pattern for a community' is expected to have the following characteristics, all of which can help to enhance community safety (see also Urban Villages Forum 1992):

- A population small enough to make up an identifiable 'community' where people will mostly recognise each other, but large enough to support a range of neighbourhood services and facilities (Alexander et al. 1977).
- A strong sense of place, with basic amenities within easy walking distance of all residents. This will define the physical design and spatial coverage of the neighbourhood (see Alexander et al. 1977).

- A variety of uses, such as shopping, leisure and community facilities alongside housing, so that people don't have to travel far out of their neighbourhood for day-to-day needs and activities. This would also encourage more social interaction, stability and cohesion.
- A choice of tenures (both residential and commercial) and housing types to enable a mixed and balanced community, with neither concentrations of disadvantage nor privilege. Also a variety of housing types, so that old and young, families and singles, able and less able can all live as neighbours, and people can stay in the same area throughout their lifetimes.
- A high level of involvement by local residents in the planning and onward management of the new development. This gives people a sense of control and ownership, and means that they have a stake in the future wellbeing of their community.

All these measures should contribute to a safe and sound neighbourhood (or cluster of neighbourhoods) with good informal social controls and active surveillance possibilities, in order to inhibit crime and antisocial activity (see Bursik and Grasmick 1993).

Above all, an 'actual neighbourhood' has to have a stable population where the majority of people feel they are settled and have a long-term commitment to maintaining an acceptable quality of life in that neighbourhood (see Hirschfield and Bowers 1997). If people regard the neighbourhood as a transit camp or temporary home, then they are unlikely to invest time and effort in developing networks and will not care too much about undesirable aspects of life in the area. This is noticeable in areas occupied by large numbers of students (passing through) or families living on unpopular housing projects who are hoping to be transferred to somewhere better. In some respects this requirement for stability militates against the increasing mobility of the job market. In the future people may have to make a conscious choice between staying in a friendly and active neighbourhood and reducing their promotion chances, or living a transitory life full of insecurities in all senses of the word.

## 4.8   Boundaries and edges

The major remaining urban village or actual neighbourhood issue is that of the 'edges' of the development and what happens in adjacent areas. This is one major difference between the urban village and its rural equivalent. In the country, a village will almost certainly be surrounded by fields, which act as a neutral and relatively safe buffer zone. In the town or city, it is likely that the actual neighbourhood will be mostly surrounded by other populated or activity areas, from whence predatory incursions may occur. Edges of neighbourhoods are often the most vulnerable to crime, because easy forays and escapes are possible and strangers or irregular activity are less apparent than in the core. The crude solution is to build a wall around the neighbourhood and indeed this happens in the USA and in areas of extreme sectarian conflict such as parts of Belfast and Londonderry. There are early signs of this approach in Britain with, for example, the Brindley Place development in central Birmingham and a number of exclusive (in both senses of the word) residential developments in the home counties, enclosing their residents behind a continuous barrier of walls and access controlled gates.

Gating is a drastic solution with many undesirable side effects, not least of which is the creation of a divided society and the gradual erosion of the civil liberty to enjoy all urban spaces as a member of the general public (Minton 2002). Walled-in neighbourhoods or gated suburbs can also heighten fear among residents who may feel they are under permanent siege and are frightened to emerge from their fortified enclave (Ellin 1997). A more humane and inclusive approach to the edge problem is to install symbolic barriers (using different surfacing materials or a finger park for example), although there is some uncertainty about their efficacy in deterring potential offenders (Shaftoe and James 2004). The best solution is to make sure that any urban village is part of a comprehensive community safety plan for a town or city and not an isolated oasis in otherwise hostile territory. This brings us back to the fourth, but less noted, principle expounded by Oscar Newman in his groundbreaking book, *Defensible Space* (1972) – the right juxtaposing of housing with safe zones in other areas.

Lynch (1960) suggests that edges of neighbourhoods can be 'uniting seams' rather than isolating barriers. This can be the case when an edge is defined by a substantial routeway to a town core or the country, or where it is a linear provider of services that could not be sustained by single neighbourhoods. So in fact the edge or seam can be an asset rather than a liability, offering access routes and major attractions, such as cinemas, restaurants and sports centres.

## 4.9 Key principles for sustainably safe places

To make our built environments more liveable, we need to ensure that they *are* safe and they *feel* safe – two different issues. The analysis given in section 4.7 leads to five key principles for creating locations that can minimise fear and maximise safety:

1. *Quality.* Cheap mass housing, leisure and retail centre solutions have proved to be expensive in the long run. Some schemes built in the 1960s have already been demolished, or expensively refurbished. Nearly all the places and spaces that have proved to be viable, safe and attractive in the long term were built to high standards of material and durability. Quality environments seem to promote good quality behaviour especially if they are well maintained and supervised. If places start to deteriorate, unless they are quickly and competently repaired and renovated, they will rapidly spiral into decline under an onslaught of vandalism and misuse (see Zimbardo 1973). There is also the psychological proposition that brutal, neglected environments encourage (or at least do not inhibit) brutal and uncaring behaviour.

2. *Diversity (and self-sufficiency).* Viable and thriving neighbourhoods need to be able to accommodate a whole range of occupants and activities. Single use, monolithic areas have proved to be less safe and secure than mixed use neighbourhoods (Shaftoe 2000). Diversity should extend to housing (for all ages, tenure types and incomes) and core amenities (shops, workshops, leisure, care and education), so that the neighbourhood is self-sufficient without being totally insular.

3. *Identity.* The neighbourhood should be the right size (probably no more than 5,000 people and one kilometre from end to end), on a human scale and have enough particular character to give it a clear identity that residents and users can relate to and 'bond' around. This bonding can lead to a sense of common cause, which in turn establishes trust and the accumulation of social capital (Putnam 1993, 1995). This links to the next principle.

4.  *'Ownership'*. Through involvement and control of the neighbourhood's destiny, residents should feel that they have a stake in the neighbourhood's present and future conditions and quality of life. In this way they will care for their neighbourhood and their neighbours and are more likely to ensure that other people behave accordingly (or that something happens if they don't).

5.  *Stability and continuity*. If residents and users are not settled, then they are unlikely to invest much time and effort in ensuring that it becomes, or remains, a good place to live. Through choice of living arrangements and lifetime homes, people should be encouraged to remain in their area. The same stability and continuity should be offered by service providers in the area. For example, the community constable should remain working in the same area for as long as possible (at least three years) and, ideally, would live there too (as happens in Japan and used to happen in the UK). By the same token, teachers, social workers and youth workers should be given incentives to stay in the same area so that they can get to know each other and the local population.

### 4.10   Access to goods and new opportunities

Another environmental variable that has implications for crime control is the changing range of opportunities to offend offered by the increase in moveable goods and more accessible environments. This is one of the downsides of our materialistic society. Some people have gone so far as to say that the only reason there has been a crime increase in the last 50 years is because there are more things to steal! There is no doubt that our environment now contains more stealable items than ever before and it is significant that new portable consumer goods are generally the items most likely to be stolen (see Clarke 2000). Today, the most popular targets for thieves are mobile phones, leading to an upturn in robberies, particularly against young people; ten years ago, this was simply not a problem because the product hardly existed. In an attempt to entice customers to buy, most retail outlets have much more accessible displays than they did some years ago. In the 1950s you had to know exactly what you wanted if you went to a grocers or an outfitters, because you had to place your order over a counter directly to a shop assistant. The most blatant environmental opportunity for crime must be that provided by parked cars and their contents. Vehicles of a value equivalent to many people's annual salary are left unsupervised in public places for hours on end. Even though car security improvements have reduced the ease with which newer cars can be stolen, this does not prevent the theft of car contents by simply smashing a window, grabbing and running. Increased flaunting of material wealth and gadgets is almost inevitably going to provoke a predatory backlash when this occurs in a climate of increasing economic polarisation (see social strain theory discussed in Chapter 3).

### 4.11   Crime and urban regeneration

A nationwide study commissioned by the Joseph Rowntree Foundation (Burrows and Rhodes 1998) found that the most widespread source of neighbourhood dissatisfaction is crime. Lower down the list come factors such as leisure facilities, rubbish, public transport, schools and general appearance of the environment. It is odd, therefore, that most urban regeneration programmes (from the Task Forces of the 1980s, via the Single Regeneration Budget of the 1990s, to the New Deal of the new millennium) downplay crime prevention as an explicit aim. Crime inevitably crops up if local people are consulted and given an open-ended question about priorities that need tackling, but generally urban regeneration bodies feel more comfortable majoring on training, job creation and environmental improvements. Of course, all these measures will ultimately help to reduce crime, but these linkages are not necessarily made explicit. Furthermore, it is often the threats and ravages of crime that deter new employers, cause the closing down of existing ones and make the environment look so degraded. The dilemma may be that talking explicitly about crime problems in an area, as a priority for action, is a sensitive subject for residents and agencies, as it may further stigmatise that area. But this is unlikely to be the real reason why crime and insecurity are only indirectly addressed in many regeneration schemes. Currently there is a serious shortage of people who have comprehensive skills and knowledge in the field of crime prevention, both at the strategic and implementation level.

Crime compounds the predicament of the poor in run-down

neighbourhoods, not simply because it impoverishes and injures them, but also because it erodes 'community'. Paul Harrison (1983: 282) writes:

> It is not just the facilities which suffer; it is the solidarity of the community itself. Redevelopment, migration and the rapid turnover of people seeking better accommodation means there is precious little of that to start with. But crime dissolves it even further. The climate of fear engenders a defensive egotism of survival in which everyone looks after themselves. A new code of ethics emerges: that thy days shall be long, thou shalt not question strangers on the stairs; thou shalt not look if thou hears screams or shattering glass; thou shalt not admonish youths for vandalism; thou shalt not help the victim of an attack.

### 4.12   Policy implications

If crime is primarily an urban problem and one of the worst quality of life factors for citizens, then the blunt policy conclusion might be to 'close down' cities and start afresh in the country. In the USA, this has happened by default as whole inner-city areas have been abandoned by those who can afford to relocate to rural communities. Mao Zedong attempted to return people to the country as part of the Cultural Revolution in China, but it is interesting to note that the flow has now reversed with a vengeance. In most Western European countries we just do not have the physical option to ruralise the population even if this was considered a good idea from a quality of life point of view. Cities have numerous advantages from cultural, governance and ecological standpoints, so the challenge for policy makers is to make them more liveable, rather than eradicate them. Although the biggest variations in crime rates are between urban and rural locations, different cities in different countries have remarkably different levels of crime, so there is the possibility to learn about what makes some cities safer than others (see, for example, Schneider and Kitchen 2002).

If urban (and rural) places and spaces are to be made safer, it will be essential to address both the environmental issues (discussed in this chapter) and the personal/social motivational issues discussed in the previous chapter. This requires a strategic vision and programmes of implementation that go beyond the narrow partisan interests of particular professions and agencies. We need models of intervention that are comprehensive, context-appropriate and timely; as will be discussed in the next chapter.

# 5

# Crime Control Models and Frameworks

## 5.1  Overview

People like simple solutions, but we have to grasp the complex nature of crime and offending, if we are to have any hope of creating safer communities. This chapter discusses various conceptual and policy frameworks within which effective crime control might function. As discussed earlier, the origins of crime, criminality and insecurity are found in such a dense web of interacting causes (everything from the breakdown of cultural norms, via urbanisation, to the construction of external doors), that to learn anything useful about why and how some places seem to be more successful at preventing crime than others, we need analytical models that will help us to tease out significant factors that could be replicated. A number of typologies or analytical templates have been developed to classify and compare crime prevention measures. Some of them are explained below. None of these frameworks can be used as the definitive 'container' for thinking about crime prevention, but, between them, we may get a better understanding of the multi-dimensionality of crime and attempts to control it.

## 5.2  Four overlapping considerations in developing a comprehensive crime control strategy

### 5.2.1  *Deterrence, opportunity reduction and criminality prevention*
Effective crime control strategies need to deter people from breaking the law, primarily through the efforts of the criminal

justice system, but also by reducing the ease with which crimes can be committed (situational crime prevention). Such policies, premised as they are on deterrence and opportunity reduction, take a classical view of human nature. However, for a comprehensive crime prevention approach that embraces the positivist theories of human behaviour, we also need to do things that will reduce the reasons why some people are inclined to offend in the first place (social crime prevention).

Cohen and Felson (1979) suggested that a crime was likely to occur when somebody motivated to offend converged with a potential victim or target in the absence of a capable guardian. The conclusion from this is that we could intervene in any one of three ways to reduce crime:

1.   reduce people's motivation to commit crime
2.   make targets or victims less vulnerable
3.   increase the presence and responsiveness of capable guardians (police, wardens, active citizens, carers and so on).

This makes a lot of sense for most locational crimes but is less appropriate for crimes where the offender and victim are one and the same person, such as drug misuse. A variation of this 'triangle' is used by some crime prevention through environmental design (CPTED) proselytisers who put the offender, the victim and the location as the three points amenable to remedial intervention. This is a useful template for property crimes from premises and, to some extent, vehicle crime, but is less relevant in the case of crimes such as domestic violence and child abuse. A diagrammatic representation, which is rather more complex than the two 'triangles' just described but seems to cater for most crime occurrences, is shown in Figure 5.1.

Figure 5.1 shows that there must be an opportunity, but there doesn't have to be a potential victim (although in many cases there will be). The location can be a target (as in a parked car or vandalised bench) or merely the context (as in the case of high rates of drug abuse or domestic violence on a disadvantaged housing estate). The linear sequence from motivated offender to offence suggests that there would be advantages in aiming interventions at the earliest point in the sequence, as this would obviate having to address the later stages, that is, if we could reduce the motivation

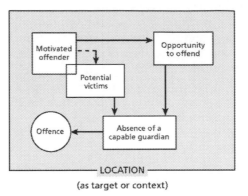

(as target or context)

**Figure 5.1**    Factors leading to a crime occurrence

of people to offend in the first place, we would not have to put so much effort into reducing opportunities, safeguarding potential victims and deploying guardians.

### 5.2.2    *Primary, secondary and tertiary points of intervention*
Intervening at three points in the risk cycle is more likely to be effective than single point interventions. Primary crime prevention is directed at the population as a whole and may include security and personal safety advice, plus universal interventions such as health visiting and inclusive education. Secondary intervention targets 'at-risk' neighbourhoods and groups with ameliorative strategies. Estate Action and the New Deal for Communities are English examples of neighbourhood programmes, while anti-truancy projects or mentoring schemes for young people are examples of secondary prevention work with groups. Tertiary crime prevention is the kind of work that probation officers try to do with offenders under their supervision, to help them stay out of trouble in the future.

Van Dijk and de Waard (1991) added a vertical axis to this model which makes it possible to isolate whether the level of crime prevention intervention was targeted at offenders, situations or victims, as shown in Figure 5.2.

Thus, by way of example, primary prevention aimed at potential future offenders (that is, all of us) might consist of moral education programmes in schools, secondary prevention aimed at poten-

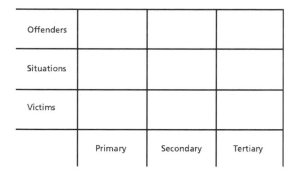

|  | Primary | Secondary | Tertiary |
|---|---|---|---|
| Offenders |  |  |  |
| Situations |  |  |  |
| Victims |  |  |  |

**Figure 5.2**   Crime prevention matrix

tial future offenders might consist of a detached youth project in a deprived neighbourhood and tertiary prevention might involve a probation officer mediating a meeting between a young offender and his or her burglary victim, in the hope that the burglar will realise the full consequences of his or her actions and thus desist from further offending.

Graham and Bennett (1995) came up with a three-part classification for preventive approaches: criminality prevention; situational crime prevention; and community crime prevention. This classification has similarities to the vertical grid of van Dijk and de Waard's typology, although 'victims' could only loosely be equated with 'community'. In fact the community category in Graham and Bennet's classification is rather loose, as it embraces not only community organisation but also some defensive and criminality prevention measures where these are contained 'within a community-based framework of action'.

Perhaps the most useful classification (for practical rather than academic analysis) is the grid developed by Marnix Eysink Smeets in Holland (1995). He calls this classification 'putting crime behind bars' and it is shown in Figure 5.3. Using this 'behind bars' scheme, it is possible to compare the type and quantity of crime prevention activity in various countries.

### 5.2.3   Short-, medium- and long-term inputs and outputs

If people are suffering daily from the effects of crime, they want something done *now*. This is an understandable demand, which needs some kind of response. There are some immediate things

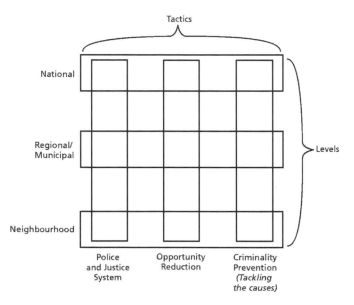

*Source*: Smeets 1995, reproduced with permission

**Figure 5.3**   Putting crime behind bars

that can be done to make people feel safer, such as improved
lighting or extra security patrols. But these measures make up only
a part of the picture and are unlikely to achieve sustainable
improvements. At the same time, plans need to be launched for
medium- and long-term interventions which are more likely to be
sustainable because they will start to address the 'root causes' of
crime. Medium-term measures may include design and management changes and long-term measures may include parenting,
child development and education interventions.

*5.2.4   National, regional, local policies, strategies and interventions*
Crime ultimately impacts on individual victims, but these individuals live in neighbourhoods managed by local authorities and area
police forces who are affected by regional trends, national policies
and international developments (such as the effects of drug traf-
ficking, mafia groups, globalisation and economic migration).
Figure 5.4 illustrates the various radiating influences that impact,
in varying degrees, on the individual, whether potential victim or

**Figure 5.4** The bigger environmental picture

offender. Ideally, all these levels (or ripples) should be addressed when developing and managing an effective crime prevention policy.

The sheer complexity of crime problems and attempts to prevent them means that *all* the above frameworks could be used to locate types of intervention and identify gaps. The multifaceted layers of these frameworks also point to the need for a range of professions and agencies, as well as the inhabitants of local communities, to be involved in crime prevention. One of the most significant developments in crime control policy over the last 25 years has been the increasing recognition that preventing crime is not just a job for the police and the criminal justice system (see Home Office 1984, 1990).

## 5.3  Crime control – by whom, for whom?

In crime prevention and community safety initiatives, the value lies not just in *what* is done but also in *how* it is done. Just as the causes and patterns of crime are extremely complex and interactive, so any strategy to tackle local crime problems must involve an intricate web of interacting resources, services and processes. Sweeping changes introduced in a standard package are likely to be less effective than a range of improvements carefully attuned to local circumstances (see Smith and Heal 1984; Osborn 1993).

Analysis of the research and experience to date can provide us with a menu or toolkit: a range of security and social options for crime prevention. It can also provide a philosophy: the effectiveness of neighbourhood crime prevention is related to the degree to which local people acquire control over and commitment to the development of their neighbourhood community and the degree to which various agencies and interests can collaborate within a neighbourhood.

Using the 'tools' on their own is not necessarily effective. A well-known experiment in Northumbria, which involved fitting extra security hardware to houses on a problem estate, was evaluated as being 'not totally positive in its effects' (Allat 1982). Many people did not use the hardware and the overall crime rate did not drop as significantly as had been expected. Equally, the philosophy of local control cannot be successfully applied as an end in itself:

> Least convincing have been those analyses which have asserted that the fact of participation by the poor, in itself, will significantly alter the conditions deplored, as for example the belief that civic participation in itself leads to a reduction in deviant behaviour. (Frieden and Morris 1968: 178)

Further variables, which overlay both the methods and the philosophy, are the *focus* and the *level* of intervention to prevent crime. In some forms of action, the focus is tightly aimed at reducing levels of crime or risk (for example a burglary prevention project, women's safe transport); in others crime reduction will be a welcome spin-off of broader social improvement aims (for example a family centre or youth activities programme). Many programmes and activities that incidentally prevent crime may not even have crime prevention as an aim; for example, a holiday playscheme in an area with high juvenile offending is set up to occupy children constructively, but may act as a secondary crime prevention measure in reducing the incidence of crime by this group. An anti-bullying strategy in a secondary school may well cover all three levels of preventive action (described in section 5.2.3).

## 5.4   Who will make the connections?

In an ideal scenario, groups of local residents would spontaneously come together, organise their demands and strategies and, with the aid of a benign local authority with a generous budget, they would implement a crime prevention plan based on a rational analysis of what would be appropriate for their particular area. Such spontaneous organisations do sometimes arise in response to social action issues, usually as a result of a 'triggering' crisis (the formation of the Craigmillar Festival Society in Edinburgh or Knowle West Against Drugs in Bristol, for example). However, in the face of a rising crime problem, people are as likely to retreat defensively as they are to organise openly. Given that neighbourhood crime is a problem both for local people and the agencies servicing that neighbourhood, it would be fatalistic in the extreme to wait for a spontaneous organisation to crystallise. It would be both more rational and efficient to have somebody 'set the ball rolling' by doing the necessary investigations and making the necessary connections.

Section 17 of the Crime and Disorder Act 1998 in England and Wales (which requires partnership working in cities and districts, to devise and implement crime prevention strategies) finally galvanised what had hitherto been a patchy and mostly voluntary establishment of local community safety strategies. In France many municipalities had been developing local strategies for the previous 20 years in response to the French government's 'carrot' of *Contrats de Villes* which had significant sums of money on offer. Other countries had tried a mixture of carrots (funding) and sticks (legislation), although England and Wales are unique in waving a stick without offering enough carrots – a sore point among many overstretched and underresourced local authorities.

The most enthusiastic supporters of section 17 of the Crime and Disorder Act in most areas were the police. Indeed the police do valuable work in this area, but, as high-profile agents of law and order, they are not necessarily best placed to take on some of the subtle negotiations characteristic of a comprehensive community safety approach. Fortunately, most local authorities in Britain now have dedicated community safety officers and they have been able to take on crime auditing and strategy development as a core task.

At the time of writing many crime audits have merely drawn on recorded crime figures and strategies have concentrated on the more obviously manageable crime problems at the expense of the more acute and intractable. Thus crimes and problems such as opportunistic thieving through open windows or doors, vandalism of a particular area, theft from cars or night-time street disturbances might be prioritised, because the police in particular have ready-made strategies for dealing with such problems. If a crime prevention officer can make some impact on these highly visible, easily solved crimes, he or she may *seem* to be very effective. However, if other more serious (intractable) crimes are not being tackled, the work will remain tangential to the process of improving overall community safety in a municipality or district. Examples of these more intractable problems might be: dealing in hard drugs; crime resulting from drug dependency; robbery from the person; aggravated burglary in homes and shops to acquire goods and money to buy drugs; domestic violence; and violent assault (often affecting young men in an area).

Bottoms and McWilliams envisaged crime prevention work as being an essential facet of the probation officer's role in their 'Non-treatment paradigm for probation practice' (1979), and this position was reiterated by the Association of Chief Probation Officers in a statement it published in June 1988. Unfortunately probation officers are under considerable pressure to cope with the rising numbers of convicted offenders, and, as crime prevention work is difficult to quantify in terms of tangible outputs, it tends to lose out to the 'numbers game' of processing offenders through the courts. Both probation officers and local authority social workers are often reluctant partners in longer term crime preventive activities. The main reason is that both social work and probation departments are overstretched, dealing with acute problems – people referred to them, who need immediate help. Individual caseloads are growing and there is little time or resources to spare for chronic, longstanding issues of crime and community safety.

In view of the above, it is unlikely that the prime mover of a more eclectic crime prevention approach would be based in a probation or social work department and this is being borne out in the low profile being taken by social services and probation in the new Crime and Disorder Reduction Partnerships. This is unfortunate, as social workers and probation officers could play a key role in the long-term prevention of future criminality and, indeed, like the police service, when the probation service was first established, its primary stated aim was to prevent crime. This aim gradually frittered away and probation officers (and many social workers) are now primarily servants of the criminal justice system who help to process miscreants into and out of various institutions, or offer non-custodial surveillance and monitoring. The position of social workers and probation officers described above highlights just why neighbourhood crime prevention is so underdeveloped – it straddles several disciplines and agency functions (or falls between several stools!).

As was famously stated in the Morgan Report (Home Office Standing Conference on Crime Prevention 1991, 3.15: 15):

> The reality is that crime prevention is a peripheral concern for all the agencies and a truly core activity for none of them, even those agencies which explicitly include crime prevention within their objectives such as the police and probation service.

Very rarely does everyone pool their resources – the one approach that may prove to be most effective. There are a number of reasons for this, which will now be discussed.

## 5.5   Intervention models

This section describes some of the themes that permeate the various approaches to improving community safety and reducing crime. Much recent theorising and research has focused on four different themes that, it is argued, are key factors to be addressed when attempting to prevent neighbourhood crime. Two of these themes are about the *process* of preventing crime: partnership; and community cohesion/control. The other two are about the *content* of crime prevention strategies: zone/neighbourhood initiatives; and targeting by group/category.

### 5.5.1   *Partnership*

Every individual citizen and all those agencies whose policies and practices can influence the extent of crime should make their contribution. Preventing crime is a task for the whole community. (Home Office 1984)

The principal co-ordination needed comes down to co-ordination among different services within localised places. This is at once the most difficult kind of co-ordination, and the most necessary. (Jacobs 1961: 430)

This pooling of resources by the experts and professions, who then work in a spirit of partnership between themselves and local people, is the baseline of neighbourhood crime prevention. The trouble is that: 'each (professional group) tends to see the road to social betterment through the biasing lenses of its own profession's filters' (Webber 1968: 16). Persuading police, housing officials, youth workers, health workers, planners, architects and social workers to do more than just pay lip service to the principle of 'interagency cooperation' is a daunting task, but one that must be faced. The move towards working partnerships can be made through direct organisation, 'psychological blackmail' or political pressure, or a combination of all three, depending on the circumstances.

Unfortunately, in many cases, barriers are erected between agencies and professionals, to inhibit effective partnerships. I would suggest that some of the barriers might be:

- different cultural views or professional attitudes to dealing with crime problems; for example housing managers might have a different attitude to dealing with young vandals than youth workers would
- tightly demarcated job and departmental remits that do not allow for sharing tasks and overlapping of activities
- budgetary arrangements which cannot accommodate pooling of resources or funding of work which might benefit another department or agency
- status or power differentials between different agencies can result in unequal partnerships and people from voluntary organisations or community groups feeling overwhelmed by the big spenders such as housing departments, police and education.

In local situations where these barriers have been overcome, there is evidence to suggest that this has contributed to the creation of safer neighbourhoods (Shaftoe 2002b).

Partnership working is not just about a bunch of people from different agencies and disciplines delivering a group project. This will be part of the output from a partnership to the communities it serves, but a large amount of delivery of community safety improvements will still have to come directly from the various participating agencies (see Figure 5.5). To varying degrees, most partnerships are still beholden and accountable to the central administrative, management and financial systems of the various agencies and departments represented. So, however good a partnership working arrangement may be, the centres of the various agencies are still crucial in delivering a full range of effective services and may need to change themselves to facilitate this.

### 5.5.2 *Developing community cohesion and control*

The Japanese experience (see Clifford 1976; Thornton and Endo 1992) has illustrated the apparent correlation between crime reduction and community cohesion. In Britain, there is a proportionally lower crime rate in rural areas than in cities, which, as already discussed, may be to do with the greater stability and social cohesiveness of the former. Much community development work is centred on generating social interaction and integration.

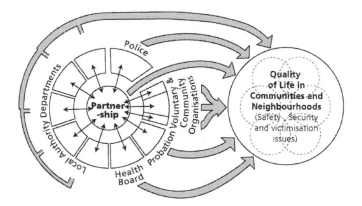

**Figure 5.5** Model of how partnerships and agencies deliver safer communities

However, community development workers have discovered that you cannot hold people together unless they can anticipate a direct benefit coming out of such cohesion, such as improved quality of life and/or more control over their own circumstances (see Loney 1983). 'Experience shows that crime prevention programmes which stimulate local enthusiasm, and so encourage the community to feel a sense of ownership towards the programmes, are more likely to last' (Home Office 1990).

With regard to community engagement, some criminologists and social scientists suggest that nothing can be done at the micro-level until there is a fundamental redistribution of power and resources at the macro-level. Although structural conditions of our society clearly perpetuate many of our social problems, there is still scope for a constructive, small-scale redistribution of power and resources – what Bottoms and McWilliams (1979) refer to as 'micro-structural and socially integrative amelioration'.

In the 1980s and early 1990s the 'new realist' criminologists led by Lea and Young (1993) have recognised the importance of taking *localised* action to create safer communities, not least because crime causes so much suffering to people who may already be disadvantaged. Community control, with professionals acting as partners rather than executives, seems to be a key element in rehabilitating disadvantaged communities. At the neighbourhood level, this empowerment of the local community can range from the token (community councils) to the total (tenant management cooperatives such as the one at Cloverhall in Rochdale and the regeneration programme run in Bradford by the Royds Community Association). In Britain, the USA and Norway, when problem estates have been handed over to the tenants, complete with maintenance budgets and allocation rights, there have been dramatic improvements in the physical condition and quality of life on these estates (Ward 1974; Birchall 1988; Power 1988). According to a Department of the Environment (1994) account of Cloverhall Tenant Management Co-operative:

> Crime and vandalism has almost disappeared. There were only a couple of break-ins in 1993. Cloverhall remains a prime example of how tenants taking charge . . . can help protect investment in an estate and give tenants a sense of pride and ownership.

Two other community responses to the problem of crime and insecurity suggest that community may not always be the rosy feel-good factor that we presume. In Northern Ireland 'community justice' involves local people with paramilitary associations sentencing and punishing alleged delinquents. A number of young car thieves have been shot through the knees by paramilitaries eager to initiate their own drastic form of community crime prevention. The rapid increase in the number of gated communities in divided countries such as South Africa, Brazil and the USA serves to remind us that communities can be exclusive as well as inclusive. It could be argued that gated communities represent an abandonment of any attempt to prevent crime through social measures and are reversing the civilising process of the last few hundred years by re-enclosing the privileged in fortified bastions and citadels. Before the British get too smug about this, it has been reported that two-thirds of one of the country's major house builder's new developments in the Thames Valley area are gated (London *Evening Standard* 18/12/98).

### 5.5.3 *Zones and neighbourhoods*
When it comes to developing a crime reduction strategy, practitioners and partnerships tend to take two approaches: targeting geographical areas and/or targeting at-risk groups and crime categories.

Chapter 4 demonstrated the extent to which crime and place are related, so it is unsurprising that many crime strategies target high crime areas. There is much sense in this zoning approach, which has also been used to focus efforts to improve health, education and the environment. Critics, however, have pointed out that this can lead to a condition dubbed 'zonitis', where numerous overlapping, but not necessarily coterminous initiatives are layered on top of each other in a confusing and uncoordinated manner. From a crime prevention point of view, there is a risk that such an approach could result in some crimes merely being displaced over an arbitrary administrative border. A zonal approach can also lead to a wasteful amount of competitive tendering, where the managers of individual neighbourhoods have to complete vast application forms explaining why their neighbourhood is more deserving of funding (from local or national government, or the European Community) than the one next door. Despite these caveats, there clearly are approaches that demand a neighbourhood approach, be this redesign, local service management or community development, and this recognition is behind the British government's Neighbourhood Renewal initiative – the successor of a number of other zone-based approaches (some of which are described in section 7.7).

In addition to the locational implications of situational crime prevention, research has revealed that the number of children in a neighbourhood, proportional to the total population, is one of the most significant factors in explaining differing levels of petty crime and vandalism (see, for example, Poyner 1982; Page 1993). This example highlights the importance of achieving the right social mix. Of course it is not just an age mix that needs attention. Most problem, or so-called sink, estates are a result of housing allocations whereby individuals and families with little choice and more than their share of difficulties tend to end up concentrated in one or two areas.

The work of Morris (1957) in Croydon and Baldwin and Bottoms (1976: 176) in Sheffield indicates that housing departments 'reinforce rather than initiate the process of segregation'. Both writers note that people tend to self-segregate through the housing market, insofar as those who have the power of choice will avoid undesirable areas, which are then left to those desperate enough to accept any kind of roof over their heads. We thus end up with the familiar city patchwork of good and bad areas. This polarisation was dramatically increased during the right-to-buy scramble initiated by the Conservative government in the 1970s. Over the ensuing three decades, good quality council housing has virtually disappeared (bought up and sold on by fortunate tenants). Most council housing that remains in the rented sector is now 'housing of last resort' (the less desirable flats and houses in notorious areas) in the style of American public housing projects – the unpopular housing that nobody but the desperate will move to. This division of the population into ghettos tends to provoke prejudice and conflict, as well as concentrating particular problems disproportionately in certain areas. The controversial issue lies in the degree to which social engineering should or could be applied in order to facilitate social integration. (The American school 'bussing' policy highlighted this dilemma.) But how do certain neighbourhoods spiral into decline, acquiring a reputation which is then difficult to shake off (Skogan 1990)? A number of factors may have led to this, including:

• the original reasons for which the housing was built, for example slum clearance or for workers at a mine which has long since closed, which will determine the social and economic character-istics of the first settlers
• if council or housing association owned, the allocation policies used
• if owner-occupied or privately rented, the level of income needed to buy into the area
• the way that those with mobility (high points for a transfer, or willing and able to sell at a knock-down price) will choose to leave a bad area
• whether the households coming into the district will be those with little choice over where they live (one offer only from the council, or can't afford to live anywhere better)
• local patterns of deprivation and unemployment
• how images of areas build up. Does it look bad? Do the majority of people steer clear of the place?
• the reputation of a neighbourhood – do people describe it in jokey or denigrating terms?

To resolve dilemmas of social mix, the most promising develop-ments are likely to be in the direction of passive social integration. These are planning methods in which neighbourhoods are designed to accommodate quotas of different social and age groups. This can be achieved through mixed housing types (for example, a certain percentage of large family houses, supported accommodation and pensioners' flats – see Newman 1980), or by mixed housing tenure (combinations of local authority, housing association, private, self-build and commercial tenures). It is clearly easier to achieve this heterogenisation at the time of large-scale redevelopment, but it is also possible to hive off parts of problem estates to housing associations, tenants' cooperatives or even private developers. This latter approach has been taken at Castlemilk in Glasgow and Niddrie House in Edinburgh.

*5.5.4 Targeting groups and categories*
When attempting to prevent crime, the alternative, or indeed com-

plementary, approach to focusing on particular neighbourhoods or zones is to concentrate efforts on at-risk groups or particular crime categories, across a whole city, borough or state.

Research has drawn attention to the fact that certain categories of people are more likely to get into trouble than the average person (West 1982; Rutter and Giller 1983; Wilson and Herrnstein 1985; Graham and Bowling 1995; Farrington 1996; Goldblatt and Lewis 1998). Those most at risk of future offending are the male adolescent who has already been in trouble, children who have experienced a very disrupted family environment and school pupils who display difficult behaviour in class or regularly truant. These categories of people are usually already known to social service agencies. It would therefore be logical to ensure that the kind of work already being done with these people was linked to any overall crime prevention strategy. Thus, childcare and family work, probation and detached youth work projects could all legitimately incorporate crime prevention as an extra dimension of their aims, without distorting their existing intentions (perhaps through social skills training or focused groupwork (see Nursey 1984; Priestley et al. 1985). These are the secondary and tertiary levels and focuses of intervention referred to earlier.

Some social workers and youth workers are suspicious of crime prevention because it sounds either too mechanistic, too symptom-oriented or too reactionary. Some feel that the criminal act is a problem for society (symbolised by the police, the courts and the establishment), rather than for the individual offender, and they therefore perceive activities aimed at reducing crime as being repressive. However, it cannot be ignored that the criminal act is a real problem for individuals living in high crime neighbourhoods, and that victimisers are often also victims themselves (Home Office 2000).

More valid criticisms of direct crime prevention work with target groups relate to issues of labelling and what Stanley Cohen (1969) refers to as 'net-widening'. Because we are talking about trying to prevent something from happening, we will inevitably prejudge certain categories of people as being at risk of offending and, to be on the safe side, we will be tempted to widen rather than narrow the cast of the net. In this way we may subtly introduce discriminatory social control measures over a wider range of groups and individuals than is actually necessary for the control of crime. This is one of the ethical problems in crime prevention. However, safer communities are better places for everyone to live in, and most effective crime prevention measures have wider social benefits, so by targeting at-risk neighbourhoods and people, we could help them to lead a better quality of life in the long term. As part of a durable community safety strategy, these targeted individuals and groups should benefit from better facilities, opportunities and support systems, rather than police persecution and surveillance by social service agencies.

High priority crime problems (as perceived by the public and politicians) can be tackled as 'themes', rather than as problems in particular neighbourhoods. Two recent examples of this approach are strategies to tackle drugs and street crime. This opens up the possibility of using national media/advertising campaigns and global approaches to opportunity reduction (for example fitting smart disabling chips to mobile phones). Critics of this approach claim that thematic approaches to tackling crime are too diffuse and thinly spread; national media campaigns in particular have been found to have a marginal effect (Rosenbaum et al. 1998; Sherman et al. 2002).

### 5.6 Cost–benefit assessment of crime prevention

In these pages there are suggestions for both new strategies and new ways of coordinating existing services. They cost money but crime prevention can be cost-effective. The financial consequences of crime are enormous; the combined costs of policing, courts, prisons, insurance and the repair of vandalism run into hundreds of millions of pounds annually. Police in Avon and Somerset (England) estimated that the total 'cost' of an average burglary (including victim losses and police investigation time) was £1,900. The Home Office has estimated that the average cost per person proceeded against in the courts is £2,700. The cost of an average custodial sentence is £17,500 (Home Office RDS Directorate 1999a).

On one small Scottish housing estate alone, the housing department estimated that the cost of damage to houses on the estate, through housebreaking and vandalism, amounted to £144,000 per year. This does not even include the cost of boarding up empty houses, at a cost of at least £750 per unit, which would add tens of thousands of pounds to the annual bill. Add to this the cost of insurance claims, police time, social enquiry reports, legal costs and so on and this just for an estate of 900 households! Cost–benefit analyses will usually justify expenditure on a crime prevention measures as long-term saving (see DoE 1989; Osborn 1993). We all pay for these huge costs, either directly, as victims of crime, or indirectly through taxes and higher charges for insurance and in shops (to cover losses from stolen goods).

So even one crime prevented is going to create a financial benefit. The trouble is that usually someone or some agency is going to have to spend some money to prevent that crime and the spender will not necessarily be the direct beneficiary. So, for example, by appointing extra health visitors to support young parents in high crime estates, in ten years' time there may be less juvenile delinquency, which is good news for the police and local residents, but what benefit does the Health Board directly experience? Youth projects funded by the municipality may reduce the amount of shoplifting or car theft in the summer holidays – great for shopkeepers and car owners, but where is the direct benefit for the municipality? Until we can achieve a more holistic and less compartmentalised delivery of public services (see DETR 1999), many cost-effective approaches to crime control are going to be dashed against the rocks of narrow vested interest.

# 6

# From Theory to Practice: Comparing, Implementing and Evaluating Policies

## 6.1 Introduction

In the last decade, criminologists and sociologists have increasingly turned their attention to crime prevention (see, for example, Tilley 1993; Crawford 1997; Gilling 1997; Hughes 1998; Hughes et al. 2002), often lured by the attractions of government or Research Council funding. Thus the concerns of comparative criminology have been focused on the crime prevention arena. This has brought some healthy critiques into an area that was in danger of being regarded as a purely technical or managerial enterprise, but has sometimes led to crime prevention being focused on through an inappropriate lens. Academics are fascinated by theory and debate but it seems that only occasionally do they make any *direct* attempt to translate their reflections and research into helping practitioners, such as police officers and social workers, to make a better job of things. To be fair, this is not what they have been employed to do (unless they are doing contract research). But those working to prevent crime on troubled housing estates and neighbourhoods (sometimes including senior staff managing multi-million pound regeneration schemes) rarely know about the latest academic findings on the value or limitations of this or that approach to crime prevention. It is even less likely that they will have heard about some successful community crime prevention initiative in Canada or Belgium, for example, unless they have had the time and motivation to explore some of the useful websites set up in other countries. (For exemplars of good practice communication from overseas, see van Limbergen et al. 1996 or the Canadian National Crime Prevention Centre's web pages at: www.prevention.gc.ca/en/.)

To take, for a moment, a reductionist standpoint, crime prevention and particularly community crime prevention (or community safety) is not really about anything that criminologists traditionally look at. It is about an absence of crime and criminals. At the root of effective and sustainable community crime prevention is a better quality of life for all and this takes it into the arena of social justice rather than criminal justice. Van Swaaningen (1997: 213–14) reminds us that crime prevention policy

> needs to be problem rather than crime oriented, and responsible authorities need to invest in city sanitation and maintenance, stimulating community activities from below and creating a facilitating rather than a control-oriented attitude among civil servants.

Or as Cain (2000: 290) succinctly states: 'The lesson is that you can't solve neighbourhood crime problems by focusing on neighbourhood crime. Rather the medium – the sociability, the organisation – is the message.' This is not a new notion; Morris and Hawkins (1970), in their seminal polemic on crime control policy, argued a very similar line. Thus, it could be argued that some of the criminological concerns about social construction, epistemology and methodology are perhaps less pressing, or at least different, when focusing on community safety. Many community-based crime prevention activities require little more than common sense to achieve their goals. For example, closing and locking the doors of your home or car when they are unoccupied are almost certainly going to reduce the risk of thefts from them, and running interesting summer activities for bored youngsters on marginalised housing estates is almost certainly going to reduce the amount of vandalism and antisocial behaviour they get up to in their spare time. This does not preclude the possibility of an interesting theoretical discussion about opportunity, displacement and diversion (for an enlightened example of this, see Crawford 1998: 68–70), but it is likely that a clear thinking lay person could see the sense in situational and diversionary measures without resort to arcane criminological texts. The one publication that attempts to bridge the gaps between theory, policy and practice – the Home Office's

*Crime Prevention News* – although containing some useful in-depth articles from time to time, tends to be debased by gushing public relations coverage of the British government's various crime prevention initiatives.

This is not to suggest that all theoretical analysis of community crime prevention should be abandoned, as was suggested by Morris and Hawkins (1970), but that there need to be more conduits between theory and research on the one hand and policy and practice on the other. Furthermore, there are undoubtedly ontological issues around what makes for a good quality of life and serious social policy considerations about whether community crime prevention is about safety for all or just the righteous (cf. Donnison 1998; Young 1998a, 1999).

Criminal victimisation and insecurity are problems common (in varying degrees) to most developed nations (Mayhew and van Dijk 1997; van Kesteren 2000). There is a remarkable symmetry of crime trends within different, although comparable countries. This often appears to be independent of national political and policy variations, but may be a reflection of increasingly global economic, social and cultural influences (Young 1998a, 1999). Although each country uses a different criminal justice system to prosecute criminals, arguably the origins of offensive behaviour and the opportunities for crime are similar throughout the world. In Europe, Canada and the Antipodes there has been a common response to the problem of crime over the last couple of decades – a shift away from overreliance on the deterrent effect of the criminal justice system as the principal means of crime control. Given what I said earlier about the nature of crime prevention, this has to be a promising development and one where we can all learn from each other as we take faltering steps towards integrating crime prevention into a broader social policy framework. (Section 17 of the British Crime and Disorder Act 1998 was a significant statutory recognition of this broader landscape.) However, there are many other countries (probably the majority in the world) where more pressing sociopolitical factors and endemic problems of violence and corruption mean that the concept of community crime prevention is a somewhat fragile vision.

Therefore the appropriateness of valid comparison and policy exchange between countries and regions in terms of community crime prevention will vary in strength according to similarities or differences in culture and overarching sociopolitical conditions. As with criminal justice policy, we have to beware of a Eurocentric (or 'Americanocentric') bias (see Cohen 1997; Cain 2000). For example, we have a considerable amount to learn from aboriginal and indigenous systems of mediation, conflict resolution, community support networks and social justice found in so-called third world and 'primitive' cultures (see Braithwaite 1989). In many ways it could be claimed that these tribes and cultures have successfully maintained the kind of community safety that our supposedly more civilised societies have lost. An interesting, but unusual, case is (or was until recently) Japan where, for the last 50 years traditional Confucian values seemed to be able to coexist with a highly advanced economic system, with consequent low levels of crime (Thornton and Endo 1992). However, recent news reports suggest that this is beginning to unravel as a new generation of young people is falling increasingly under the global influence of Western individualistic culture.

## 6.2   Compared to what?

If, as suggested above, community crime prevention has more to do with social justice than criminal justice and we want to enhance community safety in order to achieve a better quality of life for all, who should we be looking to for inspiration and models of good practice? Should we be looking at places that appear to have low levels of crime (Singapore or East Germany before the fall of the wall perhaps)? Or should we be looking at places that have achieved a fair balance between levels of crime and civil liberties (Denmark, Holland and Canada perhaps)? There is no objective answer to this, only a normative one based on what you regard as a good quality of life. Many people love the cleanliness and order of Singapore and an increasing number of ex-Soviet citizens look back nostalgically to the security of life under the old regime, but many others would prefer not to be told by the state how many children they should have, and to know that no one in their street was sending regular logs of their movements to the secret police. A slightly increased risk of having some personal property stolen seems to be a price worth paying, but many people would not agree. This normative relativity could lead to stalemate in terms of using comparative experiences to inform policy change, but I will proceed on the basis of what I think constitutes a 'just society' (and see Donnison 1998).

Many countries may pay lip service to concepts of social justice, but their policies are often at odds with these worthy aspirations and it is not always clear whether this is based on ignorance or deliberate political choices. For example, politicians of many Eastern European countries remain to be convinced that more efficient policing and more prisons are not the keys to crime prevention. In the USA many politicians still think they can 'lock away' the crime problem by building more prisons and handing out stiffer sentences (see Currie 1998). In Britain, despite a commitment by the government to try to tackle the 'causes' of crime, more effort and expenditure is still being spent on getting tough with offenders.

By contrast, France has taken a 'social inclusion' approach to crime prevention for many years (see Shaftoe 1997; Pitts 1998), yet has still experienced youth rioting on peripheral estates outside Paris, Lyons and Marseilles in the last few years, and has had to introduce local guardians into state schools in the face of rising violence and criminality in the classroom.

Some of the countries with the most impressive community crime prevention initiatives are often the ones who are quietly and conscientiously getting on with it, such as Denmark, Finland, Canada and New Zealand. In many of these countries the philosophy is to 'think nationally, act locally' to prevent crime and create safer communities for their citizens. They are carrying out sophisticated, multilayered programmes, aspects of which are transferable and replicable, at least to other countries with similar governance and culture. This is, arguably, because community crime prevention is so inextricably connected to other social policy interventions (cf. van Swaaningen 1997). Therefore countries that are most fertile to comparison and policy transfer are generally those with similar socioeconomic and political systems.

Before I compare policy and practice across different countries, it is worth pointing out that there are a number of polarities and tensions that affect individual countries' starting points for community crime prevention. As Crawford (1997), Hughes (1998) and others point out, enhancing community safety is not a neutral, technical activity but is riddled with a priori values, moral assumptions and political attitudes. Some of these background tensions or polarities are discussed briefly below:

- *Solidarity or individual responsibility?* Some crime prevention activities are prioritised according to the fundamental policies and culture of the country concerned. For example, in France neighbourhood crime (or *délinquance* as they call it) is seen as a symptom of the failure to achieve *fraternité* and every effort is made to counteract this by engaging in reintegrative activities for those perceived to be excluded from the French *solidarité*. By contrast the US constitution and culture sanctifies individual rights and freedoms above all else, so that whether or not you become a victim is primarily your responsibility rather than the state's.

- *Sticks and carrots.* Even where there might be a consensus about how to prevent crime, there are noticeable variations in how policy is converted into practice. At one extreme you have the British Crime and Disorder Act which 'requires' local authorities to prevent crime but a government that only offers resources on a competitive winner/loser basis to achieve this. At the other end of the spectrum, countries such as Denmark, Belgium and France offer the 'carrot' of sums of money and on-site expertise as an incentive for local authorities to come up with local crime prevention 'contracts'.

- *The problems of political ebbs and flows.* Crime prevention practice on the ground is hugely susceptible to changes in national political complexion. For example, in France the socialist government in the 1980s invested hugely in social crime prevention activities, most notably aimed at young people from disadvantaged backgrounds. For some years this reversed the rising crime trend characterising other European countries (see King 1988). In the 1990s the French government lurched to the right, public expenditure on combating social exclusion was reduced and, perhaps not coincidentally, crime rates rose. In New Zealand, the election during the 1990s of a right-wing government led to the slashing of welfare programmes and privatisation of public services. New Zealand's property crime rate escalated subsequently, in parallel with increased inequality. The right-wing British government that steered the country through the 1980s and early 1990s cut welfare at the same time as it increased expenditure on the police and prisons (about the only two public services they invested heavily in). Many assumed that New Labour would reduce this dependence on general deterrence and redirect resources towards long-term social prevention. A smattering of pilot projects has been instigated (for example Sure Start, New Deal for Communities) but, presumably under populist pressure, there hasn't been any significant reorientation away from reactive criminal policy.

- *Theory-driven or practice-driven?* There is a noticeable variation between countries in relation to their reliance on empiricism or theory to drive their crime prevention strategies. Superficially there appears to be a divide between the Anglo-Saxon pragmatism of 'doing what works' and the Latin cultures' desire to base action on theory and principle. It may not just be professional predilections that lead to theory- or practice-driven policies in different countries. It may also, as Mawby (1999) points out, be based on access to data. Government administrations in countries such as Britain, the USA and Holland generate huge amounts of statistics, which provide nourishing food for criminological and sociological digestion. Many academics in Southern Europe and other parts of the world have leaner or even empty statistical tables to feed from, and so are thrown by force of circumstance to theorise about that for which there are no available facts. Of course any meaningful practice is bound to be based on theory (although the reverse is not necessarily inevitable) and given the normative platform upon which community crime prevention has to be built, there must always be an underpinning theory, even if it is not made explicit.

It is difficult to use any standard criteria of success or effectiveness in community crime prevention, when 'success' or 'effectiveness' are both subjective and likely to influence and be influenced by other social policies and personal circumstances. Absolute levels of per capita victimisation would appear to be an obvious benchmark. Yet some countries which appear to have low victimisation rates (say, Greece) have relatively underdeveloped community crime prevention programmes compared with some countries that are doing more (Denmark for example). So perhaps we should measure success and effectiveness by whether victimisation rates are going down. But this would mean that the USA is doing better than Holland. Yet Holland has a more developed and comprehensive set of strategies for community crime prevention than most other countries, so maybe the benchmark should be the degree of sophistication of interventions.

Into the mix of cross-national crime prevention comparisons one has to add the predisposing factors that may make it easier for some countries to maintain lower crime levels without even having to adopt specific crime prevention strategies. Norway and Switzerland are apparently cases in point. Both of these countries are characterised by relative prosperity and equality, comparatively stable population networks and only moderate urbanisation. Criminologists and sociologists will agree that such conditions are not breeding grounds for crime and that civilised societies should strive for policies that lead to such a good quality of life for the majority. However, in the immediate term, such lofty aspirations are of limited help to countries such as Holland with the highest urban concentration in the West and England with high population mobility and relative poverty.

There is also a possible downside to countries with little crime – they tend to be characterised by conforming pressures, often imposed by draconian means. Switzerland would be regarded by some as an oppressively conservative culture, and looking internationally, Japan may have the lowest crime rate of any advanced industrialised society, but its citizens are culturally pressurised from the cradle onwards. Russia, Poland and the Czech Republic had much lower crime rates under their former communist regimes and crime-free Singapore would not be as it is had not the government intervened in very personal matters – who your neighbour is, how you live, the noise you make, how you spit or what language you use.

Perhaps this highlights the futility of comparing nations according to some kind of league table of community crime prevention value. As Nick Tilley (2002) points out, many local interventions, applied from the preventive palette, work for some people in some circumstances and are likely to achieve, at best, incremental improvements. By their very nature most, if not all, community crime prevention interventions are context-specific. Even within a country region or town, 'what works' in one locality will not automatically work in another locality (see Osborn and Shaftoe 1995). However, this is not to say that as every nation, region, city, village and neighbourhood is unique, there is no point in looking outside our own back yard for inspiration and good practice. On the contrary, nearly all progress is achieved by looking over the horizon, then thinking laterally and adapting locally.

Clearly, it is difficult to compile consistent information categories about crime prevention for each country, but, by way of an overview, here are some general comparisons of policy and practice. Arguably, the countries with the most developed crime prevention policies and quantity of practice are France, Denmark, Holland, Canada, Australia, New Zealand and the UK, along with Finland, Sweden, Belgium and Germany. All these countries have both central and local government requirements or incentives to prevent crime, rather than just controlling it through the criminal justice system. They also, to varying degrees, have a research, guidance and evaluation infrastructure. In most cases these are provided by a national crime prevention council, but in the cases of Holland, France and the UK, national government departments are the prime movers. This high level of crime prevention policy and practice could be partly a reflection of the scale of neighbourhood crime in those countries. Indeed countries such as Austria and Switzerland, which appear to have comparatively low crime and insecurity problems, also seem to engage in little explicit crime prevention activity. Does this suggest that we would be better off studying the culture and social policies of places like Austria and Switzerland rather than the crime prevention policies of higher crime countries (Clinard 1978)?

In some countries, the intensity of crime prevention activity is unevenly distributed. Two examples of this are Spain, which has a disproportionate amount of activity in Barcelona, and Italy where more seems to be happening in Turin and the Emilia-Romagna region than in other cities or regions. This suggests that the municipalities or regional administrations are taking the lead, rather than a proactive central government, as it is difficult to believe that Barcelona and Turin have significantly higher crime problems than Madrid or Rome.

Generally speaking, the countries with less developed crime prevention policies and practices tend to rely on the police as the principal protagonists and aim their practice at the criminal justice system and tertiary prevention (that is, preventing offenders from *reoffending*). The more sophisticated countries tend to have a separate national crime prevention board or department which, although linked, is separate from the police system. All the Scandinavian countries have national crime prevention councils. France has an inter-ministerial delegation on crime prevention, while in Holland crime prevention is subsumed under the Ministry of Justice. A number of Central and Eastern European countries have established national crime prevention boards or councils (Estonia, the Czech Republic and Hungary, to name three). These tend to be located at the highest inter-ministerial level but (unlike France, Belgium or Denmark) have no obvious resources or power to support or implement activity on the ground.

France is probably the leader in criminality prevention, closely followed by Denmark which has a very pragmatic, 'can do' approach to crime prevention. Sweden tends to have a rather more academic approach that is heavy on controlled experiments and rigorous evaluation. Perhaps these differences between Scandinavian neighbours are a reflection of how the two national crime prevention councils are staffed. In Denmark the prevention council is mostly staffed by seconded police officers; in Sweden they are mostly social science researchers. Britain is historically known for its focus on opportunity reduction, but is veering towards a greater interest in 'root cause' criminality prevention. Holland has a thoroughly eclectic approach and, through the sponsorship of the Ministry of Justice, has also put a lot of effort into monitoring and evaluation.

The youngest European partner to go wholeheartedly for crime prevention is Belgium, which was doing virtually nothing preventive in the 1980s, but since then has put massive political, strategic and financial resources into a range of initiatives (see van Limburgen et al. 1996). Australia has made great strides in researching and evaluating effective crime prevention interventions. The Australian National Crime Prevention Program, based in the attorney general's department, evolved in the late 1990s from the National Campaign against Violence and Crime. As well as research, the programme promotes and funds practical initiatives such as pilot projects, local prevention activities, communication and training (see www.crimeprevention.gov.au).

### 6.3  Sharing crime prevention policy and practice

In the light of all this, what possibilities for transfer of learning might be suggested? Can we assume that the universality of human nature and the broad similarity of Western nations' social and political systems offers us a level playing field for comparison, so that it is as likely that we will be inspired by a crime prevention project in Rotterdam or Toronto as by one in the neighbouring suburb to where we are living or working? The simultaneous fascination and frustration of crime prevention practice is that no one has come up with (or is likely to come up with) a single all-embracing technique that can be applied anywhere and everywhere (Osborn and Shaftoe 1995). Although the process of researching, planning and implementing crime prevention measures may be universal, the actual solution must be fine-tuned to local circumstances (Lab 2000). But the more we can find out about what has worked elsewhere in particular circumstances, the more comprehensive will be our palette of possibilities for solving our own unique crime or insecurity problem.

This palette can include comparisons at every level of political administration. National policies do not, in themselves, deliver community crime prevention, but, if well formulated, can provide the background structure, in which community safety can flourish. Sections 2 and 3 of the Crime and Disorder Act 1998 in England and Wales (requiring local authorities, the police and other public service agencies to work together to audit, implement and evaluate local crime prevention strategies) have noticeably raised the profile and interest in community crime prevention, even if there is a more sluggish development of actual community safety improvements on the ground. National policies in France and Belgium have provided both an enabling framework for local action, and (unlike England and Wales) non-competitive additional resources for community safety activity in contracted locations.

In the Emilia-Romagna region of Italy and Catalonia in Spain, regional crime prevention approaches have been developed in the absence of national policies. It will be interesting to see if the regional government offices in England and the devolved administration in Wales become more independent and divergently attuned to the different dynamics of their respective regions, or if they just remain appraisers and enforcers for central government.

Within urban policy spheres there seems to have been an increasing interest in using the city as a unit of comparison. In crime prevention terms this was mirrored by the establishment of the *secu-cités* network, under the auspices of the European Forum for Urban Security. The idea is that politicians and local government officers from the various subscribing cities visit, meet and generally exchange good practice.

Ultimately community crime prevention is actually delivered at the neighbourhood level. So, in theory, this is where the most vibrant exchange of policy should be occurring. In practice this level appears to be most weakly linked internationally. There are a few international practitioner and community representative exchange networks and visits but generally fieldworkers and resident activists get their international comparative news filtered by senior management and politicians, if they get it at all.

In view of the above observations, it is surprising that there is not a greater international exchange of research and practice in community crime prevention. I believe that there are a number of barriers to cross-fertilisation, some banal and some more substantial, but none insurmountable. Of the banal barriers, I suggest they include language differences, national pride and traditional rivalries, and the myth that 'people are different in X country'. Some middle ranking barriers include the fact that international exchange is most often undertaken between politicians and academics (at conferences and through journals) rather than between public service officers and practitioners, and the continuing assumption in some countries that general deterrence through the criminal justice system is the 'one true path' of crime prevention. Tensions exist too between Anglo-Saxon pragmatism (shoot first and ask questions later) and Latin philosophising (That's all very well in practice, but will it work in theory?). Some more substantial barriers are rooted in adherence to different theories of crime causation and the varying national politics about communal solidarity (for example France) versus individual responsibility (for example the USA).

Despite these potential barriers, there is a bewildering array of overlapping umbrella organisations for sharing and disseminating crime prevention experience. The main ones are described below (see also the key websites listed at the end of the book).

- The International Centre for the Prevention of Crime (ICPC) is a well-established organisation based in Montreal, Canada, which organises conferences and disseminates good practice, with a distinct social prevention and Francophile flavour.
- The International Society for Crime Prevention Practitioners (ISCPP) is based in Pennsylvania, USA and is focused on police

training, mostly taking a security and target-hardening approach to preventing crime.

- The International Crime Prevention Information Network (ICPIN) was established by the Dutch Ministry of Justice in the late 1980s, in cooperation with the British Home Office. ICPIN was essentially a computerised database of good practice projects. It was ahead of its time, because the internet hardly existed then and the database was difficult to access. As a result of this and the lack of continuation funding, ICPIN withered away in the early 1990s.
- The International Crime Prevention Action Network (ICPAN) is based in Vancouver, Canada. ICPAN had similar aims to ICPIN but benefited from the rise of the internet. ICPAN took a decidedly social root cause approach to crime prevention in its overall ethos, arising, as it did, from the huge Towards World Change conference in Vancouver in 1996. Due to lack of funding ICPAN appears to be inactive at the time of writing.

All these international set-ups would claim to include Europe within their ambit, but, additionally, Europe has its own suite of umbrella organisations:

- The European Institute for Crime Prevention and Control (HEUNI) is affiliated to the UN and based in Helsinki. Despite its title, a lot of HEUNI work seems to concentrate on control rather than prevention and big issues (for example organised crime) rather than community crime prevention.
- The Centre for International Crime Prevention, based in Vienna, is another UN-supported institute. It is mostly concerned with international organised crime, terrorism and cross-border crime.
- The European Centre for Crime Prevention is a lower profile organisation established by the University of Twente in Holland and the University of Munster, just across the border in Germany. It has a trilingual website, which lists good practice and useful crime prevention publications/websites. It has a distinctly Northern European stance in contrast to the next umbrella organisation.
- The European Forum for Urban Security (FESU) is based in Paris and is a well-established organisation with its power base

predominantly in Southern Europe. As a result it has a strong
social action and inclusion agenda and can be less enthusiastic
about the situational approaches often espoused by the Anglo-
Saxons.

• The European Community has now added to this plethora of
crime prevention umbrella organisations through establishment
of the European Crime Prevention Network office in Brussels
(see de Waard 2002).

In addition to the organisations listed above, there is a whole raft
of further networks that aim to share information and good practice. These include 'secure cities' networks, 'crime prevention
through environmental design' associations, informal practitioner
networks and European municipal linking associations. The big
question is why do we need so many umbrellas and networks? Is
there benefit in diversity or is this all just confusing? The answer is
probably that we don't actually need so many organisations but, a
bit like the difficulty of standardising electricity plugs throughout
the world, no one centre has the ultimate mandate to act on behalf
of everyone. On the plus side, such a proliferation of databases
and networks means that there is a huge choice of menus and
sources of information, if only you can find them!

Despite the confusing plethora of overlapping crime prevention
organisations, practice does get transferred between countries and
ideas from one country often take root in another, with few people
realising they are not indigenous inventions. In section 6.4, the UK
will be used as a case study to show just how many crime prevention initiatives are explicit or hidden imports. Significantly though,
just because practices have been transferred between nations does
not mean that they are necessarily *effective* practices, even in their
originating country. Often they are adopted because they chime
with the mood of the moment or politicians think they will garner
popular support. The most extreme recent example of this was
zero tolerance which even its New York originators downplayed as
an effective and sustainable crime control intervention (see Bratton
1997a). Neighbourhood watch also suffered a critical hammering
in the USA before it really took off in the UK and other European
countries (see Rosenbaum 1988).

It is clear, from the above illustrations, that nations and regional
administrations do learn from each other about effective commu-

nity crime prevention. It is perhaps an indictment of criminologists and academics in general that, with some notable exceptions, they do not appear to be significant facilitators of this transfer of knowledge and skill, despite numerous comparative studies. Even the famous brownies (Home Office research publications), often written by contracted academics and aimed squarely at policy and practice improvement, are perceived by many practitioners as opaque and not easy to decipher, assuming they get to see them. As Downes (1988: 2) points out:

> Much, perhaps most, of the exchanges that occur on the subject of crime and its control emanate not from academic criminology but from journalistic work, and often from the ad hoc concerns of professionals and administrators in such fields as police or probation work to learn about the doings of their colleagues overseas.

The various international organisations and networks can be a conduit for good practice, but policy can also be transferred through conferences, survey reports and study visits:

- *Conferences.* A number of international conferences around the theme of crime prevention have been organised, usually by the big three crime prevention umbrella groups (The International Centre for the Prevention of Crime, The Centre for International Crime Prevention, the European Forum for Urban Security). Conferences seem like the obvious way to exchange information and experience, but they have a number of limitations. Usually there is information overload at these events, with parallel workshops meaning that it is impossible to take in everything. They are often so big that meaningful interaction is impossible and, as they are a welcome break from 'the day job', delegates may be the people with the power and the budget to nominate themselves for such events, rather than the people for whom it could be really useful in terms of transforming their policies and practices. It is often said that the most useful aspect of conferences is not the speeches or workshops, but the networking that goes on before, after and in the gaps between the set pieces.
- *Survey reports.* A number of comparative surveys of crime pre-

vention policies and practices have been undertaken and published (Katona 1994; Graham and Bennett 1995; Shaftoe 1997;
Crawford and Matassa 2000). These documents have provided
valuable data that could benefit policy makers and practitioners,
but in each case they have had limited distribution and are not
widely known.

● *Study visits and exchanges.* Many visits to study good practice in
  other countries have been arranged on an ad hoc basis. There
  has been an attempt to formalise this through FESU's *secu-cités*
  scheme, but individual municipalities have to be paid-up
  members of FESU to participate in this. Recently the EU provided twinning funding to allow crime prevention specialists
  from Western European countries to spend time giving on-site
  advice to former Soviet states.

Overall, it can be seen that there are numerous formal and
informal conduits for policy and practice exchange. Any overarching attempt to facilitate all cross-national policy transfer in
crime prevention may be unachievable or inappropriate, but there
still seems to be scope for some international organisation to
provide a clearing house or one-stop shop. Inevitably, a number of
the organisations who might take on this role (notably the big three
mentioned earlier) have overlapping and possibly competing
remits and variable ideals of what constitutes good practice,
making cooperation an added difficulty.

## 6.4    Cross-national influences

To illustrate just how much indigenous crime prevention activity is
in fact adapted practice from elsewhere, the example of the UK
will be used in this section. Nearly everything done in Britain to
prevent crime at the neighbourhood level has been imported or
adapted from elsewhere. Undoubtedly the biggest influences on
British crime prevention policies have come from the USA. Given
the USA's high crime rates, particularly in relation to violence, this
is initially rather puzzling, especially as some of our near neighbours, notably France, Holland and Denmark, have successfully
introduced policies and practices that appear to be eminently
replicable. As ever though, the facility of a common language
cannot be underestimated in the influence it gives to policy, prac-

tice and cultural exchange. And, to their credit, the Americans are much better than most nations at doing proper evaluations of the projects and initiatives they invest in (see, for example, Sherman et al. 1997; Walker 1998), so that, as a result, we have stronger evidence from them about the effectiveness of a particular intervention. First the USA gave us the war on poverty, then we bought its neighbourhood watches, early childhood intervention programmes, crime prevention through environmental design principles, zero tolerance and, latterly, ideas about building social efficacy and social capital at the neighbourhood level (Sampson et al. 1997).

The unfortunately named 'war on poverty' was an attempt by liberal American reformers in the 1960s to improve the lot of the poor and reduce delinquency through community development and 'maximum feasible participation'. The idea was adapted by the British in a number of Community Development Projects (CDPs) in deprived areas. Although some significant gains were achieved, the programmes on both sides of the Atlantic stumbled and eventually had their funding withdrawn when they (inevitably) became politicised and confrontational (Moynihan 1969). It would appear that the policy makers had not realised that if you give 'power to the people' (Alinsky 1971), power and control has to be relinquished by the establishment, who turned out to be very reluctant to do so. Thus, stung by the political fomentation of these programmes, the British and American governments subsequently invested in crime prevention approaches that were less likely to challenge the organisation of state control.

In the 1960s and early 1970s, some Americans (Jacobs 1961; Jeffery 1971; Newman 1972) had looked at the influence of the design and organisation of the built environment on levels of crime and criminal opportunity. The subsequent emergence of the concept of 'crime prevention through environmental design' (CPTED) became a powerful policy tool, which continues to this day both in the USA and the UK. The great attraction of CPTED is that it appears to be value-neutral – it offers a technical set of guidelines which, if implemented, will, it is claimed, keep criminals away from their potential victims, through the use of defensible spaces, symbolic barriers, natural surveillance and buffer zones (covered in section 4.2). Although many CPTED principles make good common sense, many of them are acts of faith rather than scientifically proven in their effectiveness (Atlas 1999) and their apparent effects can be overridden by more pressing social and ecological factors.

The idea that crime could be designed out was developed into the concept of 'situational crime prevention' by the Home Office in England and Wales (see Clarke 1997 and section 4.3 in this book). The principle of situational crime prevention has been described earlier as a 'non-theory' because its aim is merely to make crime more difficult or risky to commit. Evaluations of situational crime prevention measures have demonstrated that they can have some positive effect (see, for example, Ekblom 1998; Armitage 2000), but they do not address the motivation to offend in the first place and have therefore not received much of a welcome in the social crime prevention-oriented countries of Southern Europe.

The next crime prevention idea to drift eastwards across the Atlantic was neighbourhood watch. This has been wholeheartedly promoted by police forces in the UK and, as a result, is now the country's most visible and ubiquitous form of crime prevention. Unfortunately, there are some doubts about its overall efficacy (see Rosenbaum 1988; Laycock and Tilley 1995), perhaps partly because it lost some of its essence during the transatlantic transfer. Neighbourhood watch schemes in America were originally conceived as a means whereby residents in problem areas could complement local policing. Neighbourhood watch members would often patrol in pairs, wore specially issued identifying anoraks and often had access to a storefront base. The watered-down version in Britain has generally not been so proactive, has been spread thinly to include many low crime areas and has often had limited support from the police, once established. Interestingly, the apparent limited effectiveness of neighbourhood watch schemes in the UK has done little to prevent their spread, and schemes to watch industrial plants, boats, petrol station forecourts and farms have all been developed. The best neighbourhood watch associations are generally more akin to community associations, which include social network-building activities and are often led by charismatic community leaders. This brings us on to the next American import, the concept of social efficacy and cohesion.

Having realised that opportunity reduction is not the whole solution to crime problems, some Americans started to look at key social factors that differentiated areas which appeared similar demographically but varied in their levels of crime (see Sampson et al. 1997). They discovered that a key factor was the level of social efficacy or social capital in a neighbourhood. 'Social capital' refers to the density of civic engagement in an area, based on trust between social actors, embedded in shared values and social networks (Coleman 1988; Putnam 1993). Thus, the more neighbourhood residents are bonded through joint activities and face-to-face interactions, the more resistant will that neighbourhood be to predatory and violent crime, as people will be prepared to intervene to prevent crime and impose shared norms of social behaviour. So any form of community development and network building may have a crime preventive impact – the process is as important as the content. This new notion of social capital and inclusion has been enthusiastically adopted in the UK, by the various area regeneration programmes set up by the government.

Another American import influencing recent British government policy is the introduction of early developmental support programmes to at-risk communities. Although well researched in Britain (see, for example, Farrington 1996), the influence of early protective and risk factors in leading to later criminality was tackled at policy level in the USA through such schemes as Hawaii Healthy Start, Communities that Care and the High/Scope Preschool Program (see Utting et al. 1993). Subsequent British schemes such as Sure Start aim to prevent future problems through early intervention in communities with high levels of risk and deprivation, although interestingly the possible criminality prevention impact of Sure Start is not referred to within the programme – possibly another example of British compartmentalised thinking.

While on the one hand the Americans were getting all soft and liberal with early intervention programmes and building social efficacy, their most famous recent crime control export owes more to Arnold Schwarzenegger (the actor not the politician) than to Melanie Klein – zero tolerance. The appeal lies in its very name yet the difficulty of transplanting it to the UK for anything but short-term blitzes (let alone its ideological undertones) meant it burnt brightly but briefly over Middlesborough and a few other British locations (see Young 1998b; Kelling 1999). The USA has probably had the biggest influence on British crime prevention

policy and practice, but our nearer neighbours in Continental
Europe have also pioneered approaches that have subsequently
been adapted and taken up in the UK, most notably certain policies originating in France, Holland and Denmark.

The French motto of Liberty, Fraternity, Equality manifests
itself in their approach to crime prevention. The notion of social
exclusion originated in France and was identified as a cause of
crime and other social ills long before New Labour adopted the
idea. In the 1980s, France had a huge social crime prevention programme particularly aimed at excluded youth. Their efforts paid
off and crime went down in France during the 1980s, in contrast
to the upward trend in most other European countries (see Pitts
1998). This huge national social prevention strategy was delivered
by a new political conduit that ran from central government,
through the regional administrations down to the towns and cities.
Contracts to deliver crime prevention were made by central government to local administrations with the carrot of considerable
funding. The French approach prefers to use trained local people
as the *animateurs* who engage with offenders and victims. The
effectiveness of peer mentoring and peer pressure could therefore
be seen as a French influence on other countries' policies. A particular branch of this local control approach is the use of
concierges at entrances to multi-occupied dwellings, which has
been a feature of French urban life for hundreds of years and has
been adapted for use in British tower blocks (SNU 1997).

There are clear similarities between the French central–local
government approach and attempts by the British government, ten
years later, to adopt a similar strategy via the 1998 Crime and
Disorder Act. However, funding from the Home Office for community safety and crime prevention purposes has tended to be
centrally allocated to crime reduction initiatives with discreet
objectives. The recent Crime Reduction Programme, for example,
provides money for burglary reduction initiatives, projects aimed
at reducing violence against women, targeted policing projects,
and CCTV schemes, amongst others, rather than contracted
funding to local authorities to reduce crime comprehensively in
particular localities (as in France).

The recruitment, training and employment of local unemployed
people as city guards in Holland has been a much-trumpeted
success. City guards provide a uniformed presence on housing

estates, the streets and public transport vehicles. They provide reassurance and advice and can call up other public services (most notably the police) if necessary. Again, there are elements of the Home Office's neighbourhood wardens programme that have been clearly influenced by the success of the city guards in Holland, although the Dutch have a broader use of their guards, including acting as conductors on trams and acting as concierges in housing blocks.

The influence of Dutch drugs policy in the UK illustrates a problematic aspect of the transference of crime prevention techniques. The Dutch approach suggests that treating drug misuse as a health and social problem, rather than primarily a criminal one, is a much more effective way of stemming drug abuse and the crime that flows from it (see, for example, Coleman 1992; Williamson 1997; Holloway 1999). This approach has had a big influence in Britain, even amongst senior police officers. However, despite a small step towards the downgrading of the illegality of cannabis, most UK politicians, no doubt influenced by their transatlantic colleagues, remain resolutely committed to the ongoing war on drugs.

Through their National Crime Prevention Council, the Danes have quietly been getting on with imaginative and effective approaches to crime prevention for many years. Their most influential work has been through their social services, schools and police scheme which brings the three main agencies likely to be involved with at-risk children and youths together to coordinate early preventive interventions. Similar approaches are being adopted in Britain under various guises and often prompted by the requirements of the Crime and Disorder Act.

Finally, Australia and New Zealand, through their pioneering work in secondary and tertiary prevention, have influenced a number of British schemes such as Community Service Orders, victim/offender mediation, restorative justice and alternative dispute resolution (see, for example, Braithwaite 1989).

So, the question has to be asked; are there any crime prevention approaches that are exclusively indigenous to the UK? Two possible contenders are community policing and the use of CCTV in public places. The selection of community policing may appear to be somewhat quixotic, bearing in mind the huge impact that community policing has had in the US, not least via the COPS

(Community-oriented Policing Services) programme introduced by the Clinton administration with the aim of putting an additional 100,000 police officers on the streets in the US.

However, what is interesting is the limited extent to which models of community policing espoused in the US bear any resemblance to those operating in the UK. Certainly their genesis is radically different. While UK police forces can point to the notion of 'policing by consent' as a concept with well-established historical roots, this is not the case in the US. There the concept of community policing was developed as a response to the perceived failures of so-called 'modern' methods of policing (see Walker 1998). These placed an emphasis upon speed of response to crime calls and mobile patrol. Concepts of community policing are notoriously vague and imprecise (Eck and Rosenbaum 1994) and while a number of developments in the US share a common nomenclature with developments in the UK, the content of community policing varies markedly between the two countries. Definitions in the US tend to focus on the community aspect of the term rather than the policing element. Thus community policing, at its most basic, can be understood as policing which involves some contact or consultation with the public; at its most developed it implies policing *by* the community, through neighbourhood social control.

Of perhaps more interest is the reimportation of community policing methods from the US into the UK, notably the support given to problem-solving and problem-oriented policing. One of the familiar complaints offered by British police officers in response to the latter is that they 'already do that'. The extent to which this is the case, at least in any routine, structured way is questionable (Read and Tilley 2000), but is perhaps an illustration of the different historical context in the two countries.

The British approach to community policing, and in particular the emphasis upon policing by consent and the use of local 'beat' bobbies, has a long history, stretching back to Sir Robert Peel's conception of crime prevention rather than crime control (Crowther 2000). After a rocky period in the 1970s and 80s British policing has mostly managed to return to the original Peelian ethos. While we in the UK tend to take for granted the notion, if not the actuality, of the 'bobby on the beat', in many countries this was (and still is) an alien concept. For example, the

Belgians and French traditionally took an 'army of occupation' approach to policing high crime areas and have only recently begun to introduce *police de proximité* with some success (see, for example, Bouchet 1999; Chalumeau 2002).

The other indigenous British invention, which may not export quite so easily, is saturation CCTV coverage of public and communal spaces. Perhaps it is the docile nature of the British, or perhaps they are more susceptible to electronic equipment manufacturers' claims, but Britain is now awash with CCTV cameras, whilst in other countries, such as Germany, Denmark and France, such installations would be seen as contraventions of civil liberties and human rights (see Fyfe and Bannister 1998; Norris and Armstrong 1999). Even the USA appears to be more cautious about CCTV, perhaps because of its high constitutional concern about individual rights and freedoms.

So it appears that many new ideas are in fact recycled and recontextualised ones, although all too often this recontextualisation owes less to an assessment about what is effective with the original approach, and more to the different situation into which the technique is transplanted. It is also worth thinking laterally – looking at initiatives that have been set up to tackle one type of problem, that might not have been directly to do with crime, to see if they can be adapted and transferred for the benefit of community safety.

It is worth looking for interesting developments in the crime prevention field elsewhere, but we should not assume that any one country will have it all. The USA appears to have an excessive influence on British crime prevention policy, but just because we speak (almost) the same language, go to the same conferences and are bombarded with American products, it does not necessarily follow that Britain is fertile soil for US policy transplants. As Kelling (1999: 56) points out: 'I understand that when one crosses the Atlantic or Pacific one is always very cautious because the extent to which ideas from one country generalise to another is extraordinarily limited.' Furthermore, there are some aspects of the American way that we may wish to actively avoid, most notably the embedded cultures of inequality and violence. Some European countries, such as Holland and Denmark, are much closer to the UK culturally and aspirationally. If we could persuade policy makers to spend more time looking East rather than West for inspiration, we might end up with a more humane, equitable and safe society.

## 6.5    Evaluation and the complexity of intervening variables

The multidimensional nature of crime and its prevention makes evaluation of projects and interventions notoriously difficult. If crime has gone down in a particular neighbourhood or a category of offending has reduced, how do you know that what you did was responsible for the reduction in crime? Do you even know that crime reduced and where do you draw the 'boundary of influence'? These and many other interacting variables turn crime prevention evaluation into a minefield of uncertainty.

The current popularity of scientific realist approaches in the crime prevention field lies in part because of its appeal in trying to make sense of 'what works' and what might be generalisable elsewhere in a complex world (Pawson and Tilley 1997). However, unless we adopt more rigorous evaluation criteria for crime prevention initiatives, it is going to be very difficult to make accurate comparisons of effectiveness (see Hope 2002). Two meta-evaluations, one in the UK (Home Office 1998) and one in the USA (Sherman et al. 1997), were groundbreaking in their coverage, but also highlighted the paucity of rigorously evaluated crime prevention interventions.

In the UK the Crime Reduction Programme, a three-year initiative launched in 1999, stressed the importance of evidence-led policy, in which the role of evaluation was central:

A common theme of the recent Crime Reduction Programme has been the implementation of schemes which are based on reliable evidence of what works and what is cost effective, and which themselves generate more of that evidence through rigorous evaluation. The successor programme – the Safer Communities Initiative – also favours an evidence-based approach. (Home Office Crime Reduction website at www. crimereduction.gov.uk/learningzone/cco.htm)

As a result material is increasingly being made available about evaluation and how to undertake it, in the form of research reports, specialist journals and, increasingly, guidance notes for practitioners (see, for example, National Crime Prevention 2002). In England, the Home Office Crime Prevention College (2002) has produced a *Passport to Evaluation* that aims to provide those on the ground with the basic techniques needed to evaluate crime reduction projects. Equally the Crime Reduction Toolkits on the Home Office's Crime Reduction website provide examples of evaluated work in various subject areas, and a checklist for evaluators (www.crimereduction.gov.uk).

Evaluation plays an important part in the 'conjunction of criminal opportunity' framework developed by Paul Ekblom at the Home Office (http://www.crimereduction.gov.uk/learningzone/ cco.htm), and in his emerging '5 Is' model:

> The 5 Is is a knowledge management framework designed to assist practitioners in improving their performance of crime prevention, by helping them select and replicate good practice appropriate to their needs and circumstances. It helps them to accurately follow the underlying principles and practical details of (properly evaluated and documented) preventive action, yet to adapt it for different contexts. (http://www.crimereduction. gov.uk/learningzone/5isintro.htm)

However, despite the increased amount of information available to assist evaluation (Tilley 2002), the extent to which this has had an impact upon practice at a local level remains questionable, with evidence of well-evaluated interventions still thin on the ground.

A simple but practical evaluation framework was used by Osborn (DoE 1994; Safe Neightbourhoods Unit 1995) to compare the effectiveness of various crime prevention measures taken on British housing estates. He measured each initiative against the following questions:

- Did crime go down? (measures changes in number of offences and victimisation rates)
- Were crime problems reduced? (measures fear and qualitative issues)
- Was the initiative responsible for the changes?
- Which specific measure led to the changes?

- Does the effect last?
- Is the initiative replicable or generalisable?

If we could start submitting a range of crime prevention initiatives to the above assessment criteria, then we would be well on the road to useful comparative learning. But it is important to note that monitoring and evaluation measurements would have to be built into initiatives from the start – like crime prevention itself, you can't achieve much after the event.

## 6.6   Conclusion

There has been a remarkable symmetry in crime trends in most Western countries during the last few decades. In most countries, crime rose sharply during the 1960s, 70s and early 1980s but levelled off and started to reduce by varying amounts during the late 1990s and into the new millennium. The exceptions to this rule are the former Soviet states, which appeared to have stable levels of crime until democratisation, since when crime rates have continued to increase.

Many researchers in the West have concluded that crime rates have not been significantly affected by the efforts of the criminal justice system (see, for example, Pavarini 1997: 87; Currie 1998) and that the most promising directions for reducing crime levels are to be found in preventive efforts, particularly at the community level. This conclusion has not always been favourably received by politicians, who, particularly in the UK and USA, have been under pressure from the general public to be more punitive and retributive towards crime and criminals. Thus more police and more prisons are still seen as the solution to crime in many countries. The evidence to the contrary can be found in much research and also in the successful practices of low crime countries such as Japan, Canada, Switzerland and Norway. To have any policy impact, this research and good practice needs to be disseminated not only to professionals but to the general public and their elected representatives. In democracies, policy is generally determined not by professional policy makers (who are limited to advising on policy and then devising implementation strategies), but by politicians who are swayed by the sentiments of the citizens who elected them. It is for this reason that we ended up with the scenario under the last UK Conservative administration, where the home secretary was in many cases pushing through crime control policies (such as 'prison works') that flew in the face of the evidence and advice supplied to him by the expert advisors and researchers employed in his Home Office. At the time of writing, a similar scenario seems to be emerging under the present Labour administration, particularly in relation to drugs, young offenders, antisocial behaviour and street crime.

Politicians tend to look over their shoulders rather than to research evidence when looking for crime control cues. But it is not just the short-term electoral system that undermines the rational flow from theory to research to practice. Every country has a huge lobby that prefers to keep things as they are. Police federations, prison officers' associations, court and probation services, the popular media and the huge private crime control industry all have a vested interest in keeping crime levels high. They don't want us to hear about successes in Holland and Norway, for example, where reduced use of incarceration has not led to an increase in crime (cf. Downes 1988).

Although community safety and crime prevention have the neighbourhood or city as the ultimate point of delivery, one cannot fully decentralise policy transfer (where, for example, workers and community representatives from a troubled estate outside Wolverhampton might learn how to make their neighbourhoods safer, from workers and community representatives on a formerly troubled housing estate outside Marseilles). It would be wonderful if such exchanges could be facilitated at the grass-roots level, but there must be good practice exchange at the national or state level too. This is because, in most cases, national or state frameworks (such as the relevant sections of the British Crime and Disorder Act or the French *Contrat de Villes*) have to be in place to enable local initiatives to flourish. You *can* introduce innovative community crime prevention programmes despite national policy, but it's hard work!

Academic researchers could do more to influence policy and practice in the field of community crime prevention by, among other things, writing critiques and proposals for changes in policy and practice that are academically rigorous but will reach a broad constituency of lay readers (cf. Currie 1993, 1998), alerting local actors to useful prevention models elsewhere, helping local groups to take advantage of national policy changes and resourcing opportunities, and giving local people the skills to work effectively in community safety. In the USA, although there is pressure on academics to produce publications to enhance scholarly status, there is a third strand that, in addition to running courses and doing research, encourages academics to engage in public and community service. The Pratt Institute Center for Community and Environmental Development in New York and the Community Service Program organised by a consortium of Chicago universities are admirable endeavours that, by transferring skills and knowledge from academic research and expertise into troubled and disadvantaged communities, actually help to improve the quality of life for citizens in these areas. Even when there is a *willingness* to learn from others' experiences and transfer these into local quality of life improvements, there are barriers to achieving this, particularly if we are looking across national boundaries for evidence and inspiration. These include the difficulty of actually finding out about what other countries, or even other localities in the same country, are doing to prevent crime and the complication of measuring success or failure. Under the circumstances, it is remarkable and encouraging that we have been able to share experience and influence each other's policies to the extent that we have.

# 7

# The Politics and Failures in Crime Control

## 7.1 Overview

This chapter looks at the various policies of the last 100 years that have attempted, often unsuccessfully, to reduce crime problems. Even where crime problems have been reduced, there have often been undesirable side effects such as infringement of civil liberties, increased fear and escalating financial costs.

Crime control is inextricably tied to political views of what constitutes a just society (see Donnison 1998). Rational and technical approaches to crime control cannot be divorced from the political context within which they operate. At best they will be under pressure to deliver results speedily and tangibly; at worst logic and good sense will be thrown out of the window because they do not fit with the prevailing political dogma.

Political swings and ideological whims over the last 50 years have, according to the line of the moment, favoured or challenged one or more of the following approaches:

- Personal and communal protection – fortification and situational prevention
- Overreliance on the criminal justice system to control crime
- Deterrence, repression and incarceration (including 'three strikes and you're out' and 'short sharp shocks')
- Incapacitation ('warehousing' offenders on the assumption that 'if they're locked up, they can't be committing any more offences')

- Retribution, revenge, public punishment and humiliation
- Policing and surveillance
- Community and social development
- Action Zones, special projects and pilot locations for crime prevention
- Blaming the victim – individual responsibility – opportunity reduction and personal precautions
- 'Ghettos for the privileged' – gated communities and private security.

## 7.2   Political whims

Like crime itself, explanations of what crime control is and how it can best be achieved change according to popular prejudice and political whim. In 1979, for example, William Whitelaw, Home Office minister at the time, argued that the only way we could stem the 'rising tide of anarchy and violence threatening to engulf our shores' was to institute a 'short, sharp shock' regime in detention centres. By 1991, however, faced with an unprecedented 16% rise in the annual recorded crime rate, Kenneth Baker, the then home secretary, told citizens that they were individually responsible for crime prevention by making sure their property didn't get stolen. By 1994 another cabinet minister had decided that much crime was caused by the 'wickedness and greed' of cultures in our country which 'reject all decency and civilised values' (see *Guardian* 21/03/94). By 1996, Tony Blair, the prime minister-in-waiting, famously declared that not only would he (like the Tories) be tough on crime, but he would be tough on the *causes* of crime too; hinting strongly that a Labour administration would aim to tackle some of the underlying social and situational factors that researchers reckon are prediposers to offending. By 2003 the Labour government was talking tough on punishment and surveillance, but the 'causes' somehow had slipped into the background once more.

At the turn of the new millennium, 'zero tolerance' was the new buzz word, even though the much cited New York zero-tolerance crime reductions were as much to do with crime prevention and community policing as with cracking down on minor crimes and incivilities (see Bratton 1997b). The zero-tolerance concept was based on the 'broken windows' idea posited by James Wilson at least 20 years earlier and field tested by Zimbardo (see Ward 1973) around the same time. It was not long before some police chiefs discovered that zero tolerance was both unsustainable and too close to *intolerance* to be a viable option.

We shouldn't underestimate the huge influence that the media wield when it comes to influencing the 'policy on the hoof' approach that so many governments subscribe to these days. Bad news sells and draconian responses to moral panics about crime waves tend to be vigorously promoted by the popular press. This in turn generates a mass hysteria to which politicians feel duty bound to respond.

## 7.3  Punishment

There is a common-sense view that punishments must have some effect upon the crime rate – potential miscreants will surely be deterred by the possibility of harsh prison sentences and public humiliation. Yet the evidence for this is far from conclusive – it is one of those instances where the reality doesn't match common sense. The famous illustration of this is from the nineteenth century, when pickpockets were executed at Tyburn in front of huge crowds. At the very moment of execution, other pickpockets were active among the crowds, committing the very offence for which the person was being hanged!

Although capital punishment is not currently included in the sentencing tariff of Western European countries, it is gradually creeping back as a sentencing option in an increasing number of American states. We have to recognise that even in the UK there is substantial popular support for this and other tough solutions, such as heavier fines and longer prison sentences. It is likely that this enduring popular desire to be tough on criminals is more rooted in anger and primitive desires for vengeance and retribution, rather than any coolly rational view of what might prevent crime. In the USA where the tide has long since turned back to a more retributive criminal policy, the sheer public expense of such policies is proving to be more of a political restraint than the actual irrationality of the policy (see Currie 1993, 1998).

In the USA there has been a concerted attempt to lock away the crime problem, by huge prison building programmes (some states now spend more on prisons than they do on education) and deterrent sentencing such as 'three strikes and you're out'. The result is a per capita prison population seven times higher than the average for Europe, one-third of young Afro-Americans under the jurisdiction of the criminal justice system, yet still a violent crime rate higher than in Europe (Stern 1998; Currie 1998). The US situation has become so pandemic that Ross and Richards (2002), two American criminologists, have written a survival guide to prison because, as they say on the jacket: '10,000 men and women enter prison each week in the United States. What if it were you, or someone you love?'

Derek Lewis (1997: 229), a former director general of the prison service in England and Wales, said of this American attempt to lock away the crime problem: 'Rarely has so much hope and money been invested over such a long period in a programme that has produced so little benefit.' The idea that the courts can deter all villains by handing out heavy exemplary sentences to the few that they catch is not supported by the research. Burglars interviewed about their thoughts and actions (Bennett and Wright 1984) either didn't think about the consequences of apprehension, deliberately put such thoughts out of their minds, believed they wouldn't get caught or thought they would be caught and punished eventually but went on offending in the meantime. Deterrent sentencing just doesn't seem to affect the crime figures in the way that common sense suggests it should.

There is an argument, often put forward by the public and the police, that if you lock up convicted criminals they will be out of harm's way and, in any case, prison is what they deserve. But prisons were built to reform criminals as well as punish them. Only recently have we finally seen official recognition of the failure of this hope. Prisons now – to many governors as well as most prisoners (but not necessarily home secretaries, see Kirby and Cooper 1994) – are at best merely lock-ups and at worst colleges of crime. Even the 'off the streets' justification has limited impact on the overall crime rate; we have already seen how few crimes result in the conviction of a perpetrator, and researchers at the Home Office famously calculated that the prison population would have to rise by 25% to cut crime by 1% (Tarling 1994). Even the 'lock-up' case for prisons has limited value. Although nobody in their right mind would challenge the importance of keeping violent, unreformed criminals off the streets, in reality such dangerous people only make up a minority of the prison population. The remainder, discounting those on remand, who may be innocent anyway, tend to be persistent 'volume' thieves, drug dealers or other property criminals. By locking them up and failing to reform them in the process, we may be providing only the most temporary respite for their poor victims, as younger siblings, peers or competitors step into their offending shoes, take over their 'turf', or, in the case of drug dealers, increase their market share of willing customers.

Of those few criminals who are caught and imprisoned, over half of them will be reconvicted within two years of release from their prison sentence (Kershaw 1999) and who knows what the other half are up to! Comparing European countries, there is no obvious connection between levels of imprisonment and levels of crime. Norway has one of lowest imprisonment rates in Europe – in fact they operate a 'waiting list' system where many convicted criminals are sent home from the court until a vacancy comes up at a suitable prison – yet it still has a lower crime rate than Britain (Home Office 1993; Christie 1993).

## 7.4 Police

Conduct any kind of crime survey asking residents what they think will best prevent crime in their neighbourhood and top of the list will be 'more police'. In Kansas City, USA they decided to test the common-sense belief that more police equals less crime. In a controlled experiment, they found that neither tripling the amount of police car patrols nor removing patrols altogether from particular areas made any significant difference to the crime rates in those areas (Kelling et al. 1974). Similarly, inconclusive results came from police foot patrol experiments in New Jersey and research by the Home Office in Britain (Hough 1996; Home Office 1998).

The reason why more police patrols doesn't result in less crime lies in the nature of crime itself. It is usually committed stealthily and not always in public places where the police are likely to be. For instance, a police officer might once every four years be within 100 metres of a place where a crime is being committed, and he or she will not necessarily see it take place. Another example is that a police officer in a patrol car is likely to encounter a robbery in progress perhaps once every 14 years (Clarke and Hough 1984) –

not that you'd believe this if you were a regular viewer of television police series. So, as with prison building, the degree of increase in the police force needed to have any appreciable impact on crime is going to be far in excess of anything that we can afford or would accept as being sensible.

It is possibly this failure to reduce crime through patrolling that prompted the police to lose interest in putting bobbies on the beat, despite an overwhelming desire from the general public to have visible policing of the streets. It also has to be recognised that random patrolling is a boring activity for (predominantly) males who joined the police because it looked like it was going to be challenging and exciting. This restlessness may partially explain the high turnover of community police officers that undermines the building up of local intelligence and trust, but another factor is the tenure system in British police forces. Allegedly as a career progression facilitator but possibly as an anti-corruption measure, police officers are systematically moved around both localities and tasks. Thus, for example, a community constable, who may just be beginning to really get to know the residents and needs of a particular neighbourhood, will be forcibly transferred to traffic duties in another area or a city-wide drugs operation. Local residents, particularly those actively involved in community initiatives such as neighbourhood watch, find this rapid turnover of nominated police officers particularly frustrating; a problem compounded by the tendency for those deployed at the soft end of policing to be called away at a moment's notice to react to emergencies and high-profile incidents. This instability of policing was a significant factor in the failure of an initiative that purchased extra community policing for a neighbourhood in York (Crawford et al. 2003). Even worse, the evaluators found that not only were the residents disappointed with the lack of visibility or permanence of 'their' constable, but fear of crime and actual criminal incidents increased over the two experimental periods.

Another popular public misconception is based on the notion of rapid response by the police. Many surveys of the public's priorities about what they want in order to reduce crime list 'faster response times by the police' second only to 'more police on the beat'. Yet the evidence shows that the speed at which police respond to a criminal incident has no influence on overall crime levels (Hough 1996). This is mainly because most crimes are over in seconds, if not a couple of minutes, and it would be practically impossible for the police to speed up their response times sufficiently to get to more crimes in progress. Furthermore, most calls reporting crimes to the police are made after the event, so the rapidity of response is irrelevant in terms of deterrent prevention.

**More police and faster response times?**

At midnight on 30 August 2001, four police officers were attending a road traffic accident in the Cliftonwood area of Bristol. A woman had lost control of her car and crashed into a wall. By coincidence, at the same time a burglar was trying to gain entry to the rear of a house overlooking the crash scene, totally oblivious to the fact that four police officers were just metres away. One of the occupants of the house spotted the burglar trying to jemmy open a first-floor window, so immediately ran to the front of the house to alert the police. The police abandoned their accident investigation and rushed round to the back of the house in time to see the burglar making a rapid escape. Despite a chase, the police officers lost the offender, who ran off into the dark. One police officer was particularly frustrated with the turn of events. He said 'This is the closest I've ever been to a burglary taking place and we still didn't manage to catch the villain!'

We expect too much of the police; even if they apprehend someone, they may not necessarily achieve a conviction. In fact, recent Home Office figures show that the police clear-up rate for crimes have fallen in many areas over the last decade. As a British police chief observed, 'expecting us to prevent crime is a bit like expecting the staff of a hospital emergency ward to stop road accidents'.

For most of the time that police forces have been in existence, detection of crime has been seen as real police work – the high-status activity that the smart officers get put on to (see Gilling 2000). This is despite the fact that Robert Peel, the founder of public policing in 1829, stated that the primary purpose of the police would be the prevention of crime. For many years, the police presumably justified their preoccupation with detection and arrest of offenders as preventing crime through deterrence of others. Unfortunately, as we saw in Chapter 3, general deterrence as a crime prevention approach has serious limitations both for theoretical and practical reasons (see Sherman et al. 2002). Another factor that kept the police focused on detection and arrest of criminals, rather than the prevention of crime, was to do with the government's measurement of police efficiency which is based on crime clear-up rates rather than crime reduction. Thus, according to this indicator of police effectiveness, there could be rampant crime in an area but as long as the police were arresting a good ratio of criminals, then they were seen to be doing a good job. It is only in the last few years that 'crime reduction' has emerged as a primary aim of good policing. As a result, there is a gradual shift towards prioritising preventive activity, which for many years was seen as a soft option for officers on the margins who could not really cut it in the car-chase and kicking-down-doors culture of real macho policing. There is also an emerging awareness amongst enlightened police officers that crime prevention involves much more than just putting bobbies on the beat or giving advice about mortise locks to householders.

We can conclude that police patrolling, rapid response, detection, arrest of alleged criminals, sentencing and prisons make little difference to crime levels. This is because, by and large, the causes of crime lie in the community, not in the shortcomings of the criminal justice system.

### 7.5   Prosperity, relative poverty and social policy

The irony is that despite the proven limitations of the pillars of the criminal justice system – prisons and policing – many politicians, journalists and members of the public still think that the only problem is that of insufficiency. They point an accusing finger at the apparent failures of an alternative strand of policy aimed at eliminating crime – the one that aims to eliminate poverty. The late 1950s and 60s in Britain and the USA was a perplexing time for some criminologists. The popular assumption that crime was a product of poverty and that, with the advent of prosperity, it would simply wither away had proved to be unfounded. During that period in the US and the UK, the only thing growing faster than per capita incomes was the juvenile crime rate. Some claimed, and still claim, that crime increases as there are more things to steal. But if we are all so prosperous these days, why should anybody *need* to steal (see social strain theory, section 3.9)?

The politics of the immediate postwar period identified the state as leader in the task of social reconstruction. This leadership involved the identification of gaps in education, training, housing, health and welfare, and the provision of appropriate state services to fill those gaps. Social problems were to be analysed by social scientists commissioned by the state and solved by state professionals who would intervene in the lives of families and communities (Pitts 1988). So why, when all these health and social fixes were being introduced, did crime continue to rise, particularly amongst young people? It was assumed that it must have been a consequence of social disorganisation and community breakdown. Juvenile crime was a product of rapid social change. Slum clearance and the creation of urban housing estates and new towns had fractured traditional community ties and eroded the controls which had previously supported parents in caring for and controlling their children. The solution was to provide more social workers, community workers, primary school teachers and youth workers to enter those communities and families in which a 'culture of poverty' still survived. This would help their residents to overcome the barriers that still inhibited them from participating in the modern age of prosperity and opportunity (Lewis 1966; Clarke 1980). The effect, and often the intention, of such policies was to remove questions of poverty, social inequality, opportunity and crime from the place they occupied on the political agenda and relocate them on a list of social anomalies to be eradicated by a scientifically informed process of 'social engineering' (Gouldner 1971; Habermas 1976).

But beneath this wave of optimism, poverty was being rediscovered (Abel-Smith and Townsend 1965). Research published in the mid-1960s revealed that rather than the classless and equal society celebrated by the Wilson government, Britain in the 1960s was characterised by discrepancies of wealth and opportunity at least as stark as they had been in the 1930s. True, virtually everybody had a higher absolute income and standard of living, but the gap between the rich and the poor had, if anything, widened. This discovery, which had been made in the USA some time before, had a profound impact on the ways in which policy makers came to think about the problem of crime.

Sadly this gap between rich and poor wasn't subsequently reduced; in fact in Britain in the 1980s and early 1990s the number of people living on less than half the average national income actually increased from 5 to 12 million, while the richest 20% of the population increased their share of the nation's wealth by 7% (www.oecd.org). This inequality gap has continued into the new millenium despite New Labour's discovery of social exclusion and the setting up of a special unit to eliminate it.

As we saw in Chapter 3, the social strain of relative deprivation – the realisation that one is destined never to achieve socially valued success goals by legitimate means – can become an impetus to delinquency. It follows from this that a society characterised by great wealth and a culture of material success, which, nonetheless, denies some of its members the opportunity to access this success and wealth, will be a society with a high crime rate.

These cycles of social policy in various countries can offer some useful lessons in the vagaries of political fashion and their impact on the quality of life for citizens. The next four sections look at political developments aimed at crime control in four countries: the USA, Britain, France and, as an influential contrast, Japan.

### 7.6   Crime and the American dream

Attempts to prevent crime in the USA, other than through the blunt instrument of the criminal justice system, can be traced back to the University of Chicago in the 1920s and experimental practices to overcome the delinquency-inducing effects of 'social disorganisation' (Shaw 1929; Park 1936). The Chicago Area Project was established to work with young people in deprived areas of Chicago and has had a huge influence on subsequent youth work and community development.

Social strain theory came to the forefront in the USA when, in 1960, Richard Cloward and Lloyd Ohlin, two social scientists at the Columbia School of Social Work, New York City, wrote *Delinquency and Opportunity*. It is about the relationship between social inequality and juvenile crime and it was destined to trigger one of the biggest and most expensive crime prevention programmes in history. Cloward and Ohlin argued that popular culture in the USA presents all citizens, irrespective of their social or economic position, with the same 'success goals' and status symbols. Popular culture also tells them that these goals can be attained through hard work and individual effort; this, in effect, is the 'American dream'.

However, the reality beyond the dream is that the opportunities to achieve success legitimately are not distributed equally. Indeed, at the bottom of the social heap, amongst the young people in the ghetto, such opportunities hardly exist at all. But the American dream or American culture generally, according to Messner and Rosenfeld (1997), is more interested in the ends rather than the means, with the consequences that one can achieve status and success 'by any means possible'. So if you cannot become rich via Harvard and merchant banking, the alternative route might involve being a 'gangsta' and dealing drugs.

In the 1960s the US government decided to launch a war on poverty which was directly influenced by social strain theory and aimed to give poor citizens (most notably young black people living in inner-city ghettos) the opportunities to achieve wealth and status without having to resort to delinquency. The central strand of the war on poverty was 'community action', the involvement of the residents of the ghetto in the planning and implementation of programmes that would create legitimate opportunities for children and young people. The war on poverty was to mobilise 'indigenous leadership'. A popular slogan of the time, 'don't agonise, organise', encapsulated the process. Problems in local communities were to be defined by local people, young and old, and in turn citizens would become politicised.

The poverty programme had two major strands; community organisation and social compensation. Community organisation was concerned with locally based campaigns for fair rents, welfare rights and access to employment. Beyond this, however, the community organisation initiatives of the 1960s also sowed the seeds for much of the equal opportunity programmes and legislation that continue to benefit socially disadvantaged Americans. Social compensation was the attempt to offer the children and young people of the ghetto the kinds of educational and recreational experiences and resources that were readily available to their more privileged peers. This was a response to the fact that socially deprived children were more prone to educational failure or drop-out and this simply compounded their overall deprivation.

At the centre of this initiative was Operation Headstart: a nationwide programme sponsored by the Federal government which aimed to offer preschool education to the children of the poor. The absence of such education was, according to many contemporary educationalists, the single most important factor in the subsequent educational failure of ghetto children. (This concept was picked up 30 years later by the British government under the similarly named Sure Start initiative for children in disadvantaged communities.) One of the most tangible outcomes of the Headstart initiative was the TV series *Sesame Street* which successfully brought a ready-made, compensatory, preschool curriculum into the home.

Costly and ambitious though it was, the US poverty programme had little impact on the distribution of political power in the USA and even less on the distribution of wealth. Ultimately it was concerned with the reallocation of welfare expenditure over a relatively short period of time and when the money was spent there was little left to show for it. The poverty programme was founded on the belief that the various campaigns and activities which went to make up the programme would consolidate into a self-perpetuating 'community politics'. Yet with no base in an established political party or trades union, no political platform beyond the fact that its supporters were poor and, by the end of the 1960s, no more friends in high places, it simply ran out of steam (Moynihan 1969). In his influential critique of the crime prevention policies of the 1960s, James Wilson (1975; Wilson and Hernstein 1985) offered a pessimistic account of the way the world worked and what, if anything, could be changed. Criticising the architects of the war on poverty for their attempt to make an impact on the ultimate causes of crime, Wilson (1975: 50) writes:

> But ultimate causes cannot be the object of policy efforts precisely because, being ultimate, they cannot be changed. For example, criminologists have shown beyond doubt that men commit more crimes than women and younger men more [of certain kinds] than older ones. It is a theoretically important and scientifically correct observation. Yet it means little for policy makers concerned with crime prevention since men cannot be changed into women or made to skip over the adolescent years.

Implicit within the ideas that Wilson criticises is the notion that, by a process of 'social engineering', a better type of human being can be produced. Wilson (1975: 209) is far more pessimistic about the power of social intervention to change human nature:

Wicked people exist. Nothing avails except to set them apart from innocent people. And many people, neither wicked nor innocent, but watchful, dissembling, and calculating of their opportunities, ponder our reaction to wickedness as a cue to what they might profitably do. We have trifled with the wicked, made sport of the innocent, and encouraged the calculators. Justice suffers and so do we all.

Wilson is a proselytiser of classical or rational choice theory (see Chapter 3). Thus, for the rational being, crime is a viable option to the extent that it helps to maximise pleasure and profit. The role of the state is to provide a justice system which inflicts sufficient pain or loss upon wrongdoers to persuade them and potential miscreants that their pleasure and profit will be maximised only if they desist from crime. The criminal justice policies which flowed from these ideas emphasised the importance of harsher punishments, including the restoration of the death penalty and the incapacitation of persistent offenders through exemplary sentences (Van den Haag 1975). These policies reached their fullest expression in the late 1980s when the US Supreme Court ruled that juveniles and the mentally handicapped were appropriate subjects for capital punishment. By the new millennium, the majority of states in the USA had *re*introduced capital punishment.

After a fallow period dominated by the self-interest politics of Ronald Reagan, the Democrats attempted to revive watered-down versions of the anti-poverty programme, with such policies as 'affirmative action' in the late 1980s. But by the late 1990s even these policies had more or less sunk amongst an increasingly repressive (for the poor) and escapist (for the rich) set of trends. The most famous crime control policies to come out of America in the 1990s were zero tolerance and three strikes and you're out; both repressive tactics which resorted to a concept of sweeping crime off the streets by heavy-handed interventions from the police and judicial system. The most remarkable thing about these two policies, coming from a nation where 'money speaks', is how unsustainably expensive they both are. Zero tolerance – saturation policing which challenges even minor infractions before they escalate into more serious crimes – proved to be only viable and therefore self-defeating in short spurts in specific locations. The three strikes policy in California – where a third conviction for however minor an offence automatically results in a prison sentence – has virtually bankrupted the state administration, where new prisons were built but no money was left to pay the gaolers.

By the 1990s some American academics were advocating wholesale cultural change (Reiman 1995; Messner and Rosenfeld 1997), involving abandonment of the American dream, as being the best way to get out of America's continuing problem with violent crime. The recent British politicians' discovery (via France) of social exclusion seems to bear a remarkable resemblance to Cloward and Ohlin's observation of the USA in the 1960s!

### 7.7   Together we can crack crime in Britain

By the mid-1960s the ideas which had informed the US poverty programme had crossed the Atlantic to challenge the dysfunctional family and psychological assumptions which informed British responses to juvenile crime. In due course the British poverty programme, a far more modest affair, was launched. It comprised the Urban Programme, Educational Priority Areas, Community Development Projects, Inner Area Studies, Quality of Life Projects and hundreds of smaller endeavours located in local authority social services and housing departments, settlement houses and voluntary organisations. In both the US and British poverty programmes, the idea that people who were socially and politically marginal should be involved in decisions which affected their lives was central. Indeed, Derek Morrell, the Home Office civil servant who was the architect of the Community Development Projects, saw the British poverty programme as a way of transforming the political process:

> The whole process . . . involved practical problems of the transfer of power from the haves to the have nots – power in the sense of the ability to effect or resist change. (CDP 1977: 56)

Like the US poverty programme, its UK counterpart failed to gain a foothold in the mainstream of British political life and was destined to share the marginality of those it strove to empower. In particular the Community Development Projects dug their own graves by becoming increasingly politicised and challenging to regional and central government. Realising this, the government rapidly ran them down. For many years thereafter, community development had a bad name and it was only from the late 1980s onwards that it was gradually rehabilitated through such schemes as the Priority Estates Project, Estate Action and, to a lesser extent, Safer Cities Projects and the Single Regeneration Budget (see below).

By the mid-1980s a far more eclectic approach to crime prevention, which included elements developed in the British and US poverty programmes, was being developed. Subsequently, a number of local authorities took a more proactive role in crime prevention and community safety by, for example, developing strategies or appointing community safety officers. What started as a voluntary initiative by some enlightened local authorities turned from a stream into a flood with the advent of New Labour's Crime and Disorder Act in 1998. This flow of British policy initiatives is described sequentially below.

*1976* – Cunningham Road Improvement Scheme 1976
     (Hedges et al. 1979)
In 1976 a group of professional researchers and community workers moved on to the Cunningham Road Housing Estate in Widnes, Cheshire. Funded by the Home Office through the Urban Aid Programme, their aim was to try and cut down the high levels of crime and incivilities on the estate by testing out the theory (based on social disorganisation and social control theories) that if people have a sense of belonging and responsibility for the place in which they live, they will want to look after it and improve it. During their three-year involvement in the area, the team consulted with local residents, helped them negotiate with the authorities for social and physical improvements to the area, and evaluated the whole process. Their conclusion was that the project had effected a reduction in crime, particularly vandalism, and had contributed to a noticeable improvement in the quality of life on the estate (Hedges et al. 1979). This was the first time that a community crime prevention approach had been implemented and evaluated in the UK and could be regarded as the source from which the next 25 years of British community safety programmes flowed.

*1978* – NACRO's Crime Prevention Unit
The success of the Cunningham Road Scheme led to NACRO (National Association for the Care and Resettlement of Offenders) setting up a dedicated Crime Prevention Unit, with funding from the government's Urban Aid Programme and local authorities who were keen to replicate the Cunningham success on their own estates. NACRO's Crime Prevention Unit worked on over 100 housing estates throughout England and Wales during the following 12 years.

*1984* – Interdepartmental Government Circular on Crime
        Prevention (Home Office 1984)
This influential circular was distributed to all police forces and local authorities in England and Wales. It was the first explicit statement by the government of the view that crime prevention 'must be given the priority it deserves and must become a responsibility of the community as a whole'. What had previously been identified as primarily a police task was now seen as something for local authorities and the general public to be actively involved in. Unfortunately, the Circular was not immediately backed up by additional government funding, the official view being that crime prevention could be supported through existing programmes and resources.

*1985* – Design Determinism: Utopia on Trial and DICE
        (Coleman 1985)
Professor Alice Coleman, a geographer at University College London, published an influential book, based on extensive research on problematic housing estates, that claimed to have found a link between housing design factors and levels of crime. Professor Coleman identified a number of 'design disadvantagement' factors that, if eradicated, should reduce levels of crime and antisocial behaviour. Although methodologically flawed, Coleman's approach was enthusiastically received in certain political quarters and led to a multi-million pound Design Improvement Contolled Experiment (DICE), which attempted to put the theory into practice on a number of housing estates. A definitive evaluation of the outcome was published by the Department of the Environment in 1997. The evaluation report stated that 'none of the DICE schemes can be judged to have been effective in meeting the (admittedly ambitious) objectives set for it by Professor Coleman'.

The report suggested that DICE had no advantages over the more holistic Estate Action programme (see below).

*1985* – Estate Action (Department of the Environment)
Between 1985 and 1994 the government's Estate Action programme aimed to help local authorities in England to fund physical and social improvements that would 'transform unpopular housing estates into places where people want to live'. Although not solely aimed at crime prevention, Estate Action was probably the most effective British government programme of the 1980s and 90s for the creation of safer communities. The programme supported schemes which included the following objectives: physical improvements to dwellings; improving local management; involving tenants; diversifying tenure; attracting private investment; and providing estate-based training and enterprise initiatives.

*1986* – The Five Towns Initiative (Home Office)
This was the Home Office's direct attempt to put the experience of Cunningham Road and NACRO's estate-based work into practice on a slightly broader scale. Five areas of five towns were identified and a crime prevention coordinator appointed for each one. The coordinator was accountable to a multiagency steering group consisting of local officers and community representatives. The coordinator's salary was paid by the Home Office for a fixed term of 18 months. Some of the schemes were more successful than others, and most of them continued under some form or other, with local authority funding.

*1987* – Crack Crime campaign (Home Office)
Since 1987 the Home Office has spent approximately £5 million annually on publicity campaigns aimed at the general public. The campaigns consisted of television advertising, posters and guidance booklets offered free to the public. The campaign seemed to reflect the government's desire to make crime prevention the responsibility of the individual, and in some cases portrayed the offender as an evil animal (magpies and jackals were used symbolically in printed and television publicity). In recent years the campaign has begun to stress partnerships and community action. It is difficult to make any conclusive evaluation of the effectiveness of such broad-based publicity approaches.

*1988* – Neighbourhood Watch (Home Office Research Findings
     1994a)
In numerical terms, neighbourhood watch (where residents of particular streets or blocks watch out for suspicious activity and keep
an eye on each other's property) has been the most successful
crime prevention initiative in Britain, but quantity is no substitute
for quality. Evaluations of neighbourhood watch have shown
reductions of crime in some well-organised areas, but there have
been two significant problems: neighbourhood watch has flourished most in areas with comparitively low crime rates; and the
schemes have a high attrition rate – starting off with considerable
activity but then petering out to no more than a name and a
number on the poice's crime prevention statistics.

*1988* – The Safer Cities Programme (Home Office)
A development of the Five Towns Initiative, the Home Office
funded up to 20 urban areas for three years at a time as Safer
Cities. The Home Office had control of the annual budget, but
priorities and activities were determined locally through a multi-
agency steering committee. The best schemes took a proactive
approach in identifying and resolving crime problems, whereas
other schemes were little more than finance brokers for existing
community projects.

*1988* – Crime Concern
Led by former managers of NACRO crime prevention work,
Crime Concern was launched with Home Office funding as a
semi-autonomous capacity building agency to support the development of local authority and community-based crime prevention.
Originally given the remit to encourage neighbourhood watch and
police-sponsored Crime Prevention Panels, these were quietly
dropped in favour of youth criminality prevention and corporate
strategies. Crime Concern has had considerable success in raising
money from big businesses and has mounted a number of high-
profile conferences.

*1980s* – The private security boom
As crime rates multiplied during the 1980s, so did the sale of commercial security equipment and private security services such as
guards and patrols. In 1988 the total amount of money spent on

security by the public was estimated to be £1.6 billion, which dwarfed the government's Home Office expenditure, at the time, of about £15 million on crime prevention.

*1990* – Secured by Design and police architectural liaison officers
Starting in the southeast of England, and gradually spreading throughout the country, police forces have issued written guidance and have appointed officers to advise on the principles of crime prevention through environmental design. This service by the police is offered to architects, planners and developers to enable them to build new structures and environments that should avoid the obvious security pitfalls of earlier designs. Homes and, subsequently, multistorey car parks can be awarded Secured by Design certificates if they meet the standards laid down by police architectural liaison officers. Although a valuable free service, 'designing out crime' advice by the police has the shortcoming of considering only one aspect of the crime risk picture.

*1991* – Safer Communities – the local delivery of crime prevention
    through the partnership approach (Home Office, the
    Morgan Report 1991)
This groundbreaking report was produced by a working party of experts at the request of the Home Office. It made a number of well-considered recommendations to improve research, training and delivery of crime prevention strategies. In particular, it identified a key role for local authorities in the promotion of community safety and, as a result, the report was not well received by the Conservative government, who at the time were trying to *reduce* the role of local authorities in most things. As a result the report was shelved and only resuscitated when Labour came into power.

*1992* – The emergence of town centre management
Concern about the deterioration of some town centres, and their possible decline into unsafe and threatening environments, has led to the appointment of dedicated town centre managers to coordinate the maintenance and improvement of public and communal areas. Generally employed by the local authority, these managers act as brokers between the statutory and commercial services, encouraging good practice in security and town centre use generally.

*1994* – The Single Regeneration Budget (SRB) – an
            interdepartmental government initiative
The 1980s and early 1990s saw a proliferation of government programmes aimed at solving a range of urban problems, including
unemployment, insecurity, physical deterioration of buildings and
environments, and social and educational deprivation. In 1994, in
recognition of the interconnectedness of such problems, all these
separate government programmes were combined under one budgetary and administrative heading. The SRB was an eminently
sensible idea (even though it disguised reduced area funding
overall) but it has not stopped a proliferation of subsequent fragmented area-based funding programmes.

*1994* – Closed Circuit Television – looking out for you (Home
            Office 1994b) and the electronic security boom
This was a good practice compendium for authorities and organisations who were considering installing CCTV to improve monitoring
and security in town centres and other public urban locations. It
heralded the government's and local authorities' love affair with
CCTV that has led to a huge proliferation of cameras in public
spaces and the allocation of the lion's share of Home office crime
prevention funding to this one situational measure. Ever more
sophisticated systems are being offered to housing authorities and
commercial managers to improve the control of access to premises
and the surveillance of people passing through or around them.
Although a few high-profile incidents have highlighted the value of
such systems, questions have still to be resolved about erosion of
civil liberties, and the problems of maintenance, obsolescence, displacement and the substitution of people presence with technology.

*1998* – The Crime and Disorder Act
For the first time local authorities, the police and other public services (notably Health Boards and probation) were required by
statute to work together to prevent crime and disorder. Most
notably, Section 17 of the Act requires area partnerships to
develop and implement three-year crime reduction strategies,
based on audit and consultation.

*2000* – The Crime Reduction Programme
Finally putting their money where their mouth is, the government

started to offer serious money to local authorities and police forces who put in bids for various types of focused crime prevention activity.

*2001* – New Deal for Communities and Sure Start
Two more government initiatives that had broad aims for social inclusion and tackling childhood disadvantage, but in both cases, there was a crime prevention agenda too. For the first time the government realised that such projects had to be supported and funded for much longer than the usual three-year project term. But the government still hadn't ditched the time and resource wasting competitive bidding that was required to access these funds.

*2002* – Tackling street crime
As a reaction to significant increases in street crime in a number of large cities in England and Wales, the government ordered police forces and local authorities to drop a lot of the other things they were doing to prevent crime and focus their attention on reducing muggings by whatever means possible. The urban areas with the highest levels of robberies had to produce plans for how they proposed to achieve the reductions pledged by politicians.

*2002 onwards* – Neighbourhood Renewal
Another attempt to focus and pool resources at the neighbourhood level, Neighbourhood Renewal contains shades of the Estate Action approach of the 1980s, but has an avowed intention to mainstream any initiatives that are seen to be effective in improving service delivery and the quality of life.

In the years following the publication of this book there will undoubtedly be new fads and fashions dominating the British crime prevention scene (see Chapter 9 for some thoughts on what form some of these might take), whilst earlier initiatives (whether successful or not) will be quietly dropped as they no longer curry political favour. The description above shows that, whereas British policies of the 1960s had aimed to 'improve the conditions of the poor' and the initiatives of the early 1980s had aimed to 'harden' the physical environment, the initiatives of the late 1980s and 90s focused increasingly upon the interplay between social and environmental factors in the aetiology of particular forms of criminality. Some of the impetus for this more balanced and socially constituted approach to crime prevention came from France.

## 7.8   The French experience: the struggle against social exclusion

In response to the violent disturbances in the ghetto suburbs of Lyons, Marseilles and other cities in 1981, the French government devised a long-term programme based on the premise that unless the desire to suppress crime is tempered by a recognition of the need to express *solidarité* with the residents of the ghetto suburbs, it would lead to greater social polarisation and even more crime. The initiative which ensued provided a vast and imaginative range of social and situational measures, including housing refurbishment, job training, arts programmes, sports development and the recruitment of older teenagers in the ghetto suburbs to act as paid youth workers. The whole structure was supported by a three-tier (municipal, regional and national) policy and management system. In the first summer of its operation the scheme involved 100,000 young people. Crime prevention committees, consisting of young people, politicians, activists, businesspeople and officials, are now a permanent feature of French political life and 'social prevention' is a permanent aspect of French social provision even if it has been tempered somewhat by subsequent political swings.

But has this made any difference? Michael King (1987: 5) a social scientist who was himself involved in these developments, argues that:

> A simple answer would be that the French criminal statistics indicate a decline . . . of the type of offences likely to be committed by young people, such as criminal damage, theft, taking cars and minor assaults. As a whole, crime in France has fallen by 10,5% during this period with a fall of over 8% between 1985 and 1986.

However, since then, the situation in France has not looked so rosy. By the early 1990s a more right-wing administration had taken control of government in France, with less interest in social investment. As the 'struggle against social exclusion' was scaled down so, significantly perhaps, did crime begin to rise again. Since then crime and social disorder in France has mirrored a number of other European countries. 'Car-jackings' – people being robbed in their cars either at traffic lights or through other means of stopping their vehicles – was first reported as occurring in France in the mid-1990s, but has now spread to other countries. There were more disturbances on peripheral estates in the 1990s (usually involving disaffected ethnic minority youths) and significant problems of violence in schools (see Beaud and Pialoux 2001). The French response was to recruit and train local people to be 'social mediators' to work in schools and neighbourhoods with disaffected young people. Latterly the French have even been adopting the crime prevention practices of their Anglo-Saxon neighbours: community policing (see Chalumeau 2002) and situational crime prevention measures, including CCTV in town centres and suburban shopping precincts (for example St Denis, outside Paris).

## 7.9  The Japanese Model

If Britain and France present a contrast, there is an even more drastic difference between Western Europe and Japan. We share similar standards of living, yet Japan is a much safer society in almost every respect. Japan's lower levels of crime seem to be attributable to its capacity for self-policing. An extremely stable and conforming society, where everybody knows everybody else and their business, the Japanese internalise a strict code of Confucian ethics from a very early age. This internalised social contract means that Japanese people dare not deviate from honest behaviour because of the shame it would bring not only upon themselves, but upon their whole extended family. This strict code of legal conduct is monitored by a decentralised police force who visit *every* household in their district annually to check who is living there and doing what. The Japanese do not see this as a state intrusion into their privacy – the neighbourhood police are seen as friends and allies. This collusion with the prevailing norm has led one critic to describe the Japanese as 'a nation of sheep run by wolves'.

Japanese criminals can also expect comparatively short prison sentences and full reintegration into society as long as they express shame and remorse for their actions. However, this can backfire on those who have been wrongly convicted. They will be understandably reluctant to apologise for something they have not done and therefore will not be forgiven. Recent reports from Japan suggest that the social contract to conform to tight cultural control is being resisted by an increasing number of young people there. One can assume that, as Western media and attitudes infiltrate what was previously a very insular society, the dominant Confucian norms are being increasingly challenged by a more individualistic expressive attitude, exemplified by the USA and other influential Western nations. As a result gangs and delinquency are on the increase and Japan's status as a relatively crime-free anomaly is being eroded.

Whether Western Europeans and Americans could ever be so amenable to the historical Eastern patterns of conformity and acquiescence is a moot point, but the Japanese experience certainly supports those who link criminality to the rising 'me' culture of the West. (For more discussion of crime prevention in Japan, see Thornton and Endo 1992.)

### 7.10  A worldwide policy snapshot

The countries mentioned above represent exceptions rather than the rule when we look at crime control policy worldwide. Canada, Belgium, Holland, Germany and the Scandinavian countries all have well-developed crime prevention policies drawing on the best of British, French and US experience, but beyond those nations, the dual strategies of policing and personal protection are the only defences against crime for the majority of the world's citizens.

In countries with stable and homogeneous communities, with well-founded cultural or religious norms (many Eastern countries for example), this basic approach to crime control more or less functions. But in countries that are not homogeneous culturally and economically and where there is rapid social change and mobility, policing and personal defence have proved to be inadequate. Countries in Latin America, the former Soviet Union states and Southern Africa are all experiencing huge crime problems, wherein the police are often as much part of the problem as they are a solution, because of corrupt and illegal practices among police personnel. In such extremes of insecurity, those that can afford to retreat behind their barricades, leaving the poorer masses to their own fate.

## 7.11 Conclusion

The new tranche of statutes and initiatives introduced by Labour in 1998 and 1999 (New Deal, the Crime and Disorder Act, the recommendations of the Social Exclusion Unit) bode well for Britain's future, but as this chapter has shown, we have seen it all before, if not in the UK, then in France or the USA. What is really needed is a fundamental shift from reactive short-term policies and projects to serious investment in long-term programmes that may only reap their full benefits 10–20 years hence. The current government will have to keep the faith and provide some serious upfront resourcing, if all its 'new' programmes aren't going to be confined to the same dustbin of history as the wars on poverty and the community development projects of the past. Politics can too often muddy the waters of crime prevention – policies are introduced as reactions to the baying mob or as photo-opportunities, rather than being based on careful research and building on what has worked already.

The Japanese experience shows us that safer communities are not just dependent on material conditions. Education and development (both at home and in school) for familial and social responsibility also appear to be key components of a predominantly law-abiding society. Powerful religious and cultural bonds may explain why some less developed countries (such as India) have low crime rates, despite high poverty and inequality. The challenge for policy makers is to ensure that education is applied in its broadest and most enlightened sense and does not drift into the murky waters of indoctrination.

Many other countries have slipped into a two-tier type of society where the wealthy protect themselves in fortified enclaves and employ armed private security guards to keep the poor and the delinquent at bay. This is clearly a viable policy option which works for a minority, but shouldn't we be asking whether this is sustainable and whether this is really the sign of a civilised society – one in which the majority of the population are excluded from the ghettos of the privileged? This discussion will be picked up again towards the end of the book.

# 8

# What Works

## 8.1 Overview

Although there has been criticism from some academics of the 'technicist' approach to crime prevention, there is much practical experience and evaluative research that can help point to the best and most cost-effective types of intervention to create safer communities. This chapter sorts the wheat from the chaff.

As we saw in the last chapter, the 1970s and 80s were gloomy times for crime control – many theorists felt that, short of a full-scale revolution, nothing could be done to prevent crime. Martinson's (1974) famously gloomy conclusion that 'nothing works' in terms of reforming offenders, compounded the pessimism. By the 1990s, spearheaded by the 'new realist' criminologists (see, for example, Lea 1992), there was a new optimism that crime reductions could be achieved in victimised neighbourhoods, through a variety of interventions and that these were worth carrying out in order to relieve the suffering of already disadvantaged populations. From this targeted and micro-spatial crime prevention thinking emerged a new breed of 'what works' technologists. These new professionals, employed either by the police (crime prevention officers, architectural liaison officers), local authorities (community safety officers) or consultancies such as Crime Concern, would investigate a particular criminogenic location or set of circumstances and, using their diagnostic toolkits, would come up with a technical solution. Crime prevention thus became a politically neutral catalogue of 'fixes' that just needed an expert to identify which prescription would cure the problem. This was (and is) all very well and has led to some useful crime reduction achievements (for further discussion, see Ballintyne et al. 2000). However, to assume that 'if it works then it's worth doing' cannot usually be abstracted from a political, ethical and moral context.

If crime control was merely to be premised on what works, we could rapidly come up with some highly effective but drastic solutions. For example, we could significantly reduce levels of crime by decriminalising many current offences, but where would you draw the line? There may be a majority of people who would favour decriminalising cannabis possession, for example, but there would be considerable ethical reservations about decriminalising acts that involved theft or violence. We could probably reduce violent crime by 90%, by strangling all males at birth apart from keeping a few caged specimens for reproduction of the species, but who would accept such a policy? In some countries (such as Nigeria and the Arab Emirates), thieves have their hands cut off to prevent further stealing – solving one problem perhaps, but creating others. Proselytisers of CCTV in Britain would have the whole country under surveillance, if the expansion of systems over the last ten years continues exponentially (see Norris and Armstrong 1999). But where do we draw the moral and ethical line and take a stand on personal freedom and civil liberties? Even at a more reasonable level of intervention, we cannot necessarily justify doing something purely on the grounds that it prevents crime. For example, some crime prevention design advisors employed by the police would like to see all public car parks and open spaces completely devoid of tress, shrubs and landscaping, lit with intense lighting and laid out on a geometric grid that gives clear sightlines throughout. This may all be good from a crime opportunity reduction viewpoint, but it is important to take other quality of life factors into consideration too.

This is not to dismiss the 'what works' technicist approach to crime prevention as being a bad idea; instead I want to assert that, because of the nature of crime, there are very few crime prevention techniques that can be implemented in a political, moral or social vacuum. It is considerably worse for crime prevention choices to be made primarily for political reasons or to pander to the moral panics of the time, rather than to make rational choices about what to do, based on evaluated success elsewhere and balanced with wider issues of personal freedom, civil liberties and social justice. What follows is a synopsis of what works, which can still be generally justified within the type of liberal democracies most of us aspire to live within.

## 8.2   Rediscovering crime prevention

We may think that crime prevention is a recent idea for crime control policy yet, if anything, it has been *re*discovered, as the quotes below reveal:

> It is better to prevent crimes than to punish them. This is the ultimate end of every good legislation, which . . . is the art of leading men to the greatest possible happiness or to the least possible unhappiness. (Beccaria [1764]/1976)

> The public is put to enormous expense; an immense number of individuals are employed; and the object of both is merely to apprehend offenders – neither to remove nor investigate the cause of their delinquency. That such a system is defective is undeniable. Besides crimes which originate in natural depravity, there are a far greater number which proceed from the want of education, from indigence and other unavoidable causes. Now the object of an enlightened and liberal system of police would be not so much to punish such crimes, but to root out the causes of their perpetration. (Wade 1820)

> Prevention, instead of being a mere secondary aid, should henceforth become the primary defensive function of society, since repression has but an infinitesimal influence upon criminality. (Ferri 1897)

What has emerged in the last few decades is not so much the *rationale* for crime prevention, more the discovery of new and different ways of preventing crime. Using research, backed up by experimental projects, some policy makers and theorists have developed effective crime prevention and community safety initiatives that have achieved reductions in crime, at least in the short to medium term. Many of these projects have been described in reports produced by government departments and umbrella organisations such as the International Centre for the Prevention of Crime and the European Forum for Urban Security. They are as varied as the problems they address and the environments in which they are based. What they tend to have in common is a broader approach to crime prevention – one which improves community safety and wellbeing rather than merely 'cracking' crime by:

1. Focusing on the role of the local authority and other public service providers as well as the police.
2. Addressing the particular needs of groups most vulnerable to or most fearful of crime, and giving them equal opportunities with the rest of us to enjoy an acceptable quality of life.
3. Highlighting the relationship between crime and the facilities, services and opportunities available in our communities.
4. Recognising that preventing crime is not just about reducing the opportunities for offending but also reducing the *motivation* to offend.
5. Recognising that crime is generally an opportunist and unrewarding activity, and that young people in particular need to be offered more attractive and constructive alternatives.

### 8.3 What research can tell us – testing of theories and evaluation of practice

An enormous amount of academic research has been undertaken into the causes of crime and criminality. The trouble is that very little of this research can be used directly by practitioners on the front line of crime control. There are a number of reasons for this:

- Most criminologists write for the benefit of other criminologists, rather than for practitioners. There is a pressure on academics to 'get published' and the specialist journals are attracted to erudite and esoteric submissions.
- Many research reports conclude with recommendations for further research, rather than practical proposals for modified practice.
- Most significantly, social research into 'slippery' subjects such as crime are notoriously difficult to isolate from other influences, so that researchers can hardly ever say that a particular change in outcome (say, a reduction in a crime level) was conclusively the result of a particular input (say, more police on the beat).

Specifically in relation to crime prevention, there are very few research studies that have had a major influence on practice. This is partly to do with the problem of isolating the cause and effect, described above, and partly because durable improvements to community safety may only become clear after many years. However, a handful of research evaluations have become highly influential in terms of preventive practice and five of these are briefly described below.

*Oscar Newman and defensible space*
Oscar Newman is an American architect who, in the late 1960s, was able to carry out an experiment in improving the design of a social housing estate whilst leaving a similar adjacent estate untouched. His modifications aimed to give people more control and surveillance over the communal spaces around their homes. Crime fell in the improved area, compared to the neighbouring estate. This improvement has been maintained to the present day, according to Newman, although he also stresses the importance of what he calls 'community of interest' (that is, community development and cohesion) (see Newman 1972, 1996). Although not the only publication on this topic (see Jeffery 1971 too), Newman's book has had an extraordinary and lasting influence in Anglo-Saxon countries. Some of the terms he coined such as 'natural surveillance' and the eponymous 'defensible space' have become taken-for-granted terms amongst the police and planners.

*The High/Scope Pre-school Program*
This is another project started in the 1960s in the USA. A control group of children were offered high-quality preschool education and activities which were designed not only to be of educational value but also to give the children control over what they chose to do. Twenty-five years later those who were part of the project have benefited in numerous ways, compared to their 'untreated' peers: they are more literate, better employed, in more stable relationships and much less likely to have been involved in delinquency and crime (described in more detail in Utting et al. 1993). The High/Scope approach has subsequently been adopted in many preschool facilities and has surely had an influence on the British Sure Start programme for young children.

*The Cambridge Study in Delinquent Development*
This longitudinal research study has followed the fortunes of a large cohort of randomly selected boys who were attending primary school in 1961/2. The study found that those who ended up involved in crime emerged from circumstances characterised by low income, poor housing, living in run-down areas, parental conflict, family breakdown, poor parental supervision, harsh and erratic discipline, high degrees of impulsiveness and hyperactivity and low school attainment (see, for example, West 1982; Farrington 1996).

*Communities that Care*
The American equivalent of the Cambridge study has taken more of an action research approach. Communities that Care (CTC) proposes a range of interventions with families, children and schools that reduce risk factors and enhance protective factors. These factors are very much in line with those found in the Cambridge study. But CTC has been much more proactive and has set up community-based schemes that implement the theory (see France and Crow 2001).

*The Kirkholt Burglary Prevention Project*
This was a Home Office action research project on a high crime estate in Rochdale. Target hardening, work with offenders and very localised neighbourhood watch were implemented. As well as the notion of overlapping interventions to reduce a particular type of crime, a significant discovery to emerge from the project was the notion of 'repeat victimisation' (see Farrell and Pease 1993). It was found that, contrary to the popular notion that 'lightning never strikes twice in the same place', burglars do and, as a result, first time victims of burglary (and some other crimes such as racial attacks and domestic violence) are statistically much more likely to become victims again. This suggests that extra precautions and security measures should be targeted on properties that have already been burgled. Despite its flagship status as an exemplary research project, there has been considerable debate and controversy about what actually did make a difference in Kirkholt, as there were a number of other regeneration and community activities going on in the area at the same time as the targeted burglary prevention work (see Hope 2002).

Other pieces of research, less famous than the above, nevertheless have some useful implications for policy and practice. A selection of these is listed below:

- *Burglars on Burglary*  A small study carried out by Bennett and
  Wright in 1984. They interviewed a number of convicted burglars, asking them how they chose a target and what would put
  them off committing a crime. The interviewees generally chose
  premises that looked unoccupied and were particularly put off
  by dogs, but not necessarily by burglar alarms (which indicated
  to them that there might be something worth stealing). The
  practical implications of this research were that it is important to
  understand offenders' psychology and the reading of environmental or situational 'cues'. A similar approach has been used
  by the consumer magazine *Which?*, that employs an ex-car thief
  to attempt to break in and start cars, as a means of testing the
  effectiveness of their security.
- *The Kansas City police patrolling experiment*  In the 1970s, as
  part of a controlled experiment, the Kansas City police divided
  the city into three comparable areas. In one area, patrols were
  doubled and sometimes tripled. In another, patrols were elimi-
  nated altogether, although the police continued to respond to
  999 calls. In the third area no changes were made. After a year,
  the police checked to see how the crime rates differed in the
  three areas. They had stayed the same in all three areas and the
  public had barely noticed the difference (see Kelling et al.
  1974).
- *Single shot solutions*  A number of evaluations of crime prevention activities have indicated that, although single measures
  aimed at crime prevention (such as lock-fitting programmes,
  lighting improvements or entry phones) can reduce crime
  occurrences, they have a more durable impact if they are combined with other measures (such as community development or
  area management changes) (see Osborn and Shaftoe 1995).
- *Broken Windows*  On a public car park in the USA, a car was
  deliberately abandoned but kept under invisible surveillance. For
  many days the car lay untouched, so the researchers removed
  the number plates and left the bonnet propped open. This triggered an almost immediate and escalating response from the
  community. The following day thieves removed the battery and

then, in rapid sequence over the next few days, all removable parts were stolen. Finally, local youths descended on the car to smash the windows and dent the bodywork. This modest experiment in auto abuse led to the concept of neighbourhood deterioration known as 'broken windows' and police preventive approaches aimed at nipping this deterioration in the bud underpin zero-tolerance strategies (see Zimbardo 1973; Kelling and Coles 1996; Kelling 1999).

*Survey research*
Apart from academic research into crime and criminality, there is another type of research that is valuable for crime prevention and community safety practice – the survey. This will usually be based on a particular locality or crime problem and simply asks a representative sample of the local or target population about their experience of crime, their fears and perceptions about safety and their thoughts about improving the situation. Not only can such surveys provide an excellent reference point for preventive action, but they can act as the 'before' stage for the subsequent evaluation of the effectiveness of any practical work undertaken. For this longitudinal research study to be significant and helpful for future practice, the implementation or work phase must be carefully monitored to check whether what has been proposed is actually undertaken as specified. Despite the obvious worth of such longitudinal research and its extensive use in developmental studies (see, for example, the Cambridge delinquency study mentioned earlier), it is remarkable how few have actually been undertaken at the neighbourhood level. Even for famous locational research exercises such as the Kirkholt project, nobody has been back to see if, ten years on, the original gains and achievements have been sustained. At best, researchers may do a follow-up survey a year after a scheme has been implemented, but unless we just regard crime prevention as being a series of short-term fixes, we need to know about the effect of changes for much longer than a year or two.

## 8.4 Meta-evaluations of what works and what doesn't

The regular complaint among researchers and policy makers is that too few crime control initiatives have been properly evaluated. As we noted earlier, evaluation of any intervention aimed at altering social and personal behaviour is bound to be difficult because we can't control for many other factors that could intervene in changing the situation or people's behaviour. Quite often, though, it is nothing to do with methodological problems and much more to do with nobody bothering to evaluate or, indeed, evaluation being deliberately avoided. Sometimes the fact that a crime prevention project has been carried out is claimed to be sufficient justification for the effort involved. New street lights have been installed or a poster campaign successfully launched – isn't such a visible output good enough in itself? Fortunately, such narrow justifications have not always sufficed and enough crime prevention programmes have been evaluated for a couple of meta-studies – one in the UK (Home Office 1998) and one in the USA (Sherman et al. 1998) – to come to some broad conclusions.

The British study suggested that the following measures should be incorporated into an effective strategy to reduce crime:

- Intensive interventions among children and young families at risk
- Increasing informal social control and social cohesion in communities and institutions that are vulnerable to crime, criminality, drug usage and disorder
- Intervention in the development of products or services vulnerable to crime so as to make them less so (for example better car security)
- Incentives to individuals and organisations to reduce the risk of crime (for example reduced insurance premiums or tax reductions where an acceptable level of security has been introduced)
- Targeting situational prevention measures on 'hot spots' and areas of high risk generally (rather than blanket increases in security)
- Reducing repeat victimisation
- Placing greater emphasis on problem-oriented policing
- Extending the range of effective interventions with offenders and drug users
- Making more use, *in appropriate circumstances*, of penalties such as fines and curfew orders with tagging
- Improving the consistency of sentencing.

The study implies that the biggest returns, in the long term, will accrue from interventions with children and families but that some other activities such as situational crime prevention are worth doing in the interim, albeit with smaller gains. The American study came to similar conclusions about effectiveness, but categorised worthwhile interventions by target groups or contexts, as follows:

- *Infants*: frequent home visits by nurses and other professionals
- *Preschoolers*: classes with weekly home visits by preschool teachers
- *Delinquent and at-risk pre-adolescents*: family therapy and parent training
- *Schools*: communication and reinforcement of clear, consistent norms; teaching of social competency skills; coaching of high-risk youth in thinking skills
- *Older male ex-offenders*: vocational training
- *Rental housing with drug dealing*: nuisance abatement action on landlords
- *High crime hot spots*: extra police patrols
- *High-risk repeat offenders*: monitoring by specialised police units; incarceration
- *Domestic abusers who are employed*: on-scene arrests
- *Convicted offenders*: rehabilitation programmes with risk-focused treatments
- *Drug-using offenders in prison*: therapeutic community treatment programmes.

Perhaps what is just as valuable for a policy point of view is to know what *doesn't* reduce crime. The British study did not look across the board at crime control failures but, under the categories of criminality prevention and policing, it found that the following were *ineffective* in reducing crime:

- Individual or peer group casework and counselling/therapy
- Corporal punishment and exclusions from school
- General information campaigns (especially in relation to sub-stance abuse)
- Diversion to leisure and recreation facilities
- Fear arousal techniques (for example 'scare them straight' schemes where ex-prisoners tell schoolchildren how awful it is in prison, or former drug addicts explain the horrors of addiction)

- Pharmacological interventions (for example putting hyperactive children on sedatives)
- Random police patrols
- Increasing the arrest rate though higher charging rates per crime
- Arresting and charging juveniles for minor offences.

The American research supports most of the failures cited above but, significantly and possibly to the dismay of some committed practitioners, adds to the list of ineffective crime control strategies:

- Neighbourhood watch programmes organised with police
- Drug abuse resistance education
- Increased arrests or raids on drug market locations
- Home detention (curfews) with electronic monitoring
- Police newsletters with local crime information
- Residential programmes for juvenile offenders using challenging experiences in rural settings
- Correctional boot camps using traditional, basic military training.

Using a more general overview, a study commissioned by the Joseph Rowntree Foundation (Osborn and Shaftoe 1995) concluded that:

- There is little evidence to show that solely using physical security and design improvement measures will lead to *sustained* reductions in crime and there is a risk that they will displace crime to another location or another form of criminal activity
- Short-term, 'quick-fix' interventions may sometimes be necessary in response to a particular crime crisis, but their effect will often evaporate quickly, with the result that there is no sustainable outcome from the investment
- Broad packages of measures, that include social, managerial and physical interventions, are more likely to be effective and sustainable, than single shot solutions (asserted also in the British meta-evaluation cited above – Home Office 1998)
- There is a strong case for holistic approaches to crime prevention, with greater emphasis on social, economic and family-based interventions
- Levels of crime are linked to economic polarisation (the

increasing gap between the prosperous majority and the socially excluded).

## 8.5 Cocktails and balancing acts

The above research suggests that to significantly prevent crime we have to intervene with a cocktail of measures that contain the right balance of ingredients. This is easier said than done, both for organisational reasons and the political desire for clean sweeps. Politicians and the people who elect them would much prefer a highly visible 'magic bullet' that will, with a single shot, make our neighbourhoods and streets safer. Thus, during the period 1996–99, nearly 80% of the entire Home Office budget for crime prevention was invested in CCTV – a specific situational deterrent, but one which was based on public faith rather than hard-nosed evidence (Koch 1998; Home Office RDS Directorate 2002a).

Cocktails of measures usually require several agencies to co-operate – planners, housing managers and youth workers, for example. Even if these different professionals are working for the same organisation (the local authority), there will be difficulties connected with different budgets, remits and operational cultures. Historically, therefore, crime prevention strategies, where they have existed at all, have tended to major on one particular ingredient, even if their policy statements have a comprehensive ring to them. In Britain, this has usually meant that the lion's share of any resources has gone into situational prevention generally and residential security specifically. Situational measures have the huge political advantage that they are visible, quantifiable in terms of outputs (for example number of replacement doors fitted), often photogenic and usually show quick results. These are all important factors for politicians eagerly searching for the next press release and photo-opportunity and for practitioners eager to please their employers and satisfactorily complete the proliferation of monitoring forms that are tied to funding streams.

## 8.6 The limits to common sense, political expediency and the popular call for retribution

From all this research, it should be comparatively straightforward for policy makers to develop strategies that would significantly reduce levels of crime. Yet, as ever, political expediency, short-term thinking and kneejerk reactions conspire against a coolly rational approach to crime control, so that we continue to throw money and resources at strategies that do not work. As we mentioned in Chapter 1, nearly everyone regards themselves as being an expert on crime control. For most people it is a matter of common sense that you control crime by putting more police on the beat, catching more criminals and punishing them more harshly. The fact that none of this is supported by research evidence is a minor inconvenience that can be dismissed as the whingeing of out-of-touch academics. Your average person in the street is understandably angry and upset about the effect of crime and fear on their lives. They are annoyed that criminals are getting away with most of their crimes and that, on the few occasions when they do get caught, they are seen to 'get off lightly'. They are also likely to object to any interventions that could somehow be construed as rewarding miscreants, such as motor projects for vehicle thieves or one-to-one tuition for disaffected school pupils.

Ordinary citizens are the experts on crime and insecurity *problems* in their neighbourhoods and the places they frequent and should be consulted accordingly. However, without the benefit of knowledge gained from prior research and good practice, it cannot be assumed that they are the experts on finding appropriate *solutions* (see Hough and Roberts 1998). Nor should it be assumed that their elected representatives know, unaided, what the best solutions would be either. For example, some ministers in the British Home Office in the 1980s and 90s implied that they knew better than their senior civil servants and researchers about how to control crime (see Lewis 1997; Koch 1998). As a result, major policy decisions were taken that flew in the face of the evidence, and thus wasted huge amounts of public money as well as causing additional suffering and frustration for citizens.

In the last few years a number of experiments have been undertaken with 'citizens' juries'. In these events, a random sample of citizens is asked to make democratic judgements about contested policy or strategic options. Experts from the relevant field give evidence to the jury and only then, fully informed, does the jury give its judgement on what should be done. Several jury exercises of this type have looked at various issues to do with crime control. In each case there has been a significant change in the jury members'

views once they have heard about the relevant research and practice evidence (see Coote and Lenaghan 1997).

## 8.7 Long-termism: investing in programmes with durable outcomes rather than projects

As we saw in Chapter 7, Britain and the US have been inundated
with crime prevention projects, programmes and initiatives for the
last 25 years or more. The problem with nearly all of these is that
they have stopped as well as started and have often stopped very
soon after they started! Programmes such as Safer Cities were
time-limited and some projects were one-off interventions. The
'what works' evidence suggests that the most successful crime
control interventions are long-term preventive ones that require
sustained application and only pay off in the long run. Sometimes,
as in the case of early childhood parenting support, one has to wait
for 10–15 years for the true value of the investment to be felt. The
other problem with projects, programmes and initiatives is that
they are special; they tend to run in parallel with existing mainstream services and when they finish, the expertise and resources
disappear along with the outgoing staff, off to find another project
that will pay them. Some of these projects recognised this problem
and consequently built in exit strategies to ensure that when the
project closed down it did not just leave a big hole. The idea was
to hand over the baton and the built-up resources to an ongoing
agency (often a local authority department or a partnership).
Sometimes this worked, but usually in some scaled down form,
because the funding was no longer as substantial. In other cases
the exit strategy consisted of the project staff trying (quite reasonably) to find another job before they ended up on state benefits.

In an ideal world, crime prevention and community safety
would not need to be delivered through special projects; it would
be an inherent part of every existing public service. In reality,
public services, in Britain and the USA in particular, have been
pared down significantly, under the justification of improving efficiency and reducing waste. So the last thing schools, health services or even the probation service, for example, want to take on is
a mainstream responsibility to prevent future criminality.

There is another fundamental problem that inhibits democratic
nations' ability to mainstream crime prevention and invest in

long-term crime control strategies and that is the periodic election
of party political representatives who need to be seen to be
offering something different from their predecessors and visibly
delivering the goods. Two detrimental consequences arise from
this: firstly, no elected representative in his or her right mind will
vote through an investment of public money that will only pay off
in 15 years' time (they will have long since moved away to their
place in the sun); and secondly, politicians actually like short-term
projects because it means they constantly appear to be doing
something new and they get more photo-opportunities that way.
A fascinating example of this is the history of urban regeneration
in Britain over the last ten years. In the mid-1990s the government of the time came to the very sound conclusion that there
were far too many overlapping funding programmes aimed at a
set of interlocking problems, including crime, in particular locations. So all these different funding schemes were subsumed
under a brand new initiative entitled the Single Regeneration
Budget (critics who did some sums noted that the total budget for
the SRB was somewhat less than the combined sums of the previously separate initiatives that it replaced). This new super-budget
could be applied holistically over a period of years and made
eminent sense to those who saw partnership working and integrated area strategies as the way out of crime and social exclusion.
When New Labour came into power it inherited the SRB, but
instead of building on the firm foundations established by the previous regime, it wanted to be seen to be doing something new. So
in the ensuing years, as well as maintaining the SRB, the government introduced a vast and confusing plethora of new area-based
initiatives including the New Deal for Communities, Education
Action Zones, Health Action Zones, Sure Start and the Crime
Reduction Programme (including separate robbery, burglary and
CCTV budgets). By the new millennium we still had the SRB,
which was supposed to cover everything, plus dozens of new
funding schemes, each heralded by press releases and photo-calls
of smiling ministers. Some public service executives in disadvantaged local authority areas spend most of their time trying to keep
abreast of and applying for new government funds, rather than
delivering the services that, if properly resourced in the first place,
might obviate the need for this plethora of initiatives. It will be

interesting to see if the British government's new approach to Neighbourhood Renewal, with mainstreaming as a key objective, will achieve any more sustainability than the various regeneration projects of the past.

## 8.8 Creating safer streets and public spaces

So far, I have mostly been talking about what makes neighbourhoods safer, with the implication being that these are primarily residential neighbourhoods. Indeed this has been deliberate, because many of the crimes that people worry about (such as burglary, car crime, domestic violence and abuse) occur in residential areas. The other area that gives people cause for concern is the street. Robberies, thefts and the threat of stranger violence mean that streets and public spaces can become areas where many people feel unsafe.

There is a burgeoning number of measures being taken to make streets safer, both in terms of perception and risk reduction. The motivation driving these measures is both commercial (landlords and retailers trying to protect their profits) and sociopolitical (local authorities and government trying to make the streets safer for voters and taxpayers). These measures range along a continuum which could be categorised according to their degree of repression (squashing, excluding or displacing the problem) or integration (accommodating, diverting or rehabilitating the perpetrators). Each type of measure will be discussed separately, although in practice a number of them may overlap or operate simultaneously.

### 8.8.1 Uniformed patrolling

Most people in Britain are reassured by the sight of the police walking the streets (but see Crawford et al. 2003), although for many years, in attempting to deal with rapid response to the rising number of crimes, police officers were increasingly deployed in patrol cars. More recently, some police authorities, in response to public opinion, have increased the number of foot patrols in their areas. Unfortunately, police establishments would have to be increased many times over to make any serious impact on the visibility and accessibility of officers on the street.

Uniformed patrolling is not just restricted to police officers – private security firms patrol commercial areas and have been making inroads into residential streets where worried householders pay a small weekly subscription to have a man with a peaked cap and an alsatian dog wandering round their neighbourhood from time to time. Some local authorities have set up their own uniformed security patrols to look after their parks and estates. Most 'privatised' public areas such as shopping malls have their own security force, as do British Rail and London Transport. At a less accountable level of patrolling are the vigilante groups, such as the guardian angels in their maroon berets and various ad hoc groupings that occasionally form as a reaction to localised frustrations. This local motivation has been harnessed in New York, where volunteer tenants of the City Housing Authority patrol their project areas in collaboration with the police. The main problem with this patchwork of patrolling is displacement. It is unrealistic to have a uniformed guard outside every building and in every public space (although they come close in Rio de Janeiro and Mexico City), so the danger is that increased security in the patrolled area will just increase the risk in an unpatrolled one.

A more holistic approach was taken by the Dutch government in the early 1990s, who launched a huge and successful programme of training long-term unemployed people to become uniformed wardens of public spaces and public transport. As well as keeping an eye on public behaviour they can also act as helpers and advisers. City guards are now a familiar and reassuring sight on the streets and trams in Holland. Instead of paying out unemployment benefit for nothing in return, the government now benefits from a safer environment for its citizens. Furthermore, many city guards have managed to move on to mainstream employment as a result of their work experience. This idea was subsequently adapted by the British government, with their neighbourhood warden initiative. Neighbourhood or community wardens have been operating in some British towns for some time, but during 2001 the Home Office actively encouraged and offered part-funding for new schemes. Community warden schemes have been criticised in some quarters as being ersatz police officers with no powers of arrest, but this misses the point. A worthwhile team of wardens will not only offer reassurance but be a point of advice, referral and even direct help. In a good scheme, the wardens should gain the confidence of the local community, be accountable to local people, be around when they are most needed and do things that residents consider worthwhile.

Uniformed patrolling can consist of a mixture of publicly employed police and private security personnel, as demonstrated in Fort Worth, Texas. Fort Worth had suffered from 'the hollowing out of the doughnut' common to many American cities, as developers and traders concentrated their commercial attentions round the edge of the city. By the late 1980s the downtown area had become virtually derelict, apart from a few bargain basement stores, and was populated by the poor, the homeless and the desperate. In a bold and imaginative move, an entrepreneurial benefactor started rebuilding the 'historic' central blocks and filled them with a hotel, cafés, restaurants and cultural attractions. In order to safely manage the public spaces in these blocks, the Fort Worth police put some of their officers on mountain bikes while the entrepreneur's company appointed a similar number of private security guards to patrol the area on bikes. The two teams work in cooperation and are virtually interchangeable as far as the public is concerned. The result is a highly visible and accessible guardianship presence on the streets, which is reassuring to pedestrians and has contributed to the renaissance of the downtown area.

Uniformed patrolling is, at best, a reassurer and a fear-reducer and may act as a deterrent to the would-be offender, assuming that the perceived surveillance is comprehensive enough (as it is in Fort Worth). At worst, uniformed patrolling can veer towards repression, where everyone is potentially a suspicious person and undesirables are hounded out of sight. By way of example, the Eaton Centre, known as the 'town square' of Toronto, is a vast enclosed shopping and recreational site covering 14.5 acres of the downtown area. The Centre is patrolled by a rota team of 50 security guards who, among other duties, enforce the exclusion of an estimated 12,000 Toronto residents who have been issued with barring notices which ban them from using the Centre (Poole 1994). Furthermore, a police substation is prominently located at one of the entrances to the Centre. Ironically, in view of the above exclusion policy, Eaton's, the owners of the Centre, filed for bankruptcy in September 1999. (For a completely contrasting approach to urban security management in Toronto, see the Dufferin Mall case study in section 8.8.6).

### 8.8.2   Electronic surveillance

Electronic security surveillance could be termed 'armchair patrolling'. Instead of having distinctively clothed people walking around an area, there are distinctively boxed electronics surveying an area, while the control person reclines in his or her televisual eyrie. The idea is simple, even if the technology is complex; one person can see all over the place simultaneously, and these images can be stored for future reference. The users of public spaces are aware that their every move is being assigned to video tape to be used as evidence against them, so they refrain from doing anything that could render them liable to prosecution. Such an approach has some effect, as long as the equipment works and the monitoring staff are properly trained and vigilant (Home Office 1994b). CCTV is being adopted wholeheartedly by an increasing number of town centre administrations in the UK, despite its large capital outlay, and provides a profitable line of business for the manufacturers and installers of electronic equipment.

An approach to security based on electronic surveillance attracts exactly the caveats listed in the final paragraph of the above section on uniformed patrolling. Furthermore, because of its technological intricacy, it is vulnerable to breakdown, malfunction or malicious damage. In fact, some key locations now have video cameras watching other video cameras to ensure they are not being tampered with! Miscreants are getting wise to the video age by donning crash helmets, balaclavas or hooded sweatshirts to avoid easy identification on video tape, and by deploying masking devices such as aerosol spray paint to blank out camera lenses. Overall CCTV schemes have produced mixed results in terms of crime reductions (Home Office RDS Directorate 2002a). At best CCTV can extend the reach of the guardians of communal/public spaces and offer a protective ring of security until a problem can be sorted out by appropriate personnel. At worst CCTV can become an intrusive, humiliating and repressive means for controlling excluded populations (see Lyon 1993; Fyfe and Bannister 1998; Norris and Armstrong 1999). A most depressing example of this can be found on a housing estate in Middlesbrough which has cameras mounted on tall spike-encircled poles on every street corner, tilting, panning and zooming in on any gatherings of bored young people in the street. As one of these youngsters said: 'They spent all that money on the cameras when they could have spent it on us.'

*8.8.3   Design and physical (situational) measures*
Just as with residential areas, the design and layout of our streets
and public spaces can offer easy opportunities for certain types of
predatory crime such as street robberies, pickpocketing and bag
snatching. But is it possible to design out street crime? Situational
crime prevention measures aim to reduce the number of opportunities for offending through the design and reinforcement of environmental features. Thus, street lighting can be improved, blind
corners in pedestrian subways can be removed, bollards and shutters can be installed and buildings can be designed to look out onto
public spaces (Wekerle and Whitzman 1995). Clearly there is
some sense in trying to minimise the opportunities for crime
through appropriate design, layouts and installations. Appropriate
levels of illumination can increase community confidence and
informal social control (Home Office RDS Directorate 2002b) but
there is some debate about the efficacy of these measures alone in
reducing crime (Osborn 1993). For example, although increased
intensity of street lighting can help pedestrians to feel safer at
night, it does not necessarily reduce levels of street crime (Shaftoe
1994).

Harshly lit and heavily shuttered streets feel like hostile environments, so we may end up with fortified streets and city centres
bereft of pedestrians at night and at weekends. Design, and even
security, measures should be used to create a more welcoming and
cared-for environment, which will attract users, encourage
respectful behaviour and help to make people feel safe in an area
(Design Council 1979). For example, well-designed, see-through
or traditional-style shop shutters are better and safer than crude
galvanised metal roller shutters, which often attract abuse,
including graffiti. Pedestrian subways and underpasses, designed to
make it safer for people to cross busy roads and streets, have
turned out, ironically, to be unsafe places in themselves. In some
locations, their poor light, lack of surveillance and easy escape
opportunities have made them popular 'pinch points' for robbers
and bag snatchers. In other cases, such locations just feel unsafe
because of their claustrophobic design and lack of visibility. As a
result, some shopping and leisure locations, accessible principally
by subways and underpasses, have been adversely affected because
of people's reluctance to 'run the gauntlet'. Various attempts have
been made to make them safer, by installing cameras and mirrors

to improve visibility and surveillance, but in some cases the ultimate solution has been to seal them off (Hammersmith, London) or remove them altogether and revert to surface crossings (Birmingham inner ring). Another approach is to encourage legitimate activities in and around underpasses, to increase informal surveillance. Examples of this are retail kiosks in the complex underpass system under Edgware Road and Marylebone Road in London and the licensing of buskers in London Underground's pedestrian tunnels.

### 8.8.4 *Legal controls*

If surveillance and physical measures cannot entirely sweep offenders off the streets, then we can always resort to legal powers. At one end of the legal spectrum there are police powers to: stop and search people suspected of behaving offensively; move on loiterers; and arrest people for causing an obstruction. At the other end there are civil remedies (for example for noise control), bylaws and licensing restrictions which can be invoked by local authorities to clean up the streets. In Newport, South Wales, the Alcohol Abuse and Social Disorder Demonstration Project aimed to reduce city centre rowdyism through liquor licence controls and the revision of late night public transport arrangements. Coventry was the site of the first bylaw banning the consumption of alcohol in town centre streets and public spaces (Ramsay 1989, 1990). Such legal and licensing measures do appear to have had an effect in reducing crime and particularly antisocial behaviour in town centres, but one has to ask if the problem has not been displaced elsewhere, such as parks just outside the city centre, as appears to be the case in Coventry.

Drug dealing, prostitution and kerb crawling can make certain streets feel very unsafe for legitimate users. CCTV schemes have been seen as a possible response to these problems but again there are serious displacement issues to consider. In fact, much of the effort has been directed towards moving prostitutes and drug dealers away from residential areas rather than retail and leisure streets. Police-initiated clampdowns can offer temporary respite, but a basic principle of economics ensures that, so long as there is a demand for drugs and paid sex, a supply system will operate somehow. The South Yorkshire Standing Conference on Prostitution, for example, has the strategic relocation of street prostitution from residential areas as one of its principal aims, although its outreach work in Sheffield did include developing diversion programmes for women working as prostitutes (Local Government Association/Local Government Management Board 1996). In the same way, any strategy for stamping out drug dealing must also run in parallel with programmes that offer bored and disaffected young people attractive, legitimate alternatives to drug misuse.

As discussed earlier, the effectiveness of zero tolerance, as a sustainable approach to controlling antisocial behaviour and nuisance in the streets, has been challenged. For example, Morgan and Newburn (1997) question the approach on the grounds of practicality – a lack of police resources and the competing demands to tackle serious crime. The approach was also challenged by Young (1998b), who suggested a number of other circumstances and factors that could have influenced crime reductions. It is just as likely that the huge but less publicised growth of community policing in the USA (where the police actively engage in partnership working with local people – almost the exact opposite of zero tolerance) has been effective in lowering the nation's crime levels (see Kelling and Coles 1996).

### 8.8.5 Management

Most of the measures described above have attempted to deal with the problem of crime and insecurity through a greater or lesser degree of exclusion and repression. In other words, the offender has been made unwelcome and the offence has been made more difficult to commit. As already indicated, the risk with these measures is that there will be a displacement to a different place or type of crime, as no attempt has been made to deal with the motivation to commit crime or mediate with those likely to offend. In reality, there are very few career criminals; people who end up committing offences often do so out of boredom, frustration, desperation or as a byproduct of a personal problem such as an addiction, psychopathology or homelessness. For even the most hardened recidivist, the criminal act is only a very occasional part of their daily life. Many offenders are bored young people who would engage in more legitimate pursuits if they were given the chance (Graham and Smith 1994).

Instead of excluding undesirables and creating, in the process, an environment that is undesirable to everyone, there is a current move towards making our streets and town centres more attractive, in the hope that crime and antisocial behaviour will be 'crowded out' by the range of legitimate activities and behavioural norms of the majority of law-abiding citizens (Bianchini 1994). At the same time, it is important to engage with the minority who are displaying unwelcome or desperate behaviour – they may need help, diversion or intensive support. Enlightened strategic management of downtown areas can make them more attractive, liveable and vital, at the same time as reducing the density (if not the actual number of incidents) of crime and antisocial behaviour. Programmes that *only* focus on crime reduction may be too narrow most of the time and there is the risk that they end up impoverishing the urban realm. This revitalisation of streets and public areas in Britain is being spearheaded by town centre managers. Although their primary focus is to improve the economic fortunes of town centres, these managers are aware that crime and insecurity are big disincentives to potential users (KPMG/SNU 1990; Coventry Safer Cities Project 1992).

The 24 Hour City concept is a relatively new approach to revitalising streets and town centres (Comedia 1991; Montgomery 1994; Bianchini 1994). One of the first initiatives to be publicised was the More Hours in the Day initiative lunched as part of Manchester City Council's Olympic bid in 1993. A review of British initiatives (Stickland 1996) showed that improving night-time safety was the principal reason for introducing the 24 Hour City concept. Increased safety is seen to derive from the improved natural surveillance provided by increases in the numbers and range of people using the streets, including older people who are otherwise less in evidence after dark. The 24 Hour City initiatives adopted by local authorities include: licensing initiatives, such as staggering closing times to avoid concentrations of people and increasing the number of late-night licences; bridging the gap between offices closing and the start of entertainment activities by, for example, shops closing later; the stimulation of café and restaurant activity; and the promotion of street entertainment and festivals.

### 8.8.6 *Integration and absorption*
The notion of inclusion and neutralisation of crime and insecurity described in the management approach above can be taken one

step further. As intimated before, criminals are usually people with needs or difficulties. Therefore it is quite possible to engage with such people to help them fulfil their underlying needs or resolve their difficulties, thus diverting them from crime or antisocial behaviour. In Britain this approach has offered some promising innovations, although they have generally been piecemeal, relying on charitable initiatives and local goodwill. Often their primary aim is humanitarian, but with crime prevention or disorder reduction as a bonus byproduct. Examples include the alcohol-free bar run by the Salvation Army in central Swindon, the Centrepoint shelter for homeless runaways in Soho, London and even the *Big Issue* magazine sold by the homeless as an alternative to begging. In some Continental European countries this integrative approach to crime and disorder reduction holds greater sway. For example, in Lille, France, a group of delinquents who used the entrance to a metro station as their operating base was contacted by a team of detached youth workers. As a result, they ended up making a video about youth problems in the city centre and most of them were helped by social workers to reintegrate into normal community life (King 1988). A project in Rotterdam, Holland recruited young people who were loitering and intimidating shoppers in a central street and offered them a meeting place, support and activities in an adjacent building (Safe Neighbourhoods Unit 1993b). In the USA, the Travelers and Immigrants Aid of Chicago operates the Neon Street Clinic, where homeless and runaway young people can receive comprehensive advice and assistance from a range of professionals, or just 'hang out' in somewhere warm and dry until they are ready to use the services available (Dryfoos 1990).

Perhaps one of the most inspiring examples of an integrative approach to crime control comes from the unlikely source of a shopping mall management company in Canada. Set in one of Toronto's less salubrious but most cosmopolitan neighbourhoods, Dufferin Mall is the main local retail centre and thus attracts a cross-section of the local population. In the early 1990s, the Mall was experiencing serious crime problems, as a result of theft and violent/ threatening behaviour by gangs of young people who were using the Mall, and particularly the food court, as a place to hang out. Many local people, particularly women, were avoiding the Mall because they regarded it as a dangerous place. Rather than filtering out all those but serious shoppers, the management of

Dufferin Mall made a conscious and successful effort to engage socially as well as commercially with all its users and the surrounding community. Their philosophy, as explained by David Hall (1996) the manager at the time of these changes, is that 'the better the quality of neighbourhood life, the better the business environment – a reciprocal relationship placing an onus on business to assume its full share of responsibility for ameliorating social problems – business giving back to the community that supports it'. The practical outcome of this commitment was a huge range of integrative and involving activities, including a community newspaper, youth work, play facilities, literacy programme educational outreach work with school truants and excludees and drop-in centres in some of the shop units for a number of different advice and counselling services. The Mall has achieved significant reductions in crime and disorder – a 38% drop in reported crime over a five-year period (Wekerle 1999) – and is now hugely popular with local people, showing the sound commercial sense of such an inclusive approach to the whole population.

### 8.8.7   Criminality prevention

The ultimate extrapolation of the diversion approaches cited above would be to intervene with individuals at a point before they became a threat on the streets. Not everybody who hangs out on the streets is a thief, robber or vandal, so it is important to know why some people commit street crimes whilst the majority do not (see Barker 1993). People who become hustlers and thieves have usually experienced a range of predictive factors earlier in their lives. These predictors include growing up in disrupted families or institutions, school failure, mixing with delinquent peers, low skills and low self-esteem (Farrington 1996). A number of preventive interventions can facilitate the pro-social development of young people, notably education work in schools, peer influence programmes (where slightly older children or adolescents are trained to offer a positive role model to their younger peers through drama workshops or buddy schemes) and intensive rehabilitation programmes with young offenders, to prevent recidivism (Graham and Bowling 1995). Clearly these approaches take us into a broad area of social policy, but it is impossible to isolate problems of crime from the wider socioeconomic context within which they occur. For example, it is no coincidence that the countries with the biggest problems of street crime tend to be the ones with the biggest socioeconomic inequalities within their population. It is important to note, though, that it is not necessarily absolute poverty that affects levels of crime – some of the poorest nations are the safest. But equally, some of the wealthiest nations, such as Norway, Switzerland and Japan have low levels of street crime, although the gap between rich and poor in these three countries is much smaller than in many other developed nations. The other general quality to note in these low crime countries (both rich and poor) is that they tend to have stable and cohesive social systems. One might be tempted to conclude that safe streets are a product of fair, ethical and integrated societies with commonly held norms of behaviour. This may be true but it is also possible to achieve urban security through the tyrannical imposition of norms of behaviour imposed by the few on the many (cf. some Middle Eastern and Southeast Asian countries); which brings us back to the policy dichotomy of repression or integration.

### 8.8.8 *Sustainability*
When people think about what is meant by 'sustainable neighbour-hoods and communities', they may initially be considering factors such as non-polluting public transport and recycling schemes. However, no amount of physical or environmentally sustainable measures will be of any value, if people are too afraid to go out onto the streets. A holistic sustainability package must therefore incorporate measures to improve the safety and security of public areas. Physical sustainability is pointless without social sustain-ability. People want to feel safe using the street. This sense of safety and freedom from predatory crime is an overriding pre-cursor to most other built environment management and design considerations.

## 8.9   Summary: thinking globally, acting locally

Most of the approaches and measures described above to reduce and prevent crime have to be delivered at a neighbourhood or locational level. However, if this is to happen effectively, appropri-ately and consistently, it must be based on a district or regional strategy and supported by national policy. This understanding of the need for a consistent thread running from central government, via regions and municipalities, down to local neighbourhoods has been the foundation of French crime prevention policy since the early 1980s. It has only been implemented in Britain since the late 1990s and is still nothing but a distant glimmer in the USA. Clearly, as we have seen, there are many things that work in reducing crime and improving the sense of safety. However, we cannot assume that what works in one place or context will automatically work in another – the complex dynamics of social and environmental conditions militate against off-the-peg solutions. Furthermore, single interventions or changes are less likely to have an overall sustainable effect in preventing crime than a cocktail of context-specific initiatives that address both the opportunity and the motivation for crime.

# 9

# Future Prospects

**Plate 9.1**    CCTV control room

## 9.1   Overview of the future

People often predict the future by extrapolating from the recent
past. If we look at trends in social conditions and crime control in
the advanced Western nations and extrapolate forward from these,
we are likely to come up with a gloomy scenario, not unlike the one
at the opening of this book. We can anticipate a population almost

197

entirely intoxicated by drugs of one kind or another (legal, such as alcohol and sedatives, or illegal such as cocaine and amphetamines). There will be two types of citizen – those who, through their wealth and influence, have made it into the secure residential and working compounds and those who have been excluded from prime property areas. This segregation will be monitored by electronic surveillance and enforced by low-paid and poorly trained private security agents. Of course this is not an inevitable future dystopia, but the trends in Britain and America are certainly pushing in this direction.

The fascinating thing about futurology is that it is usually wrong, because you cannot extrapolate from the past – human ingenuity and global forces are just too unpredictable (Gray 2002). *Homo sapiens*, unlike other animal species, has the ability to reflect and the potential to consciously override 'natural' proclivities (Dawkins 1976). We can be reasonably confident that, although many things will change in the future, not everything will. Humans are the most adept species at inventing things and reorganising our lives, yet human nature itself hardly changes at all. We are products of a very slow process of evolution and natural selection (see Ridley 1996). So, for example, we still have only two arms each, even though it would probably be useful for pickpockets to have more and we can only run slightly faster than our ancestors tens of thousands of years ago, even though speed of escape would be a real advantage for many criminals.

In terms of the future therefore, it may be useful to put our predictions and recommendations into different categories: those things that will change (mostly technological and scientific developments); those things that will only change very slowly (human nature and evolution); and those things that are within our gift to change or maintain (organisational, managerial, social policy and governmental aspects). This is the logic of the following sections. I will also look at the various emerging trends in crime control policy (alluded to in the first paragraph) to see what impact these are likely to have in the future.

## 9.2   Opportunities and their reduction

If we look at new technical and scientific developments and the general direction these are taking into the consumer market, we can predict the following:

- *Smarter, smaller and cheaper security products.* The general trend within electronic security equipment is the miniaturisation of more sophisticated systems, which can then be mass produced at lower prices. High-definition security cameras, for example, can now be fitted into a casing not much larger than a cigarette packet. Electronic surveillance systems that had to be professionally installed and cost thousands of pounds can now be set up by the accomplished householder for a few hundred.

- *Integrated alarm networks.* Stand-alone alarm sounders will be increasingly superseded by home systems that are linked to a staffed emergency control centre, or ones that automatically dial recorded alarm messages to selected people.

- *Image recognition and target tracking.* Entrance doors will be released by facial or palm recognition of legitimate users, catalogued in a dedicated computer linked to a camera. Sequenced cameras will be able to track the progress of targeted individuals through buildings and their surroundings. Offenders and stolen items will trigger the release of visible or invisible dye as a deterrent and identification device. More cars and valuable products will have built-in radio transmitters that will broadcast their location if stolen.

- *Smart microdots for property marking.* Instead of ultraviolet pens or etching, almost invisible microdots will be bonded to individuals' property. These microdots will be personalised with owner information and contact details, held on a central computerised database. Eventually they might even alert a central control point if the property is moved out of a predetermined geographical location and satellite positioning systems could identify the new location (such a device is already available for cars).

- *Virtual occupancy and triggered lighting.* Householders will be able to draw curtains and switch on lights by sending remote instructions from their mobile phones. People at work or at control centres will be able to check, via their personal computers, whether all access points of distant buildings are securely locked (using signals from remote electronic sensors). People (and cats) on the prowl around buildings at night will increasingly find themselves swathed in floodlighting triggered by their infrared body heat.

However, simple is still best. The more sophisticated the security equipment, the more there is to go wrong. Over 90% of all burglar alarm soundings are false ones, often triggered by equipment faults or human error. The best solutions are elegant, simple, easy to maintain and reliable, with only enough security to counteract the likely level of threat. You can crack a walnut with a sledgehammer but you can usually achieve a better result with a more modest piece of equipment attuned to the task.

## 9.3   The changing nature of crime and criminal behaviour

A tabloid newspaper summarised some recent research with the headline: 'Crime rises because there's more to steal.' This is certainly part of the truth, but, as well as the increased quantity of consumer goods, there are different things to steal and new ways to steal them (Ekblom 1997). For example, 40 years ago there were no thefts of videos, mobile phones and computer chips because they didn't exist. Clarke (2000) has coined the term 'hot products' to describe the fact that, at any one time, thieves will prefer to steal certain items, usually because of a combination of stealability and demand on the illegal 'fencing' market. New products can also, inadvertently, become aids to criminal opportunity. Sliding patio doors, when first introduced, permitted burglars just to lift them out of their runners to gain access to homes, and rechargeable cordless electric drills have been a godsend to criminals undertaking more sophisticated access to property. Offenders also learn fast to avoid easy identification from video surveillance cameras by wearing hoods, baseball hats or crash helmets and dark glasses.

Technology alone cannot solve our security needs – there has to be a human response at some stage in the chain. In the future we can either go for a high-tech/low staffing scenario, or we can aim for more labour-intensive solutions. As we lose faith in technological fixes such as unstaffed railway stations with automatic barriers and ticketing machines, there may be a swing of the pendulum back to the re-employment of people into services that had been automated or abandoned, such as park keepers, night watchmen and residential caretakers. This has the added value of offering more opportunities to unskilled people who are overrepresented in the pool of unemployment. This approach has already been espoused in Holland, where thousands of city guards have been recruited to act as supervisors on public transport and patrol public and communal areas in order to reassure, advise and refer.

## 9.4  Crime and human nature

Wilson and Herrnstein's (1985) book *Crime and Human Nature* is vulnerable to criticism by many, on the basis that it offers too much of a pessimistic, deterministic view of people's propensity to offend. However, one only has to observe the selfish and often violent behaviour of very young children to realise that, in their unformed state, humans have no problem being offensive towards others. This is unsurprising if one examines human behaviour from an evolutionary point of view; those who have survived and thrived are those who have looked after themselves and their off-spring, if necessary at the expense of others. However, it has also become apparent that we have the best chance of surviving and thriving if we live successfully and cooperatively in groups and communities (Ridley 1996). Learning theory has clearly demon-strated that we can override most genetic inheritances and evolved predispositions and it is for this reason that there is so much interest in the potential of teaching and learning, particularly in the early stages of childhood development, to prevent antisocial behaviour. But it is not just what we can internalise in individuals that will help us to achieve a safer society; it is also the way that the society, or subsets of it, is organised.

High crime areas and high crime countries are characterised by a lack of trust between citizens and between citizens and the agents of social control. It follows therefore that 'reliable trust' is a fundamental prerequisite of a safe society. By this I mean people trusting others in the sure knowledge that they won't be let down or disillusioned. Trust is expressed through lowering your defences because you know that the trusted person will not take advantage of your subsequent vulnerability. The abuse of trust is most blatantly manifest in the manipulation of the confidence trickster, who persuades the victim to drop their defences and then robs them. If we could reliably trust our fellow citizens, we would need far fewer locks, police and security. But it only takes a few abusers of such trust to make it necessary for us all to be on our guard (Ridley 1996). We are in the best position to reliably

trust those who we know as friends or acquaintances, but there is
a limit to how many people we can recognise. Ridley suggests that
this number is about 150, although Alexander et al. (1977) suggest up to 500. The development and management of small living
clusters or 'actual neighbourhoods' could be the starting point for
a safe and secure communal system. These 'socially and environmentally engineered communities' could offer a viable and more
humane alternative to the separatist future that the combination
of the free market and new technology seems to be pushing us
towards.

### 9.5    Organisation and management

Despite the encouraging evidence that mixed but socially cohesive
neighbourhoods, where people recognise and support each other,
are more resistant to crime (see, for example, Sampson et al.
1997), there are a number of difficulties in implementing such
actual neighbourhoods. Above all, there is the understandable
desire of those with choice and means to select their own preferred
living environments. Many people like to live in the aspirational
suburbs where all neighbours are of the same social class and
family status (Sennett 1996). They don't want to live next to
poorer people, students or hostels for people with learning difficulties. Significantly though, most people on low incomes
wouldn't complain if they were offered accommodation in a prosperous neighbourhood! Even among the less well-off sectors of
society there are respectable working-class neighbourhoods and
sink estates. Nobody wants to live next to a problem family with
kids excluded from school and perhaps dabbling in drugs. There
seem to be two stark choices: either we can let the free market
heighten the polarisation of neighbourhoods into rich and poor,
black and white, families and singles (US style) or we can go for a
social interventionist approach where there are incentives for
people to live in mixed areas and people with needs get proper
levels of support and supervision (Scandinavian style). One
encouraging trend in England is the return to the cities. For most
of the past half-century people with choice have headed for the
suburbs, with the consequent abandonment of the central core to
the poor and the homeless. Recently there has been a noticeable
reverse in this trend in cities such as Bristol and Norwich where

there has been a deliberate policy to make city centre living an attractive and realistic proposition. (Scotland and most other European countries have always managed to maintain a good mix of inner-city housing.) Such an approach on its own has a valuable function in terms of extra informal surveillance at all hours. Combine this with a planned community infrastructure (as in Bordesley urban village in Birmingham) and there is a real possibility of re-establishing the actual inner-city communities championed by Jane Jacobs (1961).

Putting aside (for the purposes of this discussion) new-build urban villages such as Poundbury in England and Seaside in the USA, there are some notable examples of existing neighbourhoods that have been redeveloped physically and rehabilitated socially, where crime has been reduced and the perception of safety increased. A common thread that runs through these success stories is the input of local people in the revival of their neighbourhoods and the control they are able to exert both over the redevelopment and the management and maintenance of the improvements. Another common thread seems to be a sense of human scale whereby people can identify with and feel part of a community, where they are known and can recognise neighbours and where many of their needs are catered for within the neighbourhood. In other words, people feel that they belong to an actual neighbourhood rather than a conglomeration of buildings and spaces that have no personal or social meaning to them.

It could be argued that the model villages developed during Victorian times by philanthropically inclined industrialists for their workers were ahead of their time in providing healthy and safe environments. The well-known ones in the UK include: New Lanark (Robert Owen), Bournville, Birmingham (Cadbury), New Earswick, York (Rowntree) and Port Sunlight, Wirral (Lever Brothers). These model villages were all built to high standards, with integral community facilities, village greens and, significantly, they still remain popular, desirable and safe areas to live in. For example, New Earswick, built by Joseph Rowntree for his chocolate factory workers, is still a clearly defined community, despite being swallowed up by suburban residential expansion. The Joseph Rowntree Housing Trust continues to invest in appropriate facilities for the area and has recently built a new community centre and a small group of 'lifetime homes', enabling residents to stay within their homes in the village even when they grow old and frail. So maybe the future is to be found in the past!

In Bradford, the Royds Community Association is trying to rebuild communities out of alienating tracts of social housing. This is a resident-led and controlled rehabilitation programme covering three formerly disadvantaged peripheral housing estates with a combined population of 12,000. The Community Association secured a £108 million SRB over seven years and ensured that improvements to the area were defined, determined, managed and implemented (60% of the construction workers are residents of the area) by local people. Part of the strategy is to divide up the huge area of housing into identifiable communities with defining physical features such as public art and village centres. As neighbourhoods have been improved, crime levels fell 30–90%. As the chair of the Royds Community Association said: 'people are now taking responsibility for their own actions and their children's actions' (Design against Crime 2002; People for Action 2003).

All the demographic trends indicate that we are living in an increasingly urbanised world and this is unlikely to reverse in the foreseeable future. The city has numerous advantages, both from the point of view of sustainability and civilisation generally (see, for example, Rogers 1997). It is paramount therefore that we reverse the decline into fear and insecurity experienced by the inhabitants of many conurbations. If we fail to create and maintain actual neighbourhoods where people feel safe and secure, by default we will deteriorate into the alternative scenario of inner-city abandonment, segregation and gated communities. One of the most significant worldwide lifestyle developments of recent years has been the flight of the better-off in many countries to fortified neighbourhoods (Blakely and Snyder 1997). These gated communities (as they are often euphemistically termed) purport to provide safe sanctuary for those who can afford to live there. Such developments now constitute a major proportion of all upper income new-build housing in Brazil, USA and South Africa. As well as providing controlled access, some of these secure compounds are also patrolled by armed private security personnel. In South Africa it has been suggested that by retreating into gated communities, the better-off citizens have created a new apartheid based on wealth rather than skin colour (Landman

2000). An alternative to fortified segregation is unlikely to emerge spontaneously (Minton 2002). If we want a more humane alternative future, it will need to be planned and enabled by central and local government, with the support of the majority of the electorate.

## 9.6 Mainstreaming crime prevention

Many public and social service agencies do not regard their function as being the prevention of crime, even when their actions clearly are having this result. Thus, the youth service (through detached workers) and the Health Board (through health visitors) do not describe themselves as being crime prevention agencies; indeed they would probably resist such a label. It could be argued that, if a byproduct of their interventions is reduced crime, it does not matter that they do not regard themselves as agents of crime control. But, in fact this is problematic for two reasons. Firstly, it means that such agencies do not make the most of their crime preventive activities, as they do not regard this as being what they are about. So possibilities for refining what they do to enhance crime preventive outcomes are not taken up. Secondly, it means they are less inclined to work in concert with other, more explicit crime prevention agencies, such as the police and local authority community safety departments. Even the agencies that you would expect to have crime prevention at the top of their agenda – the police and probation service – are so caught up in *responding* to crime that they have little time or inclination left to devote to *prevention*. A lack of strategic vision is to blame here, with the result that officers are so busy processing offenders that they do not have the opportunity to step back and see what can be done to tackle the front end of this production line for human misery.

One of the key challenges for the future is to persuade relevant public service agencies and departments to incorporate crime prevention considerations into their mainstream functions. In England and Wales the legislative underpinning is there (in Section 17 of the Crime and Disorder Act) and some joint progress is being made, but in many areas the rhetoric of multi-agency collaboration has not produced much substance.

## 9.7  Policy and governance

Many things can be achieved at the personal level to reduce criminal behaviour. Many things can be achieved at the neighbourhood
and district level to create safer communities; but there are some
big issues affecting crime and insecurity that can only be tackled
through big political and cultural shifts. Whether these shifts will
occur in the future is a matter of choice and deliberation about the
kind of society we want to live in. In democratic societies, at least
in principle, the majority of citizens can influence policy directions, although, as the ongoing debate about capital punishment
suggests, these popular pushes can be emotional rather than
rational (see Stenson and Sullivan 2001). Culture is a rather more
complex and intransigent animal, although we have witnessed
some major cultural shifts in the last few decades, for example a
reduction in the moral grip of religion-based values and a move to
a more materialistic culture. As these examples demonstrate, cultural shifts can be bad for crime control as well as good.

Crime in most European and American cities is at an unaccept-
ably high level compared with 30–40 years ago. If we are to reduce
crime significantly we will have to revise or reverse policies that
appear to have exacerbated the proclivity to offend in many
Western countries:

- unemployment and increasing relative poverty, combined with
  erosion of social security benefits (such as the non-availability of
  benefit to 16- and 17-year-olds)
- cutbacks in subsidised youth and leisure facilities by cash-
  starved local authorities, which may result in young people grav-
  itating onto the streets and into city centres where, through
  boredom and frustration, they start behaving antisocially
- reductions in public guardians such as road sweepers, park
  keepers, stationmasters, bus conductors and so on, who had
  their core tasks replaced by automation or neglect, but whose
  incidental role of public surveillance and reassurance has been
  lost
- cutbacks in social house building have led to increases in
  vagrancy and homelessness, particularly amongst the young, the
  age group most likely to become involved in offending
- the move towards out-of-town shopping and recreational facili-

ties has resulted in the decline and neglect of some town centres, and their desertion by the more privileged car-owning majority (but how long will it be before the street criminals head out to the greenfield sites too?)
- commercial and planning considerations have led to monolithic uses and zoning within urban areas, with the results that certain streets and neighbourhoods are minimally occupied and rarely watched over at certain times of the day or week
- designs and developments to fulfil one need can create new offending opportunities, for example multistorey or basement car parks, pedestrian underpasses, access hinterlands around shopping malls and park-and-ride schemes (where cars are left unattended for eight hours a day), areas blighted by redevelopment proposals, road schemes or structure plans.

It should be apparent from the above list that many of these problems are not soluble at a local level; in many cases, there would have to be a shift of national policies. Many of the policies that have led to the above criminogenic problems were made for entirely different reasons (often to do with commerce or urban development). At the time they were made, the policy makers were just thinking about the results for their own particular interest, whether this was cutting public expenditure or new spatial planning. If we are to avoid generating more crime opportunities and delinquent responses in the future, all those involved in public policy planning will have to consider these potentially undesirable consequences and factor these into their cost–benefit analyses.

Another policy dichotomy we will have to resolve is the balancing of freedom and intrusion (see Clutterbuck 1997). Effective control of crime has to be reconciled with people's fundamental freedoms of lifestyle, mobility and privacy. A crime prevention programme could be so intrusive as to seriously restrict these freedoms (constant surveillance, restricted access and so on). On the other hand, we have to remember that uncontrolled crime is also intrusive and can severely restrict personal freedom, for example on some problem estates, residents are reluctant to leave their homes unoccupied for fear of burglary. Not only that, but attempts to increase crime fighting in the conventional manner can actually worsen the situation; as Wilkins (1974) warns: 'If crime and criminals are pursued with too much enthusiasm by law

enforcement agencies, then the law-abiding citizen may end up
changing his fear of crime for a fear of the police – not a very
desirable trade-off.' On the same theme Wilson (1975: 98) comments: 'The harder the police try to catch criminals the more they
are likely to rub raw the sores of community discontent.'

The whole concept of crime fighting is criticised by Clarke and
Hough (1984: 20), who note: 'It may not be helpful to think in
terms of a "war on crime" fought between criminals and the
Police, as this may increase unnecessarily public anxieties and fear
of crime.' At the minimum, then, we are talking about crime prevention as being a lesser evil, in terms of intrusiveness. Furthermore, a sympathetically designed crime prevention package, with
particular emphasis on social strategies, could not only work with
the minimum of intrusiveness, but could additionally help to
improve the quality of life, by expanding legitimate opportunities,
increasing facilities and raising community morale. In this way,
improved community safety can liberate rather than repress. And
it is important to remember that:

> Crime prevention is just one aspect of the quality of life . . . A
> preoccupation with crime prevention may create the kind of
> heavily fortified environments in which people (given a choice)
> do not want to live. And the kinds of environments they prefer
> (witness the premium on private houses that abut parks) may
> lead to increased chances of victimisation which they are willing
> to tolerate. (Osborn 1993: 165)

So what does the future hold, based on our current condition?
To make a sweeping generalisation, we seem to be becoming a
more stressed, anxious and suspicious citizenry. Our lives are
more mobile, fragmented and unstable. We are becoming more
private and exclusive, preferring to lock ourselves away inside our
fully furnished enclaves from where we can filter incoming information and culture. This human condition is in danger of driving
us into the dystopian future described at the beginning of this
chapter, where we escape, behind private security, into a drug-
enhanced netherworld. The next two sections suggest that, if we
solely extrapolate from current trends, there is a risk that this could
become a future reality.

## 9.8 Private security and personal profit

A rather alarming response to these growing anxieties and suspicions has been the privatisation of security, offering safety to those who can afford it, while the rest of us are left to our own devices. This started with the employment of private security patrols by syndicates of residents in affluent suburbs and has progressed to the gating and walling-in of better-off neighbourhoods so that only residents and authorised persons may enter the enclave of streets.

It is said that every cloud has a silver lining and one group of people who benefit from this level of widespread fear and victimisation is the crime control industry. Many people's jobs and profits depend on crime flourishing, and we're not talking about the criminal fraternity! As Palmer pointed out as long ago as 1973: 'We become dependent on crime. It becomes part of our way of life . . . It provides as well, a livelihood for several millions who are directly employed in the abortive attempt to control it.' In addition to those employed in manufacturing and servicing domestic and commercial security, what incentive is there for those employed in probation, police, courts (including solicitors and barristers) and prisons to support or engage in crime prevention? Christie's (1993) powerful critique of the crime control industry reveals the multitude of vested interests in the growth of crime. There are three categories of employment that are not only unlikely to have any interest in crime prevention, but who directly benefit from increases in crime: criminal lawyers, prison builders and private security companies.

Criminal lawyers profit from crime whether or not their clients are eventually found guilty. All they need for a regular income is a steady supply of alleged offenders charged by the police, or victims who are prepared to sue for compensation. A small number of dedicated lawyers strive, through their casework, to create a fairer and more just society, but for the majority, crime constitutes a ready supply of raw material which they then manipulate to meet the requirements of the lucrative game of winning or losing a court case. The increasingly advertised 'no win no fee' trend in legal action blatantly reveals the gamesmanship aspect of criminal and civil law, sometimes at the expense of social and criminal justice.

Since the huge expansion of the prison population in Britain and the USA over the last 15 years or so, prison building and equipping has proved to be a profitable industry with a vested interest in crime increases. Lewis (1997) notes that in the USA 'a new private sector flourished, able to finance, build and operate new prisons quickly and cheaply'. They have their own industry magazine, chock full of advertisements for exotic items such as restraint harnesses for difficult prisoners. In Britain Reliance Custodial Services Ltd, established in 1996, 'quickly established a reputation for the provision of a high quality, reliable and secure service on which the company has continued to build' (Reliance promotional brochure), to the extent that it has now branched out into electronic tagging of offenders.

Private security is a growth industry; perhaps bigger even than crime itself. Thousands of security firms are profiting from the escalating fear of crime and they will often exploit that fear in their marketing. Every week, householders, police forces, shops and small businesses are being approached by an increasing number of firms that offer everything from heat-seeking video cameras to electronic dog barkers and trauma counselling for victims. During the recession years of the late 1980s and early 1990s, while other industries withered, security thrived. Between 1989 and 1993, the turnover of member companies of the British Security Industry Association increased by 20% to over £1.4 billion. Sandwiched between reports on chilled ready meals and special interest magazines, the November 1995 Mintel *Marketing Bulletin* had a forecast for personal and home security:

> The climate of fear engendered by the increasing incidence of crime in recent years acts as a spur to households investing in home security products. The result of these favourable indicators is to produce a market increase of 56% in real terms up until 1999.

Who said crime never pays?

## 9.9   Drugs and crime

In any future crime prevention scenario, drugs are likely to figure as a prime element to be addressed. It is important to bear in mind that problematic drugs include alcohol, particularly in Northern Europe where excessive alcohol consumption is closely linked to violent behaviour. Over the last couple of decades, many Western nations have witnessed a huge increase in problematic drug use. One of the most noticeable differences between local crime surveys I was involved in during the early 1990s and those I have been involved in during the new millennium has been the ascendancy of drugs as the major crime-related problem in most neighbourhoods. In terms of crime statistics, illegal drugs achieve a triple whammy in terms of drugs use, dealing in drugs and acquisitive and violent crime associated with drug use and dealing. Many addicts are unemployed and unemployable so the only way they can raise the cash to buy more drugs from dealers is to steal and rob. As they are either intoxicated or desperate, their offending can be quite brazen. On top of this come the turf wars and rivalries between competing drug dealers that can lead to violent confrontations, sometimes using guns and resulting in fatalities.

If we think that national crime control policies leave much to be desired and are often determined for politically expedient reasons, these shortcomings pale into insignificance compared with most national polices relating to drug use. In the same way that crime fighting can be counterproductive, so the war on drugs is doomed to failure, according to a number of commentators (see, for example, Coleman 1992; Currie 1993; Williamson 1997; Gray 2002). Most countries experienced huge increases in the distribution and use of cocaine and opiate drugs during the 1970s and 80s. The worst increases were in the USA – in 1989 there had been an 800% increase in arrests for the sale or manufacture of cocaine or heroin compared with 1980 (Currie 1993). By this time the American government was investing about $13 billion per annum in the war against drugs, mostly on policing, courts and prisons. As Currie (1993: 13) says:

> What makes the severity of the American nightmare especially frightening is that, like a fire that continues to rage after we have cut down half the forest to contain it, it has withstood the most extraordinary efforts at control.

The Americans assumed that drugs were something that, with enough effort, could be stamped out, conveniently ignoring their disastrous experience of trying to stamp out that other dangerous drug, alcohol, in the earlier part of the twentieth century.

In the early 1990s the British were feeling smug about the

Americans' warning of a crack cocaine epidemic, but by the new millennium crack was indeed infiltrating some of Britain's inner-city areas. Undaunted by the Americans' failure to crush the drugs problem by the sheer weight of law and order, in the 1990s the British appointed a drugs tsar, who just happened to be a former chief constable. Despite the evidence that national campaigns to prevent crime have limited impact (see Rosenbaum et al. 1998) and the American experience of law enforcement, British drug control policy was and still is principally based on education and enforcement. Even though there have been increasing demands from the populace and even some senior police officers to rethink drugs control policy, the two major political parties in Britain will not even countenance a debate about a change in tactics towards the possibility of decriminalisation, so that drug misuse can be treated as a health and social problem rather than a criminal justice one. As John Gray (2002: 141) points out:

> Prohibiting drugs makes the trade in them fabulously profitable. It breeds crime and greatly enlarges the prison population. Despite, this there is a worldwide drugs pandemic. Prohibiting drugs has failed. Why then will no contemporary government legalise them?

'Drugs cause crime' is a common cry, but it is our political and legal attitude to drug use that creates the link to crime. I said earlier, to illustrate the social construction of crime, that one way to reduce crime would be to make everything legal. Under the current regime, addicts are likely to be double offenders, first of all for possession and secondly for committing crimes to fund their habit. Possession of a controlled drug is one of the few crimes where offender and victim are one and the same person. Given that there is a growing political concern about the rights and needs of victims, perhaps, in the case of drug misuse, we should be concentrating more on the addict as a victim rather than an offender.

It would be much more sensible to ask 'what causes drug use?' The answers to this question are similar to some answers to the question 'what causes crime?' As Coleman (1992) summarises: 'Drug addiction of all kinds will be eradicated . . . when society eradicates inequality, frustration, envy and injustice.' Although we may be able to reduce these detrimental factors in people's lives and indeed it should be the aim of enlightened social policy to do so, we will probably never eradicate them altogether. So the corollary to this is that drugs will always be with us to a greater or lesser extent. Half a century ago Aldous Huxley expressed this point eloquently, if rather depressingly in *The Doors of Perception*:

> Most men and women lead lives at the worst so painful, at the best so monotonous, poor and limited, that the urge to escape, the longing to transcend themselves if only for a few moments, is and always has been one of the principal appetites of the soul. (quoted in Williamson 1997)

But drugs are not just 'emotional anaesthetics' – they can also give pleasure. So-called 'recreational' drug users get high for the sheer pleasure that such mind alteration gives. It could be argued that for many, an added 'high' comes from the fact that when the drug in question is cannabis, cocaine or ecstasy, rather than alcohol or nicotine, this is a forbidden pleasure. So it may be that, by making the consumption of certain drugs illegal, we are actually making them more attractive and exciting. This particularly applies to young people, many of whom get a buzz from engaging in activities that attract adult censure. Thus campaigns such as 'just say no to drugs' are doomed from the start, as they fail to understand adolescent psychology (Braiker 2003).

Many people, both adult and young, will reflect on the hypocrisy and inconsistency of drugs policy: why are alcohol and nicotine – two of the most dangerous drugs, both in terms of morbidity and addiction – legal but controlled whereas other drugs are strictly illegal? The reasons are historic, cultural and economic. Alcohol and tobacco have over a number of centuries become acceptable lubricants of social interaction and generate huge revenues for manufacturers and the state. Cannabis and opium have had more chequered histories and, despite widespread use in the past and (particularly in the case of cannabis) present, are currently illegal in most countries. It will be interesting to see if the growing disapproval of cigarette smoking, both on health and social grounds, will lead to it becoming a banned substance in the future, or whether we will go the other way and decriminalise other drugs, so that overall policy is consistent with the law on alcohol and tobacco consumption.

Currently we have the worst of all worlds where there is no logic to what is legal and illegal. Proponents of the current arrangements argue that some soft drugs (such as cannabis and ecstasy) have to remain illegal because their use inevitably leads down the slippery slope towards hard drug use. At present there is no more evidence to support this than there is to show that people who smoke cigarettes, consume alcohol or drink coffee (another drug) are more likely to graduate onto hard drugs than those who abstain from such mind-altering substances (Drug Policy Alliance 2002). Ironically, any risk that recreational drug users may move on to harder intoxicants is likely to be precipitated by the very fact that they are having to deal with suppliers who have been criminalised by the law and who may therefore be able to trade in harder drugs through their underworld connections – a case of the law actually making things worse (Drug Policy Alliance 2002). Of course it is true that virtually all heroin addicts will have smoked cannabis at some time in their lives, but their heroin use is much more likely to be a response to their personal and social circumstances than to some kind of inevitable graduation from milder intoxicants.

A doomed strategy for reducing drug use is the commonly stated police and customs aim of 'taking out the dealers'. Basic economic principles ensure that, as long as there is a demand for a product, ingenious ways will be found to supply that demand. A rational approach to drug misuse reduction, resulting also in less crime, would be to work on activities that lower the demand, so that the supply chain would wither of its own accord. An example of a more rational approach to drugs control can be found in Holland. Many people throw up their arms in dismay when the words 'Holland' and 'drugs' are combined. Yet despite the country's reputation of being a kind of drugs free-for-all, the whole supply and use system is carefully controlled, managed and, in the case of cannabis, licensed (see Ministry of Health, Welfare and Sport, the Netherlands 1995; Williamson 1997). As a result of treating drug use as a health, social and management issue, rather than a primarily criminal justice issue, the Dutch have managed to stabilise both hard and soft use, while most other European countries have experienced huge increases. Their strategy removes the forbidden thrill of much drug taking and, at the same time, prevents thousands of users getting sucked into the criminal justice system where, as we have seen, many lives are stigmatised and permanently damaged (see Currie 1993).

Another approach has been tried, to varying degrees, in some countries – that of harm reduction for addicts (see Hunt 2003). The idea here is to accept that some people are addicted to drugs and try to reduce the harm they do to themselves (dirty needles, spliced drugs) and others (committing crime to fund their habit). During an experimental three-year period in Switzerland, when heroin was prescribed for addicts, drug-related crime was reduced by 60% and the addicts' health, living conditions and employability all improved significantly (Holloway 1999).

In the same way that throwing more and more money at the criminal justice system is not going to significantly reduce crime in the future, so it would seem that further attempts to prohibit and criminalise drugs use will only serve to fill our prisons rather than make any serious impact on the problem. As Richard Holloway (1999: 103) perceptively summarises:

> In open societies prohibitions that do not have the overwhelming consent of the people, are almost impossible to police and can end up corrupting the very system that is there to enforce them.

But John Gray (2002: 142) is pessimistic about any future change to our illogical drugs policies:

> Societies founded on a faith in progress cannot admit the normal unhappiness of human life. As a result, they are bound to wage war on those who seek an artificial happiness in drugs.

## 9.10 Exclusion or inclusion?

One of the political decisions we, and the citizens of many other countries, will have to make is whether we want a two-tier society, where the privileged few lead lives entirely cocooned from the mean streets of the teeming masses, or an inclusive society where everyone has the freedom to reasonably enjoy a shared environment? If we aspire to the latter, we will have to ensure that physical security measures are not so oppressive that they exclude large portions of the population from substantial tracts of the public and communal realm, with the excuse that they may at some time be inclined to commit an offence, if their movements are not monitored and restricted.

One way to minimise crime (but at a social cost) would be to give up the public realm. The original civic notion of shared spaces where everyone, whether familiar or strangers, had a right to circulate and interact could be abandoned as too risky and dangerous. This has already happened in parts of the USA where the mere act of walking down the street can lead to an interrogation by officers in a police patrol car (as some hapless British pedestrian tourists have discovered in Los Angeles). We could drive from our fortified homes to our business centre which has controlled access by vehicle only (they already have these in California, see Davis 1992) and give up altogether on street life, except perhaps for a few heavily supervised 'heritage' settlements where we could relive the historic experience of walking down pavements (the Disney Corporation has built one in Florida called Celebration).

Or we can decide that street life is the heart and soul of any vibrant and fulfilling city culture; in which case we need to ensure that our streets and public spaces are safe to walk through and linger in, for everyone. Thriving cities are premised on social and public interactions (Whyte 1988). Therefore, for cities to flourish, rather than be mere conglomerations of buildings, we need publicly shared spaces. To make them safer we can choose a number of tactics. The 'clean sweep' approach entails purging our neighbourhoods of undesirables through the imposition of physical barriers, uniformed patrolling, electronic surveillance, draconian liquor controls and, perhaps, a ten o'clock curfew for under-18s. A better alternative is surely to do everything we can to make our streets and public spaces civilised (in every sense of the word) locations, where everyone can circulate and interact and, consequently, where the pro-social majority easily outweighs the antisocial minority.

The crime control measures described in preceding chapters can be typified within a framework that covers the spectrum between repressive and integrative approaches, as shown below. The repressive approaches are generally the most obvious solutions and tend to produce the quickest and most tangible results. Integrative approaches require more imagination and a longer time scale.

| **Repression** | **Integration** |
|---|---|
| *Exclusion, zero tolerance, driving out crime* | *Inclusion, tolerance, crowding out crime* |
| • Privatisation of public space (for example enclosed shopping centres and malls ) | • Promotion of public space (for example markets, street entertainment) |
| • Gated communities and access control systems | • Actual neighbourhoods and urban villages |
| • Brute security (for example solid steel shutters and grilles) | • Subtle security (for example hinge bolts, solid doors and 'welcome' lights) |
| • Formal surveillance (policing, tagging and CCTV) | • Informal surveillance ('living over the shop', residential infill, citizens on the streets, 24-hour cities) |
| • Banning people with problems (arrests, moving on young people, curfews) | • Providing facilities and services for people with problems (drop-in centres, detached youth workers) |
| • Alcohol and busking bans | • Café culture, street festivals and cultural animation |
| • Labelling deviants and stigmatising the excluded, school exclusions for difficult children | • Extra support and social education for parents and children at a disadvantage |

It must be fairly obvious, by now, which column of approaches this author favours. However, the preference for integration rather than repression is not just based on some wishy-washy liberal notion – in the long run it is likely to be more effective and, crucially, sustainable. As Richard Holloway (1999: 17) remarks:

Fear is a potent motivator of behaviour and any civilly organised society will acknowledge its importance in deterring and punishing certain types of unacceptable conduct, but the most effective systems will generally operate on the basis of consent, not coercion; voluntary acceptance, not imposed obedience.

We may have to repress some criminal urges in the population but if we weigh down too heavily, everyone gets hurt. Better surely to take limited physical and deployment precautions but also manage our neighbourhoods and public spaces in creative and integrative ways for everyone to enjoy. It may be that a certain level of crime and insecurity is the price we have to pay for living in a society that encourages true democracy, civil liberties, free expression and cultural diversity. How we minimise that level without sacrificing individual freedom and communal rights is the challenge for enlightened nations.

### 9.11   A broader vision for social policy

The prevention of crime and the creation of safer communities are inextricably tied to wider political and cultural trends. Even changes in the prevailing belief systems of citizens will have an effect on future crime rates. On the whole deeply spiritual people (such as Buddhists, Taoists and Confucianists) and deeply humanitarian people do not get involved in crime. Influential thinkers of differing political and philosophical persuasions have wrestled with the issues of crime control and human rights for many years before this particular book was written and their comments seem to be just as relevant today, as the quotes below aim to show.

Wilson and Herrnstein (1985: 20) point out that:

> Since every known society has experienced crime, no society has ever entirely solved the problem of order. The fact that crime is universal may suggest that man's nature is not infinitely malleable, though some people never cease searching for an anvil and hammer sufficient to bend it to their will. Some societies seem better able than others to sustain order without making unacceptable sacrifices in personal freedom, and in every society the level of order is greater at some times than at others. These systematic and oft-remarked differences in the level of crime across time and place suggest that there is something worth explaining.

The problem is that 'Many of the causes of crimes which we are anxious to prevent are enmeshed in social changes which we are

**Plate 9.2** Former YMCA turned into a remand centre, the Bronx, New York

anxious to promote, and are part of the price we pay for them'
(Rees 1981: 8). It is possible to envisage crime-free societies, but
they tend to be either primitive or repressive (see Taft 1950).
Observation of post-revolutionary conditions in countries such as
Russia and China reveals that the reduction of crime does not just
depend on a drastic overhaul of the political system. Even in
Japan, which had a low crime rate for many years, there have been
persistent problems with organised racketeers and juvenile delinquency. Perhaps the best we can hope for is a sense that crime is
not dominating our anxieties and running out of control.

> The problem, like the problem of disease, is not in any final
> sense soluble, but it can be subjected to effective control. We
> cannot expect more; there is no reason why we should be satis-
> fied with less. (Morris and Hawkins 1970: 262)

However, it is worth ending with a cautionary note. Prevention
of crime is not the only goal of social policy, nor should it unduly
dominate the social policy agenda. There is a danger, particularly
in the current crime prevention boom, of expecting all aspects of
social policy to have a crime prevention outcome. After all, as

Morris and Hawkins (1970) pointed out, as a civilised society we should aim to provide decent housing, a pleasant environment and opportunities for our children, for their own sake and not because they reduce crime. This overpreoccupation with crime and its consequent distortion of broad social policy goals is usually described as the 'criminalisation of social policy'. We have only to look across the Atlantic, where a lot of current crime prevention thinking originated, to see where this preoccupation can lead: an explosion of private policing, heavily fortified suburbs, gun law, massive rates of imprisonment, capital punishment and *still* the highest violent crime rate in the Western world.

The fictional scenario right at the start of this book is only a step or two from current reality, but it is not inevitable. Although technology will change rapidly, culture will shift gradually and *Homo sapiens*' basic constitution will adapt hardly at all. Our magnificent brains offer us the potential to learn, reflect and organise ourselves socially to the best advantage of civilisation as a whole. How we control crime is, ultimately, a matter of choice, but it would be good if that was an enlightened and informed choice.

# Further Reading and Websites

In this book I have tried to present the most useful facts and views about crime and preventive approaches and have attempted to challenge many of the fallacies that undermine a sensible approach to crime control. But even if I had tried to be objective and dispassionate at all times, I will inevitably (like everybody else) have selected and filtered information. Therefore, in order to get a fully balanced understanding of crime prevention, it is worth examining other texts that may confirm or challenge some of the facts and assertions found in this book. The reading recommended below spans a range of thinking from the highly theoretical to the deeply pragmatic and from liberal to conservative perspectives.

Bursik R J and Grasmick H G (1993) *Neighbourhoods and Crime – the dimensions of effective community control.* Lexington Books, Jossey-Bass, San Francisco

> An update on the social disorganisation theory of criminality, which suggests that building strong, stable communities can lead to better informal social control, which is still a valid way of preventing crime.

Clarke R (ed.) (1997) *Situational Crime Prevention – successful case studies.* (2nd edn). Harrow & Heston, Albany, NY

> Probably the best introduction to the concept of situational crime prevention, that is, changing the situation to make crime

more difficult to commit. This second edition extends situational prevention techniques into social prevention territory, by adding a new category entitled 'stimulating conscience'.

Crawford A (1998) *Crime Prevention and Community Safety – politics, policies and practices.* Longman, Harlow

An overview of the development of crime prevention and community safety in Britain, with passing comparisons with Sweden, France, Holland and Japan. Puts the topic into a political context and criticises attempts to treat it as a purely technical activity.

Currie E (1998) *Crime and Punishment in America – why the solutions to America's most stubborn crisis have not worked, and what will.* Owl Books, Henry Holt, NY

The title summarises it all. Elliot Currie is the USA's most informed liberal thinker on the subject of crime control. He is unrelenting in his attack on the existing American criminal justice system which prefers to react punitively and inefficiently rather than tackle the root causes of violent crimes that are among the highest in the world.

Home Office (1998) *Reducing Offending: an assessment of research evidence on ways of dealing with offending behaviour.* Home Office Research Study 187

A very useful meta-analysis of research into crime prevention, both physical and social. Influenced the Labour government's policy shift towards long-term social crime prevention measures.

Hughes G, McLaughlin E and Muncie J (eds) (2002) *Crime Prevention and Community Safety – new directions.* Sage, London

A collection of articles by some of the leading theoreticians in the field of crime prevention and community safety. Ties the topic into broader social science debates around risk, control, conflict and postmodernism.

Kelling G and Coles C (1996) *Fixing Broken Windows – restoring order and reducing crime in our communities.* The Free Press, New York

A very good critique of the limitations of reactive, military-style policing and the importance of community involvement, written by an academic who is considered to be right-of-centre, and was partly responsible for the idea of zero-tolerance policing.

Morris N and Hawkins G (1970) *The Honest Politician's Guide to Crime Control.* University of Chicago Press

An early, classic attempt to introduce some pragmatic reasoning into the debate about controlling crime. Mostly directs its attention at suggested modifications to legal statutes and operations of the criminal justice system.

Sherman L, Farrington D and Lab P (2002) *Evidence-based Crime Prevention.* Routledge, London

Builds on the meta-analysis of 'what works, what doesn't, what's promising', carried out for the US Department of Justice.

Skogan W G (1990) *Disorder and Decline – crime and the spiral of decay in American Neighbourhoods.* University of California Press, Berkeley

An interesting counterpoint to the Kelling and Coles book. Suggests that attempts to prevent crime and disorder through community action are least effective in the most troubled neighbourhoods and that proactive redevelopment policies are needed, along with a range of other policy initiatives, to underpin grass-roots developments.

Walker S (1998) *Sense and Nonsense about Crime and Drugs* (4th edn). Wadsworth, Belmont, CA

A brilliant digest of research showing both what is effective in dealing with the crime and drugs problems and the fallacies of some policies. It's only shortcoming is that it looks exclusively at the USA.

Walklate S (1998) *Understanding Criminology: current theoretical debates*. Open University Press, Buckingham

A thorough and clear introduction to the theories that underpin criminology and how they relate to political views and policy.

Wilson J Q and Herrnstein R J (1985) *Crime and Human Nature – the definitive study of the causes of crime.* Touchstone, New York

A powerful and well-researched account written from a conservative viewpoint. An interesting contrast to Elliot Currie's book. Reading the two of them shows just how much to do with crime control is political and debatable.

Vold G, Bernard T and Snipes J (1998) *Theoretical Criminology* (4th edn). Oxford University Press

Despite the dry title, this is an excellent digest of all the key theories about why crimes occur. It also discusses how the theories interlock or apply to various types of crime and what all this implies for research and policy.

**Key websites**

http://environment.uwe.ac.uk/commsafe/ – will give you ready access to all the other sites listed below, plus many others relevant to crime prevention.

www.crime-prevention-intl.org/english/ – the International Center for the Prevention of Crime, based in Montreal, Canada

www.urbansecurity.org/ – The European Forum for Urban Security, based in Paris

www.europa.eu.int/comm/justice_home/eucpn/ – The European Crime Prevention Network, established by the European Union www.crimereduction.gov.uk/ – the crime prevention site for the Home Office (England and Wales)

www.aic.gov.au/research/cvp/ – the main Australian crime prevention site

www.prevention.gc.ca/en/ – the main Canadian crime prevention site

www.ncpc.org/ – the main American crime prevention site

# Bibliography

Abel-Smith B and Townsend P (1965) *The Poor and the Poorest*. Bell & Sons, London

Ad Hoc Working Group on the International Exchange of Crime Prevention Information (1989) *Crime Prevention Perspectives and Practices*. US Department of Justice

Adler A (1931) *What Life Could Mean To You*. Reprinted 1992 by Oneworld Publications, Oxford

Alexander C, Ishikawa S and Silverstein M (1977) *A Pattern Language: towns, buildings, construction*. Oxford University Press, New York

Allat P (1982) *An Experiment in Crime Prevention on a Difficult to Let Estate*. Newcastle Polytechnic

Alinsky S (1971) *Rules for Radicals – a pragmatic primer for realistic radicals*. Random House, New York

Armitage R (2000) *Evaluation of Secured by Design Housing in West Yorkshire*. Home Office briefing Note 7/00

Association of London Government (1995) *Europe's Response to Youth Crime – a survey*. ALG, London

Atlas R (1999) *The Alchemy of CPTED: Less Magic, More Science!* Paper presented at the International CPTED Association Conference, Mississauga, Canada

Baldwin J and Bottoms A (1976) *The Urban Criminal*. Tavistock, London

Ballintyne S, Pease K and McLaren V (eds) (2000) *Secure Foundations – key issues in crime prevention, crime reduction and community safety*. Institute for Public Policy Research, London

Balvig F (1987) *The Snow-White Image: the hidden reality of crime in Switzerland*. Norwegian University Press, Oslo.

Barclay G (ed.) (1993) *Information on the Criminal Justice System in England and Wales*. Home Office, London

226

Barclay G, Tavares C and Siddique A (2001) *International Comparisons of Criminal Justice Statistics 1999.* Home Office, London

Barker M (1993) *The Prevention of Street Robbery.* Crime Prevention Unit Paper 44. Home Office, London

Beaud S and Pialoux M (2001) *Emeutes Urbaines, Violence Sociale.* Le Monde Diplomatique, Paris, July 2001

Beccaria C ([1764] 1976) *On Crime and Punishment.* Trans. by Paolucci H, New York

Becker H (1963) *Outsider: Studies in the Sociology of Deviance.* Free Press, New York

Belson W A and Didcott P J (1969) *Causal Factors in the Development of Stealing by London Boys.* LSE Survey Research Centre, London

Bennett T and Wright R (1984) *Burglars on Burglary.* Gower, Aldershot

Bianchini F (1994) Night cultures, night economies. *Town and Country Planning,* November

Birchall J (1988) *Building Communities the Co-operative Way.* Routledge & Kegan Paul, London

Blakely E and Snyder M (1997) Divided we fall – gated and walled communities in the United States. In Ellin N (cd.) *Architecture of Fear.* Architectural Press, Princeton

Booker C (1980) *The Seventies.* Penguin, Harmondsworth

Bottoms A and Pease K (1986) *Crime and Punishment: interpreting the data.* Open University Press, Buckingham

Bottoms A and McWilliams A (1979) A Non-treatment Paradigm for Probation Practice. *British Journal of Social Work* **9**(2)

Bouchet S (1999) Une Police plus Proche. *Journal de Paris,* 17 April

Bowlby J (1946) *Forty Four Juvenile Thieves.* Penguin, Harmondsworth

Bowlby J (1953) *Child Care and the Growth of Love.* Penguin, Harmondsworth

Box S (1981) *Deviancy, Reality and Society.* Holt Rinehart & Winston, New York

Box S (1983) *Power, Crime and Mystification.* Routledge, London

Braiker B (2003) 'Just Say No' is a 20 year old failure. *Newsweek,* 15 April

Braithwaite J (1989) *Crime, Shame and Reintegration.* Cambridge University Press

Braithwaite J (1998) Reducing the crime problem: a not so dismal criminology. In Walton P and Young J (eds) *The New Criminology Revisited.* Macmillan – now Palgrave Macmillan, Basingstoke

Bratton W (1997a) Zero Tolerance can help to beat crime. *The Electronic Telegraph,* issue 750. www.telegraph.co.uk

Bratton W (1997b) Crime is down in New York City – blame the police. In Dennis N (ed.) *Zero Tolerance – policing a free society.* Institute of Economic Affairs, London

Bright J and Petterson G (1984) *Community Based Improvements on 12 Inner London Housing Estates.* SNU, London

Brody S (1976) *The Effectiveness of Sentencing.* Home Office, London

Buikhuisen W and Mednick S (1988) *Explaining Criminal Behaviour – interdisciplinary approaches.* E J Brill, Leiden

Burrows R and Rhodes D (1998) *Unpopular Places? Area disadvantage and the geography of misery in England.* Policy Press in association with the Joseph Rowntree Foundation

Bursik R and Grasmick H (1993) *Neighbourhoods and Crime: the dimensions of effective community control.* Jossey-Bass, San Francisco

Cabinet Office (1999) *Living Without Fear – an integrated approach to tackling violence against women.* Inter-departmental Steering Group on Violence Against Women. The Women's Unit, Cabinet Office, London

Cain M (2000) Through other eyes: on the limitations and value of western criminology for teaching and practice in Trinidad and Tobago. In Nelken D (ed.) *Contrasting Criminal Justice – getting from here to there.* Ashgate, Aldershot

Chaline C and Dubois-Maury J (1994) *La Ville et ses Dangers.* Masson, Paris

Chalumeau E (2002) La police de proximité en point de mire. *Revue Urbanisme,* 323, Mars/Avril

Christie N (1993) *Crime Control as Industry.* Routledge, London

Cicourel A V (1968) *The Social Organisation of Juvenile Justice.* Wiley, New York

Clarke J (1976) Skinheads and the magical recovery of community. In Hall S and Jefferson T (eds) *Resistance through Rituals.* Hutchinson, London

Clarke J (1980) Social Democratic Delinquents and Fabian Families. In National Deviancy Conference (proceedings) *Permissiveness and Control.* Macmillan, Basingstoke

Clarke R (1997) *Situational Crime Prevention – successful case studies* (2nd edn). Harrow & Heston, Albany, NY

Clarke R (2000) Hot products: a new focus for crime prevention. In Ballintyne S, Pease K and McLaren V (eds) *Secure Foundations – key issues in crime prevention, crime reduction and community safety.* IPPR, London

Clarke R and Felson M (eds) (1993) *Routine Activity and Rational Choice.* Transaction, New Brunswick

Clarke R and Hough M (1984) *Crime and Police Effectiveness.* Research Study 79, Home Office, London

Clifford W (1976) *Crime Control in Japan.* Lexington Books, Lexington

Clinard M B (1978) *Cities with Little Crime – the case of Switzerland.* Cambridge University Press

Cloward R and Ohlin L (1960) *Delinquency and Opportunity – a theory of delinquent gangs*. Routledge & Kegan Paul, New York

Clutterbuck R (1997) *Public Safety and Civil Liberties*. Macmillan – now Palgrave Macmillan, Basingstoke

Cohen L and Felson M (1979) Social changes and crime rate trends: a routine activity approach. *American Sociological Review*, 44(4): 588–608

Cohen S (1969) Community control – a new utopia *New Society*, 15 March

Cohen S (1988) *Against Criminology*. Transaction Books, New Brunswick

Cohen S (1997) Western crime control models in the third world: benign or malignant? In Beirne P and Nelken D (eds) *Issues in Comparative Criminology*. Ashgate, Aldershot

Coleman A (1985) *Utopia on Trial*. Hilary Shipman, London

Coleman J (1988) Social capital in the creation of human capital. *American Journal of Sociology*, **94**

Coleman V (1992) *The Drugs Myth – why the drug wars must stop*. Merlin Press, London

Comedia (1991) *Out of Hours: a study of the economics and life of town centres*. Gulbenkian Foundation

Community Development Projects (1977) *Gilding the Ghetto*. Home Office, London

Coote A and Lenaghan J (1997) *Citizen's Juries: theory into practice*. Institute for Public Policy Research, London

Cornish D and Clarke R (1986) *The Reasoning Criminal – rational choice perspectives on offending*. Springer Verlag, New York

Coventry Safer Cities Project (1992) *City Centre Community Strategy*. Home Office Safer Cities Report

Council of Europe (1999) *European Sourcebook of Crime and Criminal Justice Statistics*. Council of Europe, Strasbourg

Crawford A (1997) *The Local Governance of Crime – appeals to community and partnerships*. Clarendon Press, Oxford

Crawford A (1998) *Crime Prevention and Community Safety – politics, policies and practices*. Longman, Harlow

Crawford A and Matassa (2000) *Community Safety Structures – an international literature review*. Criminal Justice Review Group, Northern Ireland Office

Crawford A, Lister S and Wall D (2003) *Great Expectations: contracted community policing in New Earswick*. Joseph Rowntree Foundation, York

Critcher C (1975) Structures, cultures and biographies. In Hall S and Jefferson A *Resistance Through Rituals*. Hutchinson, London

Croall H (1992) *White Collar Crime*. Open University Press, Buckingham

Croall H (1998) *Crime and Society in Britain*. Longman, Harlow

Crouch S, Shaftoe H and Fleming R (1999) *Design for Secure Residential Environments.* Longman, Harlow

Crowther C (2000) *Policing Urban Poverty.* Palgrave Macmillan, Basingstoke

Currie E (1993) *Reckoning – drugs, the cities and the American future.* Hill & Wang, New York

Currie E (1998) *Crime and Punishment in America – why the solutions to America's most stubborn social crisis have not worked, and what will.* Henry Holt, New York

Davidson R (1981) *Crime and Environment.* Croom Helm, London

Davies M, Croall H and Tyrer J (1998) *Criminal Justice – an introduction to the criminal justice system in England and Wales.* Longman, Harlow

Davis M (1992) *City of Quartz.* Verso, London

Dawkins R (1976) *The Selfish Gene.* Oxford University Press

Department of the Environment (1989) *Handbook of Estate Improvement Part 1: Appraising Options.* HMSO, London

Department of the Environment (1994) *Estate Action Update.* DoE, London

Department of the Environment (1997) *An Evaluation of DICE Schemes.* Regeneration Research Summary no 11. DoE, London

Design against Crime (2002) *Housing by Royds Community Association.* Design and Innovation Research Group, University of Salford (readable online at: www.artdes.salford.ac.uk/dac/)

Design Council (1979) *Design against Vandalism.* Heinemann, London

DETR (1999) *Cross-cutting Issues Affecting Local Government.* Department of the Environment, Transport and the Regions, London

van Dijk J and Mayhew P (1992) *Criminal Victimisation in the Industrialised World – key findings of the 1989 and 1992 International Crime Surveys.* Directorate for Crime Prevention, Ministry of Justice, the Netherlands

van Dijk J and de Waard J (1991) A two dimensional typology of crime prevention projects. *Criminal Justice Abstracts,* Sept

van Dijk J, Mayhew M and Killias M (1990) *Experiences of Crime Across the World – key findings of the 1989 International Crime Survey.* Kluwer, Deventer, the Netherlands

Ditton J and Duffy J (1983) Bias in newspaper reporting of crime news. *British Journal of Criminology,* **23**: 159–65

Donnison D (1998) *Policies for a Just Society.* Macmillan – now Palgrave Macmillan, Basingstoke

Downes D (1988) *Contrasts in Tolerance – Post-war policy in the Netherlands and England and Wales.* Clarendon Press, Oxford

Downes D and Rock P (1982) *Understanding Deviance.* Clarendon Press, Oxford

Drug Policy Alliance (2002) *RAND study refutes claims that Marijuana is 'gateway' to cocaine and heroin.* www.drugpolicy.org/news/

Dryfoos J (1990) *Adolescents at Risk – prevalence and prevention.* Oxford University Press, New York

Duprez D and Hedli M (1985) *Le Mal des Banlieues? – Sentiment d'Insecurité et Crise Identitaire.* Logiques Sociales l'Harmattan, Paris.

Eck J and Rosenbaum D (1994) The new police order: effectiveness, equity and efficiency in community policing. In Rosenbaum D (ed.) *The Challenge of Community Policing.* Sage, Thousand Oaks, CA

Eck J (2002) Preventing crime at places. In Sherman L, Farrington D and Lab P (eds) *Evidence-based Crime Prevention.* Routledge, London

Ekblom P (1997) Gearing up against crime: a dynamic framework to help designers keep up with the adaptive criminal in a changing world. *International Journal of Risk, Security and Crime Prevention*, **2**(4): 249–65

Ekblom P (1998) *Situational Crime Prevention: Effectiveness of Local Initiatives. In Reducing Offending.* Research Study 187, Home Office, London.

Ellin N (ed.) (1997) *Architecture of Fear.* Architectural Press, Princeton

European Forum for Urban Security (1996) *Police Forces in Europe and Urban Safety.* FESU, Paris

Eysenck H (1964) *Crime and Personality.* Rev. edn 1977, Paladin, London

Farrell G and Pease K (1993) *Once Bitten, Twice Bitten: repeat victimisation and its implications for crime prevention.* Home Office, London

Farrington D (1996) *Understanding and Preventing Youth Crime.* Joseph Rowntree Foundation, York Publishing Services

Felson M (1994) *Crime and Everyday Life.* Pine Forge Press, Thousand Oaks, CA

Ferrero G (1911) *Criminal Man According to the Classification of Cesare Lombroso.* London

Ferri E (1897) *Criminal Sociology.* New York

Foster J and Hope T (1993) *An Evaluation of Priority Estates Projects.* Home Office, London

France A and Crow I (2001) *CTC – the story so far: an interim evaluation of communities that care.* Joseph Rowntree Foundation, York

Freeman R (1983) Crime and unemployment. In Wilson J Q (ed.) *Crime and Public Policy*, Institute for Contemporary Studies, San Francisco

Freud S (1980) *Introductory Lectures.* George Allen & Unwin, London

Frieden B and Morris R (1968) *Urban Planning and Social Policy.* Basic Books, New York

Fyfe N and Bannister J (1998) The eyes upon the street – closed-circuit television surveillance and the city. In Fyfe N (ed.) *Images of the Street – Planning, Identity and Control in Public Space.* Routledge, London

Garland D (1997) Of crimes and criminals: the development of criminology in Britain. In Maguire M, Morgan R and Reiner R (eds) *The Oxford Handbook of Criminology*. Clarendon Press, Oxford

Garland D (2001) *The Culture of Control – crime and social order in contemporary society*. University of Chicago Press

Gauntlett D (1995) *Moving Experiences – understanding television's influences and effects*. University of Leeds

Gelsthorpe L and Morris A (eds) (1990) *Feminist Perspectives in Criminology*. Open University Press, Milton Keynes

Georges-Abeyie D and Harries K (eds) (1980) *Crime – a spatial perspective*. Columbia University Press, New York

Gilling D (1997) *Crime Prevention – theory, policy and politics*. UCL Press, London

Gilling D (2000) Policing, crime prevention and partnerships. In Leishman F, Loveday B and Savage F (eds) *Core Issues in Policing* (2nd edn). Longman, Harlow

Gilroy P (1982) Police and thieves. In Centre for Contemporary Cultural Studies *The Empire Strikes Back*. CCCS, Birmingham

Gladwell M (2001) *The Tipping Point – how little things can make a big difference*. Abacus, London

Glueck S and Glueck E T (1956) *Physique and delinquency*. Harper, New York

Goffman I (1961) *Asylums*. Doubleday, New York

Gottfredson M and Hirschi T (1990) *A General Theory of Crime*. Stanford University Press

Gouldner I (1971) *The Coming Crisis of Western Sociology*. Heinemann Educational, Oxford

Graham J and Bennett T (1995) *Crime Prevention Strategies in Europe and North America*. European Institute for Crime Prevention and Control, Helsinki

Graham J and Bowling B (1995) *Young People and Crime*. Research Study 145, Home Office, London

Graham J and Smith D (1994) *Diversion from Offending: the role of the youth service*. Crime Concern, Swindon

Gray J (2002) *Straw Dogs – thoughts on humans and other animals*. Granta, London

Habermas J (1976) *Legitimation Crisis*. Heinemann, London

Hall D (1996) *The Dufferin Papers*. Dufferin Mall Marathon Realty Co., Toronto

Hall S, Clarke J, Critcher C, Jefferson T and Roberts B (1978) *Policing the Crisis*. Macmillan, Basingstoke

Harrison P (1983) *Inside the Inner City: life under the cutting edge*. Penguin, Harmondsworth

Hebert H (1993) The people's peepshow. *Guardian*, 23 November

Hedges A, Blaber A and Mostyn B (1979) *Community Planning Project: Cunningham Road Improvement Scheme – final report.* SCPR, London

Heidenson F (1985) *Women and Crime.* Macmillan – now Palgrave Macmillan, Basingstoke

Heidensohn F and Farrell M (1993) *Crime in Europe.* Routledge, London

Henry S and Lanier M (2001) *What is Crime? Controversies over the nature of crime and what to do about it.* Rowman and Littlefield, Lanham, MA

Her Majesty's Inspectorate of Constabulary (1998) *Beating Crime*, London, Home Office

Her Majesty's Inspectorate of Constabulary (2000) *Calling Time on Crime*, London, Home Office

Hillier B and Shu S (2002) *Do Burglars Understand Defensible Space? New evidence on the relation between crime and space.* Space Syntax, Bartlett School of Arcitecture, London (readable at www.spacesyntax.com)

Hirschfield A and Bowers K (1997) The effect of social cohesion on levels of recorded crime in disadvantaged areas *Urban Studies*, **34**(8): 1275–95

Holloway R (1999) *Godless Morality – keeping religion out of ethics.* Canongate Books, Edinburgh

Home Office (1984) *Circular on Crime Prevention*

Home Office (1985, 1988, 1992, 1994, 1996) *The British Crime Surveys.* HMSO

Home Office (1990) *Crime Prevention – the success of the partnership approach.* Home Office, London

Home Office (1993) *The 1992 British Crime Survey.* HMSO, London

Home Office (1994a) *Participation in Neighbourhood Watch: findings from the 1992 British Crime Survey.* HMSO, London

Home Office (1994b) *Closed Circuit Television – looking out for you.* Home Office, London

Home Office (1998) *Reducing Offending: an assessment of research evidence on ways of dealing with offending behaviour.* Research Study 187, Home Office, London

Home Office (2000) *The 2000 British Crime Survey.* Home Office Statistical Bulletin 18/00, London

Home Office Crime Prevention College (2002) *Passport to Evaluation: an introduction to evaluating crime reduction initiatives and projects.* Easingwold, York

Home Office Research, Development and Statistics Directorate (1999a) *The Cost of Criminal Justice.* Home Office, London

Home Office Research, Development and Statistics Directorate (1999b) *Information on the Criminal Justice System in England and Wales – Digest 4.* Home Office, London

Home Office Research, Development and Statistics Directorate (2000a) *Youth Crime – findings from the 1998/9 Youth Lifestyles Survey*. Home Office, London

Home Office Research, Development and Statistics Directorate (2000b) *Recorded Crime Statistics: England and Wales*. Home Office, London

Home Office Research, Development and Statistics Directorate (2002a) *Crime Prevention Effects of Closed Circuit Television: a systematic review*. Research Study 252, Home Office, London

Home Office Research, Development and Statistics Directorate (2002a) *Effects of Improved Street Lighting on Crime: a systematic review*. Research Study 251, Home Office, London

Home Office Standing Conference on Crime Prevention (1989) *Fear of Crime*. Home Office, London

Home Office Standing Conference on Crime Prevention (1991) *Safer Communities – the local delivery of crime prevention through the partnership approach* (the Morgan Report). Home Office, London

Hope T (2002) The road taken – evaluation, replication and crime prevention. In Hughes G, McLaughlin E and Muncie J (eds) *Crime Prevention and Community Safety – new directions*. Sage, London

Hope T and Shaw M (eds) (1988) *Communities and Crime Reduction*. HMSO, London

Horton C (1995) *Policing Policy in France*. (has a chapter on crime prevention) Policy Studies Institute, London

Hough M (1996) The police patrol function: what research can tell us. In Saulsbury W, Mott J and Newburn T (eds) *Themes in Contemporary Policing*. Independent Committee of Inquiry into the Role and Responsibilities of the Police, London

Hough M and Roberts J (1998) *Attitudes to Punishment: Findings from the 1996 British Crime Survey*. Research Findings 64. Home Office Research and Statistics Directorate, London

Hughes G (1998) *Understanding Crime Prevention*. Open University Press, Buckingham

Hughes G and Edwards A (eds) (2002) *Crime Control and Community – the new politics of public safety*. Willan, Cullompton

Hughes G, McLaughlin E and Muncie J (eds) (2002) *Crime Prevention and Community Safety – new directions*. Sage, London

Hunt N (2003) *A Review of the Evidence-base for Harm Reduction Approaches to Drug Use*. Department of Social Science and Medicine, Imperial College, London

Husain S (1990) *Neighbourhood Watch and Crime – an assessment of impact*. The Police Foundation, London

Jacobs J (1961) *The Death and Life of Great American Cities*. Random House, New York

Jeffery C R (1971) *Crime Prevention through Environmental Design.* Sage, Beverly Hills

Jones S (1990) *Young People Admitting to Crime in Mid-Glamorgan.* Cardiff, Mid-Glamorgan Social Crime Prevention Unit

Jones T, Maclean B and Young J (1986) *The Islington Crime Survey.* Gower, Aldershot

Joyce P (2001) *Crime and the Criminal Justice System.* Liverpool University Press

Junger-Tas J et al. (1994) *Delinquent Behaviour among Young People in the Western World: first results of the international self-report delinquency study.* Kugler, Amsterdam

Katona G (ed.) (1994) *Survey on Crime Prevention in Europe – Data from 27 European States.* Institute for Law Enforcement, Management, Training and Research, Budapest

Katz P (1994) *The New Urbanism – towards an architecture of community.* McGraw-Hill, New York

Kelling G (1999) Broken windows, zero tolerance and crime control. In Francis P and Fraser L (eds) *Building Safer Communities.* Centre for Crime and Justice Studies, Kings College, London

Kelling G and Coles C (1996) *Fixing Broken Windows – restoring order and reducing crime in our communities.* Free Press, New York

Kelling G et al. (1974) *The Kansas City Preventative Patrol Experiment.* Police Federation, Washington DC

van Kesteren J, Mayhew P and Nieubeerta P (2000) *Criminal Victimisation in Seventeen Industrialised Countries – key findings from the 2000 International Crime Victims Survey.* Ministry of Justice, The Hague, Netherlands

Killias M (chair of specialist group) (1995) *European Sourcebook of Criminal Justice Statistics – draft model.* Council of Europe, Strasbourg

King M (1988) *Making Social Crime Prevention Work: the French experience.* NACRO, London

Kirby T and Cooper G (1994) Tories ignore crime study. *The Independent,* 24 April

Koch B (1998) *The Politics of Crime Prevention.* Ashgate, Aldershot

KPMG/SNU (1990) *Counting Out Crime – the Nottingham crime audit.* Nottingham Safer Cities Project

Det Kriminalpraeventive Rad (1994) *Co-operation for Prevention in Local Areas.* Crime Prevention Council, Copenhagen

Kuhlhorn E and Svensson B (1982) *Crime Prevention.* National Swedish Council for Crime Prevention, Research and Development Division, Report no 9, Stockholm

Lab S P (2000) *Crime Prevention – approaches, practices and evaluations.* Anderson, Ohio

Landman K (2000) *An Overview of Enclosed Neighbourhoods in South Africa*. CSIR, Pretoria, South Africa

Lawson M (1995) Liking violence. In *Battered Britain*. Channel 4, Broadcasting Support Services, London

Laycock G and Tilley N (1995) *Policing and Neighbourhood Watch: Strategic Issues*. Crime Detection and Prevention Series paper 60. Home Office, London

Le Grand J and Robinson R (1984) *The Economics of Social Problems*. Macmillan – now Palgrave Macmillan, Basingstoke

Lea J (1992) The analysis of crime. In Young J and Matthews R (eds) *Rethinking Criminology: the realist debate*. Sage, London

Lea J and Young J (1985) (rev. edn 1993) *What Is To Be Done About Law And Order*. Penguin, Harmondsworth

Leitner M, Shapland J and Wiles P (1993) *Drugs Usage and Drugs Prevention – the views and habits of the general public*. HMSO, London

Lewis D (1997) *Hidden Agendas – politics, law and disorder*. Hamish Hamilton, London

Lewis O (1966) The culture of poverty. *Scientific American* **215**(4)

Lilly R, Cullen, F and Ball, R (1989) *Criminological Theory: context and consequences*. Sage, London

van Limbergen K, Walgrave S and Dekegel I (1996) *Promising Practices – crime prevention in Belgium: 10 examples*. Permanent Secretariat for Prevention Policy, Ministry of the Interior, Belgium

Linklater J, Pitts J, and Smith P (1994) *Safer Schools: an organisational development approach*. Longman, Harlow

Local Government Association/Local Government Management Board (1996) *Crime – the local solution*. LGMB, London

Lombroso C (1911) *Crime – its causes and remedies*. London

Loney M (1983) *Community against Government*. Open University Press, Milton Keynes

Lynch K (1960) *The Image of the City*. MIT Press, Boston

Lynch K (1981) *A Theory of Good City Form*. MIT Press, Cambridge, MA

Lyon D (1993) An electrical panoptican – a social critique of surveillance theory. *Sociological Review*, **41**(4)

Mack, J (1964) Full time miscreants, delinquent neighbourhoods and criminal networks. *British Journal of Sociology*, **15**

Maguire M (1997) Crime statistics, patterns and trends – changing perceptions and their implications. In Maguire M, Morgan R and Reiner R (eds) *The Oxford Handbook of Criminology*. Clarendon Press, Oxford

Maguire M, Morgan R and Reiner R (eds) (1997) *The Oxford Handbook of Criminology*. Clarendon Press, Oxford

Mayhew P, Aye Maung N and Mirrlees-Black C (1992) *The 1992 British Crime Survey*. Home Office Research Study 132.

Martinson R (1974) What works? Questions and answers about prison reform. *The Public Interest* 35: 22–54

Mathiesen T (1974) *The Politics of Abolition*. Martin Robertson, London

Matthews R and Young J (eds) (1986) *Confronting Crime*. Sage, London

Matthews R and Young J (eds) (1991) *Realist Criminology*. Sage, London

Matza D (1964) *Delinquency and Drift*. Wiley, New York

Matza D (1969) *Becoming Deviant*. Prentice Hall, New York

Mawby R (1999) Approaches to comparative analysis: the impossibility of becoming an expert on everywhere. In Mawby R (ed.) *Policing Across the World*. UCL Press, London

Mayhew P (1980) *Designing Out Crime*. Home Office, London

Mayhew P and van Dijk J (1997) *Criminal Victimisation in Eleven Industrialised Countries: Key Findings from the 1996 International Crime Victimisation Surveys*. Wetenschappelijk Onderzoek – en Documentatiecentrum, Ministry of Justice, The Hague, Netherlands

McClintock F H (1963) *Crimes of Violence*. St. Martins Press, New York

McGuire J and Priestley P (1995) *Reviewing 'What Works' – past, present and future*. Wiley, Chichester

Menninger K (1968) *The Crime of Punishment*. Viking Press, New York

Messner S and Rosenfeld R (1997) *Crime and the American Dream*. Wadsworth, Belmont, CA

Merton R (1968) *Social Theory and Social Structures*. Free Press, New York

Mills C Wright (1959) *The Sociological Imagination*. Penguin, Harmondsworth

Ministry of Health, Welfare and Sport (1995) *Dutch Drugs Policy in the Years to Come*. Factsheet V-12-E, Ministry of VWS, Rijswijk, the Netherlands

Minton A (2002) *Building Balanced Communities – the US and UK compared*. Royal Institute of Charterd Surveyors, London

Montgomery J (1994) The evening economy of cities. *Town and Country Planning*, November

Morgan R and Newburn T (1997) *The Future of Policing*. Routledge, London

Morris N and Hawkins G (1970) *The Honest Politician's Guide to Crime Control*. University of Chicago Press.

Morris T (1957) The Criminal Area. Routledge & Kegan-Paul, London

Morris A, Giller H, Szued M and Geech H (1980) *Justice for Children*. Macmillan, London

Moynihan D P (1969) *Maximum Feasible Misunderstanding – community action in the war on poverty*. Free Press, New York

Muncie J (1999) *Youth and Crime – a critical introduction*. Sage, London

NACRO (1991) *Crime and Social Policy – papers from an international seminar*. National Association for the Care and Resettlement of Offenders, London

National Crime Prevention (2002) *Principles for Evaluating Community Crime Prevention Projects*. Australian Government Attorney General's Department, Canberra

Nelken D (1994) Whom can you trust? The future of comparative criminology. In Nelken D (ed.) *The Futures of Criminology*. Sage, London.

Nettler G (1982) *Explaining Criminals*. Anderson, Ohio

Nettler G (1984) *Explaining Crime*. McGraw-Hill, New York

Newman G, Clarke R and Shoham S (eds) (1997) *Rational Choice and Situational Crime Prevention*. Ashgate, Aldershot

Newman O (1972) *Defensible Space – people and design in the violent city*. Architectural Press, London

Newman O (1980) *Community of Interest*. Anchor Press/Doubleday, New York

Newman O (1996) *Creating Defensible Space*. US Department of Housing and Urban Development, Washington, DC

Newman S and Lonsdale S (1996) *Human Jungle*. Ebury Press, London

Norris C and Armstrong G (1999) *The Maximum Surveillance Society – the rise of CCTV*. Berg, Oxford

Nursey A (1984) *Skill Training with Offenders*. University of East Anglia, Norwich

Nye F I (1958) *Family Relationships and Delinquent Behaviour*. John Wiley & Sons, New York

Osborn S (1993) *Crime Prevention on Council Estates*. Department of the Environment, HMSO, London

Osborn S (1998) Evaluating crime prevention initiatives. In Marlow A and Pitts J (eds) *Planning Safer Communities*. Russell House, Lyme Regis

Osborn S and Shaftoe H (1995) *Safer Neighbourhoods? – successes and failures in crime prevention*. Safe Neighbourhoods Unit, London

Page D (1993) *Building for Communities: a study of new housing association estates*. Joseph Rowntree Foundation, York

Pain R (2001) Crime. space and inequality. In Pain R, Darke M and Fuller D (eds) *Introducing Social Geographies*. Arnold, London

Palmer S (1973) *The Prevention of Crime*. New York

Park, R E (1936) Human ecology. *American Journal of Sociology* **42**(1)

Pavarini M (1997) Controlling social panic: questions and answers about security in Italy at the end of the millennium. In Bergalli R and Sumner C (eds) *Social Control and Political Order – European perspectives at the end of the century*. Sage, London

Pawson R and Tilley N (1997) *Realistic Evaluation*. Sage, London

Pearce F (1973) Crime corporations and the American social order. In Taylor I and Taylor L (eds) *Deviancy and Politics*. Penguin, Harmondsworth

Pearson G (1982) *Hooligan – a history of respectable fears*. Macmillan – now Palgrave Macmillan, Basingstoke

Pease K (1991) The Kirkholt project: preventing burglary on a British public housing estate. *Security Journal* 2(2)

People for Action (2003) *Transforming Housing Associations – Royds Community Association*. People for Action, Birmingham (readable online at: www.o2.org.uk/Briefings)

Phillips C and Sampson A (1992) Taking Action Against Perpetrators of Racial Attacks on Housing Estates. Home Office (unpublished)

Pitts J (1988) *The Politics of Juvenile Crime*. Sage, London

Pitts J (1990) *Working With Young Offenders*. BASW/Macmillan, Basingstoke

Pitts J (1993) Thereotyping: criminology, anti-racism and black young people. In Cook D and Hudson B (eds) *Criminology and Racism*. Sage, London

Pitts J (1998) The French social prevention initiative. In Marlow A and Pitts J (eds) *Planning for Safer Communities*. Russell House, Lyme Regis

Platt T and Takagi P (1981) *Crime and Social Justice*. Macmillan, London

Poole R (1994) *Operation Columbus: travels in North America*. West Midlands Police, Birmingham

Power A (1988) Housing, community and crime. In Downes D (ed.) *Crime and the City*. Macmillan – now Palgrave Macmillan, Basingstoke

Poyner B (1982) *Crime Prevention through Environmental Design and Management: an overview*. Research Bulletin 13, Home Office, London

Poyner B (1983) *Design Against Crime: beyond defensible space*. Butterworths, London

Priestley P, McGuire J, Flegg D, Hemsley V, Welham D and Barnett R (1985) *Social Skills in Prison and Community*. Routledge, London

Putnam R (1993) The prosperous community – social capital and public life. *American Prospect* **13**

Putnam R (1995) Bowling alone: America's declining social capital. *Journal of Democracy*, **6**(1): 65–78

Ramsay M (1989) *Downtown Drinkers – the perceptions and fears of the public in a city centre*. Crime Prevention Unit Paper 19. Home Office, London

Ramsay M (1990) *Lagerland Lost? An experiment in keeping drinkers off the street in central Coventry*. Crime Prevention Unit Paper 22. Home Office, London

Ravetz A (1980) *Remaking cities – contradictions of the recent urban environment*. Croom Helm, London

Read T and Tilley N (2000) *Not Rocket Science? Problem-solving and crime reduction*. Crime Reduction Research Series Paper 6. Home Office, London

Rees T (1981) *The Concept of Crime*. Research Bulletin 72, Home Office, London

Reiman J (1995) *The Rich Get Richer and the Poor Get Prison – ideology, class and criminal justice*. Allyn & Bacon, Boston

Ridley M (1996) *The Origins of Virtue*. Viking, London

Robert P and van Outrive L (1993) *Crime et Justice en Europe – état des recherches, évaluations et recommandations*. L'Harmattan, Paris

Rock P and McIntosh M (eds) (1973) *Deviance and Social Control*. Tavistock, London

Rogers R (1997) *Cities for a Small Planet*. Faber, London

Rogerson R et al. (1990) *Quality of Life in Britain's Intermediate Cities*. Dept of Geography, University of Glasgow

Rosenbaum D (1988) A critical eye on neighbourhood watch: does it reduce crime and fear? In Hope T and Shaw M (eds) *Communities and Crime Reduction*. HMSO, London

Rosenbaum D, Luvigio A and Davis R (1998) *The Prevention of Crime: social and situational strategies*. Wadsworth, Belmont, CA

Ross J and Richards S (2002) *Behind Bars – surviving prison*. Alpha Books, Indianapolis

Rutherford A (1986) *Growing out of Crime*. Penguin, Harmondsworth

Rutter M and Giller H (1983) *Delinquency: trends and perspectives*. Penguin, London

Safe Neighbourhoods Unit (1993a) *Crime Prevention on Council Estates*. HMSO, London

Safe Neighbourhoods Unit (1993b) *Not Afraid to Trade – business and crime prevention in Hackney*. London, SNU

Safe Neighbourhoods Unit (1995) *Housing-related Crime Prevention*. Safe Neighbourhoods Unit, London

Safe Neighbourhoods Unit (1997) *High Hopes – an evaluation of concierge, controlled entry and similar schemes for high rise blocks*. HMSO, London

Sampson R, Raudenbush S and Earls F (1997) Neighbourhoods and violent crime: a multilevel study of collective efficacy. *Science*, **277**: 918–24

Sanderson J (1992) *LLB Criminology Textbook*. HLT Publications, London

Schneider R and Kitchen T (2002) *Planning for Crime Prevention – a transatlantic perspective*. Routledge, London

Schur E (1975) *Radical Non Intervention*. Prentice Hall, New York

Scottish Executive (2000) *A Report on a Research Project Examining the Experience of Violence and Harassment of Gay Men in the City of Edinburgh*. Scottish Executive, Central Research Unit

Scottish Office (1994) *Planning for Crime Prevention*. Planning Advice Note 46, Scottish Office, HMSO, Edinburgh

Searle J (1995) *The Construction of Social Reality*. Penguin, London

Sennett R (1996) *The Uses of Disorder – personal identity and city life*. Faber & Faber, London

Shaftoe H (1994) Inner city Bristol lighting improvements. In Osborn S (ed.) *Housing Safe Communities – an evaluation of recent initiatives*. Safe Neighbourhoods Unit, London

Shaftoe H (1997) *Creating Safer Communities in Europe – a crime prevention sourcebook*. University of the West of England, Bristol (accessible online at: http://uwe.ac.uk/commsafe/environment.)

Shaftoe H (2000) Community safety and actual neighbourhoods. In Barton H (ed.) *Sustainable Communities – the potential for eco-neighbourhoods*. Earthscan, London

Shaftoe H (2002a) The camera never lies but, in truth, is it any use? *Community Safety*, **1**(2): 27–30

Shaftoe H (2002b) *Southmead – is it getting better? An evaluation of community safety initiatives*. Cities Research Centre, University of the West of England, Bristol

Shaftoe H and James S (2004) *Do Symbolic Barriers Prevent Crime?* Faculty of the Built Environment, University of the West of England, Bristol

Shaftoe H and Pitts J (1994) *Taking Offence: crime and community safety – the facts and the debate*. University of the West of England, Bristol

Shaw C (1929) *Delinquency Areas*. University of Chicago Press

Shaw C and McKay H (1942) *Juvenile Delinquency and Urban Areas*. University of Chicago Press

Sherman L, Gottfriedson D and Mackenzie D et al. (1998) *Preventing Crime: what works, what doesn't, what's promising*. National Institute of Justice, Washington

Sherman L, Farrington D and Lab P (2002) *Evidence-based Crime Prevention*. Routledge, London

Shover N (1998) White collar crime. In Tonry M (ed.) *The Handbook of Crime and Punishment*. Oxford University Press

Skinner B F (1953) *Science and Human Behaviour*. Macmillan, New York

Skogan W G (1990) *Disorder and Decline – crime and the spiral of decay in American Neighbourhoods*. University of California Press

Smeets M E (1995) *Crime Prevention: The Dutch experience*. Reader for seminar in Edinburgh, hosted by the Safe Neighbourhood Unit

Smith D (1984) *Police and People in London*. Policy Studies Institute, London

Smith L and Heal K (1984) *Crime Reduction: towards a preventative strategy*. Home Office Research Bulletin 17 HMSO, London

Sparks R (1992) *Television and the Drama of Crime – moral tales and the place of crime in public life*. Open University Press, Buckingham

Stenson K and Sullivan R (2001) _Crime, Risk and Justice: the politics of crime control in liberal democracies._ Willan, Cullompton

Stern V (1998) _A Sin Against the Future: imprisonment in the world._ Penguin, Harmondsworth

Stickland R (1996) _The Twenty Four Hour City Concept: an appraisal of its adoption and its social and economic viability._ Department of Urban Planning, University of Nottingham

Sutherland E and Cressey D (1943) _Principles of Criminology._ J B Lippincott, Philadelphia

van Swaaningen R (1997) _Critical Criminology – visions from Europe._ Sage, London

Taft D (1950) _Criminology – a cultural interpretation._ New York

Tarling R (1994) _Analysing Offending: data, models and interpretation._ HMSO, London

Taylor H (1999) Forging the job: a crisis of 'modernisation' or redundancy for the police in England and Wales, 1900–39. _British Journal of Criminology,_ **39**(1): 113–35

Taylor I and Taylor L (1971) Soccer consciousness and soccer hooliganism. In Cohen S (ed.) _Images of Deviance._ Penguin, Harmondsworth

Taylor I, Walton P and Young J (1973) _The New Criminology._ Routledge & Kegan Paul, London

Thorndyke E L (1898) Animal intelligence. _Psychological Review Monograph,_ Supplement 2 (8)

Thornton R and Endo K (1992) _Preventing Crime in America and Japan – a comparative study._ Sharpe, New York (extract in reader)

Tilley N (1993) Crime prevention and the safer cities story. _Howard Journal,_ **32**(1): 255–72

Tilley N (ed.) (2002) The rediscovery of learning: crime prevention and scientific realism. In Hughes G and Edward S (eds) _Evaluation for Crime Prevention._ Willan, Cullompton

Toch H (ed.) (1979) _Psychology of Crime and Criminal Justice._ Holt, Reinhart & Winston, New York

Toch H (1980) Foreword. In Georges-Abeyie D and Harries K (eds) _Crime: A spatial perspective._ Columbia University Press, New York

Toynbee P (1994) The channels of fear, The _Guardian,_ 3 June

Toynbee P and Walker D (2001) _Did Things Get Better? – an audit of Labour successes and failures._ Penguin, Harmondsworth

Urban Villages Forum (1992) _Urban Villages – a concept for creating mixed use urban development on a sustainable scale._ Urban Villages Group, London

Urmson J O and Ree J (1989) _The Concise Encyclopedia of Western Philosophy and Philosophers._ Unwin Hyman, London

Utting D, Bright J and Henricson C (1993) _Crime and the Family –_

*improving child-rearing and preventing delinquency.* Occasional Paper 16. Family Policy Studies Centre, London

Van den Haag E (1975) *Punishing Criminals.* Basic Books, New York

Vennard J and Hedderman C (1998) *Effective Interventions with Offenders.* Research Study 187, Home Office, London

Vold G and Bernard T (1986) *Theoretical Criminology* (3rd edn). Oxford University Press

Vourc'h C and Marcus M (1993) *Security and Democracy* – Report by the Analytical College on Urban Safety. European Forum for Urban Safety, Paris

Vourc'h C and Marcus M (1995) *Nouvelles Formes de Criminalite Urbaine, Nouvelles Formes de Justice.* European Forum for Urban Safety, Paris

de Waard (2002) *The European Crime Prevention Network: introduction for members of the European Parliament.* EUCPN, Unit B-1, Police and Customs Co-operation, Brussels

Wade J (1820) *The Black Book.* John Fairburn, London

Walker S (1998) *Sense and Nonsense about Crime and Drugs – a policy guide.* Wadsworth, Belmont, CA

Walklate S (1998) *Understanding Criminology: current theoretical debates.* Open University Press, Buckingham

Ward C (ed.) (1973) *Vandalism.* Architectural Press, London

Ward C (1974) *Tenants Take Over.* Architectural Press, London

Webber M (1968) Comprehensive planning and social responsibility. In Frieden B and Morris R (eds) *Urban Planning and Social Policy.* Basic Books, New York

Wekerle G (1999) From eyes on the street to safe cities. *Places,* Fall

Wekerle G and Whitzman C (1995) *Safe Cities – guidelines for planning, design and management.* Van Nostrand Reinhold, New York

West D (1982) *Delinquency – its roots, careers and prospects.* Heinemann, London

West D and Farrington D (1973) *Who Becomes Delinquent?* Heinemann, London

West D and Farrington D (1977) *The Delinquent Way of Life.* Heinemann, London

Whyte W H (1988) *City – rediscovering the center,* Anchor/Doubleday, New York

Wiles P and Costello A (2000) *The Road to Nowhere: the evidence for travelling criminals.* Research Study 207, Home Office, London

Wilkins L (1974) *The Prevention of Crime.* NACRO Paper 20, London

Williamson K (1997) *Drugs and the Party Line.* Canongate Books, Edinburgh

Williamson T (2000) Policing: the changing criminal justice context – twenty-five years of missed opportunities. In Leishman F, Loveday B and Savage S (eds) *Core Issues in Policing.* Longman, Harlow

Wilson J Q and Herrnstein R J (1985) *Crime and Human Nature*. Simon & Schuster, London

Wilson, J Q (1975) *Thinking about Crime*. Basic Books, New York

Wilson J Q and Kelling G (1982) Broken Windows. *Atlantic Monthly*, March

Wolfe T (1990) *The Bonfire of the Vanities*. Picador, London

Young J and Mathews R (1992) *Re-thinking Criminology – the realist debate*. Sage, London

Young J (1971) The role of the police as amplifiers of deviancy. In Cohen S (ed.) *Images of Deviance*. Penguin, Harmondsworth

Young J (1998a) From inclusive to exclusive society: nightmares in the european dream. In Ruggeiro V, South N and Taylor T (eds) *The New European Criminology*. Routledge, London

Young J (1998b) Zero tolerance – back to the future. In Marlow A and Pitts J (eds) *Planning Safer Communities*. Russell House, Lyme Regis

Young J (1999) *The Exclusive Society – social exclusion, crime and difference in late modernity*. Sage, London

Zimbardo P (1973) A field experiment in auto shaping. In Ward C (ed.) *Vandalism*. Architectural Press, London

# Index

Printed and bound by CPI Group (UK) Ltd, Croydon, CR0 4YY